FOLLOW THE MONEY

The Tale of the Merchant of Ennis

DAVID McWILLIAMS ∿

Gill & Macmillan

AUTHOR'S NOTE

The Merchant of Ennis, his wife Elaine Flannery, Shylock, Fr O'Mahoney, Breakfast Roll Man, Miss Pencil Skirt, Mr Big, Fin Boy, Ballygarrit and the development in Rialto are purely fictional and any resemblance to any persons, living or dead, any town or any proposed or existing development is purely coincidental.

Gill & Macmillan Ltd
Hume Avenue, Park West, Dublin 12
with associated companies throughout the world
www.gillmacmillan.ie

© David McWilliams 2009, 2010
First published in 2009
First published in this format 2010
ISBN 978 07171 4807 3

Typography design by Make Communication
Print origination by Carole Lynch
Printed by CPI Cox and Wyman, Reading

This book is typeset in Linotype Minion and
Neue Helvetica.

The paper used in this book comes from the wood pulp of managed forests. For every tree felled, at least one tree is planted, thereby renewing natural resources.

A CIP catalogue record for this book is available from the British Library.

5 4 3 2 1

CONTENTS

ACKNOWLEDGMENTS

This book was written to the chorus of *'C'mon, Dad, have you not finished it yet?'* so thanks to my family: Sian, Lucy and Cal for putting up with the ogre who was no fun and lived in the attic all summer. They were always helpful and encouraging, even when reduced to feeding me at intervals through the gap between the floor and the door when things got a bit tight and tetchy. Lucy and Cal, this book is dedicated to you.

I'd also like to thank my mother who has had a difficult year but who still managed to quiz me on the book when she had other things on her mind.

Special thanks to my wonderful researchers Grainne Faller, Eoin Cunningham, Lorcan Roche Kelly and Robin Adams.

Thanks also to Ben Webb, Clare Ridge and Jonathan O'Brien. To Frank Coughlan at the *Irish Independent* and Cliff Taylor at the *Sunday Business Post* for giving me time off and generally for their support.

Thanks as always to Gill & Macmillan, my publisher Fergal Tobin, my careful and patient copy-editor Tess Tattersall and my thoughtful agent Marianne Gunn O' Connor.

I'd like to express my gratitude to all those who helped me but would prefer not to be thanked in public for various reasons. You know who you are. Thanks also to the dozens of people on Twitter for giving me so many ideas and stories.

Finally for the person who makes it all possible, my wife and editor, Sian. Sian read every word, queried every assertion, concept and proposition. And late at night over a glass of wine or a cup of tea, Sian encouraged me quietly without ever asking me to get a proper job. Nothing happens without her.

Dublin, September 2009

PART I

| FATHER AND SON

The young boy felt very secure on his new bike. He'd just got it for Christmas. When he first saw it, he realised straightaway that it was second-hand, but someone had so lovingly scrubbed and polished it that the Triumph Twenty sign sparkled. No one would know the difference and he hadn't the heart to point out that the tops of the spokes were marked with tiny flecks of rust that even the most vigorous cleaning couldn't erase.

He cycled as hard as he could and the low winter sun glimmered off the handlebars as his long shadow stretched out in front of him. He raced past the Garda Station on Rochestown Avenue and across to the hospital where the people who had bad car accidents learned to walk again. That was the reason his dad was following him in the car, his mum said, so as not to have an accident, so as to be safe.

He loved having his dad drive behind him. His dad had just made the old speedometer work. It was attached to a dynamo on the front wheel and, as the boy pedalled down the hill, the little hand pointed to 16 miles per hour. He wanted to scream out to his dad and tell him how fast he was going. He wanted to impress him. He'd be in school in no time and then he'd have to say goodbye until after the bell. His father would wait for him and then they would go the 3 miles home again, him cycling like Eddie Merckx and his dad following behind, keeping him safe.

He worked his legs until they felt like jelly and he had to stand on the pedals and freewheel to catch his breath. It was still early and the frosty air caught in his throat and made him cough. He looked behind and his dad, in his suit, smiled back from the front of his orangey-yellow Hillman Hunter.

What was going through his dad's mind as he listened to the news on the radio? All that stuff about factories closing and taxes and petrol price rises and something called the EEC which all the adults seemed to talk about.

The little boy didn't know anything about these things. All he knew was that Kenny Dalgleish was Scottish and so too were his dad's mum and dad, his grandparents, and that made him closer to Kenny Dalgleish than anyone else in his class. And that also made him closer to the best player in the world, and when Scotland won the World Cup that year—as everyone said 'Ally's Army' would—he would feel as if part of him had won it, even if Scotland wasn't Ireland, and he could explain that to his friends.

His dad fixed his tie in the mirror at the traffic lights and, when the boy looked around, his dad pulled a funny face that made both of them laugh.

He hated traffic lights because then you had to start all over again and he was already boiling in his duffle coat and Leeds Utd hat, with his schoolbag strapped to his back and the big flask weighing it down. Traffic lights weren't fair.

Every morning now his dad woke him. At first it was strange having him in the house. He used to leave before the rest of the family had even stirred, gone into the black dark of morning, the way the other dads on the road must've done. The boy would only see him on really cold mornings if the car didn't start and everyone would have to get up and push it until it spluttered and coughed its consumptive way into life. It was like the boy down the road with the stammer and all the effort it took him to start the sentence, stuttering and gulping for air, and then finally out came the word and then he continued speaking non-stop as if he knew that when he stopped he'd have to start the whole torture again.

At the first spark, his dad would jump in and off it went with a friendly quick double toot, his dad laughing in the mirror at them as they waved, black exhaust fumes belching from the stuttering jalopy.

But now his dad was home in the mornings. In fact, he could be home all day if he wanted to be, although you wouldn't know it, because every morning before half-seven he put on his suit, tie and London Fog Mac as if he were going to work.

He told the little boy that he had a new job in Bray with 'our uncle Joe'. But in reality he had nowhere to go. So he went with his son to school, pretending to the whole road that he was just going to work as he always did.

He must've stayed out all day, traipsing around, replying to job adverts, trying to remain busy. Later he told his son, when he got old enough to understand, that he had rejection letters piled high. He never gave up writing these letters for jobs he wasn't qualified to do. Most places told him that, at 45, he was too old. These must have been dark, dark times.

His mother kept it all from him as he was the youngest and just liked having his dad about so this was the best of all worlds for him. But he could tell from the hushed conversations in the kitchen after he'd gone to bed that this was serious. Sometimes he pretended to be asleep but he waited on the stairs in the dark and listened. But it all sounded so boring to a 10-year-old and, normally, his dad came up to sing him to sleep so life was brilliant with his dad at night and in the morning. Adults were always a bit serious anyway, the way they talked about money and people on the telly. That's just the way they were.

Luckily his mum was a teacher and there was an income in the house. But these things—like unemployment—were not supposed to happen to people like them. It wasn't in their script. Their script was one of aspiration, of upward social movement.

SUBURBAN DREAMS

Everyone on our road came from somewhere else and we were on the move. This was Ireland of the 1970s. The country had experienced a mini boom at the end of the 1960s that lasted until the mid-1970s. We hadn't heard of the 1980s yet, so there was no reason to be fearful. The future was bright.

Home was a smallish suburb—a comfortable place of bungalows, pebble-dashed semi-Ds, corrugated cement roads, scratched record collections and daily soccer games of 'three and in' on the road using gates as nets. Mostly our dads went out to work and our mothers stayed at home.

People seemed to like each other and, contrary to the more disparaging commentary on the faceless nature of Irish suburbs, there was a strong sense of community. Friendships were enduring; funerals, communions and weddings came and went and everyone attended them. If we were not quite dropping in for 'a cup of sugar', people knew each other.

These were Ireland's first instant communities, testament to the extraordinary flexibility and adaptability of all of us. We were uprooted people, thrown together, and for many of our parents, it was their first time living away from home. For the children, it was normal to go around in big packs of 10 or more. And it was normal that everyone's granddads and grannies came from all over the country.

The three-bed semi mazes that sprang up in our cities in the 1950s, 1960s and 1970s were the first real melting pots in the country. Strange as it may sound, these places were our Brooklyn, our Finsbury Park, our Bowery. Many of our parents had never seen—let alone talked to—people from different counties or even towns before. Now they were sharing driveways. Galway lived beside Wexford, Cork beside Cavan. The rooted rural culture of Kerry was tied by the shared sitting room wall to the urban, dispossessed culture of north Belfast.

We were all blow-ins from somewhere else. Nobody knew what our grandparents did for a living or who were 'our people' and we didn't care. We were all uprooted, looking to create a new life.

Typically, the parents had left small towns and villages in the 1950s and early 1960s to come to Dublin to find work. They paired up quickly and got married. Had they not ended up in Dublin, they would have moved on to Coventry, Toronto or New Jersey.

People here were gelled together by the promise of a better life for themselves and their children. We lived in the future.

WHAT'S IN A NAME?
From places like this, the aspiring middle classes began their ascent, constantly looking upwards, anxious not to fall back down. Sure there were some people who were slipping back, having been born in swankier areas, but they were a clear minority. Most of us were on the march, on our way up. And it felt that way until the 1980s stopped us in our tracks.

If the 1980s were about survival, the decade or two before were about social improvement, as people tried to carve out their niche and re-invent themselves in the great suburban tapestry of self-improvement.

My parents moved into this suburban estate in 1958. A pope had just died. At the first meeting of the residents, one of the more devout new neighbours suggested that the place be called Pope Pius the Twelfth Road. Well, there was uproar. An Orange Lodge would have taken it better. Despite possibly 90 per cent of the residents being religious, mass-going Catholics, the thought that you might call the place after a pope, a priest or a patriot triggered hysterics in the social anxiety gauge which chimed away inside the head of every aspirant housewife.

Council house estates were named after popes, not private roads. In the end, someone from the upwardly mobile instant community came up with the thoroughly English—and therefore, posher—name of Windsor Park. It was passed by the road committee unanimously. The street beside us was christened with the eminently home counties' moniker of Richmond Drive and next to that was Ashton Park. With these names we had clearly distinguished ourselves from the corporation estates across the main road—Oliver Plunkett Crescent, Rory O'Connor Park and St Patrick's Road.

In such an environment, where movement upwards was the suburban dream, dads didn't lose their jobs. That was unthinkable.

IN THE CITY WHERE NOBODY GOES

My name was down for the local posh school since I was two months old. After national school, I'd be going to a school that had given the country presidents and surgeons and Fergus Slattery.

My dad must've worried that I'd be bullied when it became known that the skinny new boy with the red hair had a dad who was out of work. He was as protective as any dad, but he felt that ability to protect had been torn away.

Of course he never said anything. He kept it inside and as months went by and the rejection letters piled up, he must have been beginning to give up hope. He told me he loved me no matter what the new big boys said. I didn't understand what he meant and just wanted him to keep playing soccer with me in the back garden and driving behind me to school. I didn't mind about any big boys because we were now together all the time and that's what counted.

Dad's day was an elaborate hoax of false leads, fabricated meetings and important destinations: the crucial thing was not to be noticed. Mum told me to tell anyone who asked that Dad was a liquidator, and I suppose in a way he was when the company folded. But ultimately he was liquidating himself. However, the word sounded good. A liquidator. It sounded impressive.

One afternoon, we drove together in the orangey-yellow Hillman Hunter to a strange place. I was so excited. I now recognise it to be Werburgh Street beside Christchurch. Back then, it was 'in town'. I'd never been in town apart from trips to Santa at Cleary's so this was a huge adventure. I asked him where we were going, peering out over the dashboard at people and places that were alien to me, and funny little streets with women pushing prams piled high with clothes and children, boys of my age but hundreds of them.

This place was about as far away from our suburban road as you could possibly imagine. I couldn't wait to tell my friends at home about this odd world that existed beyond the borders of ours. I thought no one I knew had ever been to a street like this. And that was the point: no one we knew would ever come to a place like this and so this is where my father signed on and hid his failure from our world.

He looked at me as if to say, 'Please understand, son' and left me in the car. He walked, examining papers that were in his pocket, into a strange building, which had those chain-smoking women pushing those prams with the clothes. I saw my dad in the half-light of the room.

Something didn't fit. He was standing at the back of what looked like a queue. That was strange because he told me he was dropping something off to a friend who worked in the funny building in the funny street in the strange part of the city that no one we knew had ever seen. Maybe there were loads of friends dropping things off to the same friend and that was why Dad had to queue. I continued playing Colditz with little plastic soldiers, using the dashboard of the Hillman Hunter as my battleground.

Then he re-appeared, looked around, put his head down, stared at the tarmac and slunk into the car.

When I think back to it now, he was broken with shame. The shame of being redundant, the shame of being out of work, of having to put his hand out to the government for the dole, of not having the self-worth to be valued by anyone except his 10-year-old son who loved him anyway. After all, he drove behind me to school and played football in the back garden and he bought me sweets after the visit to the funny friend in the strange building in that faraway place where everyone pushed big prams that I told him would make great go-cart wheels.

'Can we come back here, Dad? Please.'

He couldn't wait to get out of the place. He looked ahead as we drove through the drizzle. I asked him about the queue; he didn't answer. Who were all those people in the half-light? And who were all those women with the prams? Dad looked so sad.

At night, when he walked the dog on his own, still in his work suit and overcoat, what went through his mind? There he was, strong, fit, honest as the day is long, and he was on the slack heap. He couldn't talk to anyone. Maybe we weren't really a community after all. We only spoke of success, of a week's holiday to Spain and the new colour TV. No one talked about failure.

Of course our neighbours must've known, as they whispered behind his back, and many of them were probably going through something similar.

But no one mentioned it, these were the suburbs—death was better than redundancy. Maybe, like the family down the road the year before, we wouldn't be able to pay our bills and we would slip down, silently sucked into the quicksand of failure. There'd be no posh school for me, and my mother's hopes and dreams, which were wrapped up in the magic letter from the priests about starting big school on the first of September, would be shattered. All because my dad was a failure. He had lost his job, no one wanted him and he was to blame.

Deep down he knew that everyone also knew. His rituals didn't fool anyone, not the suit and tie, the elaborate charade of the drive to work every morning, or the incessant public chirpiness of the privately tormented man. These neighbours were equipped with the heightened social antennae of the anxious classes. They could smell trouble a mile off.

In later years, he told me that after he'd followed me to school, he'd head to Sally Gap and walk for miles. Sometimes he'd go to Brittas or even some huge rural church where he'd sit at the back for hours trying to count down the giant slow-moving daily clock of the unemployed. Maybe there were others with him, other broken men trying to come to terms with their life in an economy that didn't work.

But back then the little boy didn't care. He had his bike and, even if it wasn't new, it was shiny and fast and he had his dad behind him, making him feel safe.

2009

This is the story of this book. It is about why good people are broken by bad economics. Today, there are thousands of people like my dad in our country. We have to help them. My story has a happy ending. Miraculously, my dad did get a new job and unemployment for him was a temporary nightmare. His self-esteem was handed back to him, by the same invisible force that took it away in the first place.

The entire episode was put into a compartment in our family's history. But he never forgot it and neither did I. We chatted about it, Dad and me, a few weeks before he passed away earlier this year. He said it was terrible to see young people idle again in Dun Laoghaire. He said he thought all that was over. He asked me what was going to happen.

'You understand all this stuff now, son. We really didn't have a clue in my time but we know now, don't we? What are we going to do now?'

Deep down, the reason I ended up choosing economics in university was not because I was naturally good at it—I was better at other subjects—but I immersed myself in the cold world of graphs, equations and charts because I wanted to understand how a good man could be diminished by a system. How did this system work? As a boy, I couldn't figure out how my dad, who was honest and hard-working, meticulous and frugal, could be surplus to the needs of the economy. Who decided this and who made Dad look so sad when we drove back in the rain from the strange place in town where he'd given his friend something? Who were these men in suits from political parties who came on the telly with their grave faces, telling my mum and dad to tighten their belts? And why did my dad turn off the TV every time they came on?

I needed to understand economics to make some sense of what had happened and to comprehend how the warm feeling of a 10-year-old boy being looked after by his dad as he cycled to school could be seen as a bad thing by everyone else. How could it be something that his dad shied away from and was embarrassed by? How could something so loving be kept from the neighbours as if it were a stain?

A GOREY STORY

Gorey is typical of the type of town that flourished in the boom and is now capsizing. Gorey has the biggest secondary school in the country, testament to the huge increase in the young population, the new estates and the vibrancy of Ireland's babybelt. From 2002 to 2006, Gorey saw its population jump by a staggering 36 per cent.[1] This is the story of many other similar towns, Naas, Newbridge, Navan and Drogheda outside Dublin, Carrigaline and Ballincollig outside Cork, Claregalway and Oranmore outside Galway and Ennis up the road from Limerick.

In the past 12 months these types of places have been hit by an economic firestorm. Unemployment in Gorey has risen by 299 per cent.[2]

These people turn up not just at the dole office but at the GP's clinic as the interlinked emotional, familial and psychological impact of the recession begins to be felt. The doctor is overwhelmed. She doesn't know what to say to them. How could she? She has gone from diagnosing type 2 diabetes, bronchitis and the flu to holding the hands of crying young mothers who don't know what to do and who just want 'it' to go away.

Her clinics are jammed from morning to night. The recession has changed the profile of her patients. Instead of a massive increase in the poor and the old which she would have expected, she is now flooded with new patients, with new ailments. For the first time, the majority of her patients are young, apparently healthy parents who can't cope with the shock of being laid off.

They are depressed, stressed and anxious. They can't pay their bills and are falling deeper into debt. Most have children. Some are divorcing and many can't see a way out. Her anecdotal observations are substantiated by research published by the Wexford local development authority. This found that over half of the people recently thrown on the dole have difficulty sleeping, one in two think that they are a failure, and 30 per cent said that they have trouble dealing with the free time they have.

These trends are being repeated all over the country. Back in Gorey, one in three said that they were depressed and this was most prevalent among parents in their thirties.

Out in our new suburbs, a new generation—the Juggling Generation—is sinking under the weight of huge debts, negative equity and the trauma of failure. They bought into the dream that they could juggle all the balls in the air, the new houses, the new jobs and the new children. They believed that the price of houses would continue rising. Why wouldn't they? Every politician and businessman in the country told them it could only go one way. The media saturated them with seductive images of a brave new world where they could just hop on the Irish bus to success. All you needed to do was gather the deposit and you would be whisked away to an advertiser's dream world of better stuff, better friends, better kitchens, better careers, better sex.

The entire prospect was held together with the most fragile gossamer assumption that credit would always be available and the banks would keep churning it out. Now that the banks are bust, the game is up and these people, the Jugglers—our neighbours, brothers and sisters, daughters and sons—are taking the brunt of the slump and are presenting to doctors looking for Prozac to ease the pain.

Like my father and others in the late 1970s, many thousands of mothers and fathers are living in that twilight world between debt, social welfare and the constant striving to do the best for their young children.

The trauma of this sudden collapse in the economy is deeply psychological. Around kitchen tables all over the country today, couples are arguing over money, while trying their best to shield their children from the reality of a dream shattered. They too are trying to disguise the shame. Maybe, like my dad, they are putting on the suit, backing the Ford Focus out of the drive, waving to the kids and driving off into suburban oblivion in order to pass the time.

One more rejection letter could send them off the cliff. People are under tremendous strain, knowing that they are behind on the mortgage, trying to keep body and soul together for the upcoming Communion and hoping not to have their own kids shown up by friends' children who have the latest iPhone.

As people lose their jobs, and unemployment rises by the thousands, affecting families, children, husbands, wives, parents, brothers and sisters, we should face the fact that this is a man-made catastrophe. We have to do everything in our power to get out of this meltdown as quickly as possible. If this means taking big risks and ripping up the rulebook, let's do it. Unemployment is the enemy and if we don't fight it, the implications for a generation will be traumatic.

The Gorey story brings me back to my dad's secret afternoon trip to the Werburgh Street dole office 30 years ago. I am once again the little boy cycling to school but now that I have the eyes of an adult, it is easier to see what we are going through.

THE FIVE STAGES

One way we can come to terms with the collapse of the Irish miracle is to regard it as a bereavement. Someone close, someone we expected to be around for a long while, has suddenly died and we all deal with death in different ways, at different paces.

The Swiss doctor and psychologist Elizabeth Kübler Ross first developed a theory of the five stages of bereavement.

When an economy has been hit by the type of disaster that has just visited Ireland, the population reacts to this type of loss similarly. We have lost money and jobs, and our houses are in negative equity. Many of us feel overwhelmed. If you are made redundant, a similar emotional rollercoaster cranks up, taking you into various stages before you recover. If you are told that your business is on the rocks or, more likely in the Irish case, if you are told that your assets should be halved to get their real value, but your liabilities have stayed the same, you need to adjust to the new reality and this takes time.

The first phase of bereavement is denial. You can't quite believe that something has happened. You avoid the news and try to get on with what you were doing in the hope that if you ignore it, it will go away. In the denial phase, you simply can't digest the enormity of what has happened, so you don't. We saw this in Ireland last year when people just could not accept what was unfolding in the economy. People put their head in the sand as the bills came in and the news went from bad to worse.

In the cycle of bereavement, the second phase is known as the 'anger' phase. Here you want to hit out at someone or something. We want to blame everyone. Consider what is happening at the moment in Ireland, The government is blaming the bankers, the bankers are blaming the developers. The man with the overdraft is blaming the banks and the banks are blaming the man with the overdraft. The Left is pointing the finger at the Right. The public sector is blaming the private sector and vice versa. Everyone blames the politicians for overseeing the disaster and they in turn are blaming the rest of us for 'losing the run of ourselves'. Pro-Europeans are blaming anti-Europeans and the farmers are blaming something called 'Dublin 4 economics'. In short, we are in the anger phase. We will make many mistakes in this phase and we will get into huge divisive rows with each other.

As the anger stage passes, the third phase begins: bargaining. This is where we try to negotiate with whoever we believe can help us. This is the stage where were try to get the dead person back or if we have just been diagnosed with a terminal illness, we promise that we'll change our behaviour in exchange for a reprieve. Similarly, if a company is in trouble the owner will also bargain, holding out for a white knight to rescue him at the end. For countries, the same thing can happen. For example, Ireland is now being kept afloat by the generosity of the European Central Bank, which is injecting cash into our bankrupt banks, but this is hardly a long-term solution. We are also bargaining with the financial markets, pleading with them to come and rescue us if we cut spending and raise taxes. The country will remain in this phase for a while.

The fourth phase is where we finally capitulate and slump into a depression. The fight is gone and we languish in our grief and loss. This phase can last for some time but it is the beginning of the recovery.

The final stage is acceptance. We accept what has happened and move on. This is where we rebuild things and many psychologists argue that we are stronger emotionally having gone through all the phases of bereavement.

Over the course of the next few years, Ireland is going to go through something similar. We will alternate between being angry, sad, frustrated and dark but ultimately we will pull through. Some of the stages will last longer than others. At the moment we are firmly in the anger phase. We are furious with those whom we deem created this problem: the bankers and the politicians who recklessly fuelled the boom. And, we are angry with ourselves for believing the hype. However, this phase will pass when we realise that we had better start bargaining very quickly as Ireland flirts with default.

At the moment the central thrust of our economic policy makes no sense. We are doing all the wrong things, for all the wrong reasons, to protect all the wrong people. No country has ever emerged from a depression by raising taxes, bailing out useless banks and putting good people on the dole. The policy of this government will turn our country into a large debt-servicing machine for a generation.

We have to make a stand and realise that the economic solution now being proffered by the mainstream is precisely the type of thinking that got us into the mess in the first place. In fact, laughably many of the people now advocating that there is now 'no alternative' are the very same people who never saw the bust coming and who told us in the boom that Ireland was different and we would experience a 'soft landing'.

Ireland is no different. There is an alternative based on sound economic theory and empirical evidence from all over the world. In every other country that has successfully engineered a recovery from debt deflation and depression, there is not one instance of a country adopting the policies our government is now adopting. We are now implementing policies for which there is absolutely no basis in economic theory. We have been taken over by economic fetishists intent on using the country as some sort of bizarre experiment. To be led up the garden path once in the past 10 years by a bunch of charlatans is a tragedy, to be led down the swanney twice by the same people is unforgiveable.

This book is about the alternative.

The little boy with the red hair on the polished second-hand bike couldn't understand the world of adults, with their worries, frowns and hushed conversations. His world was one of bike races, football matches and swimming in Seapoint every summer.

What was it like to be big? What would it be like when he put on a suit and drove behind his own son, if he ever had one? Would he too make funny faces at the traffic lights, which made the two of them laugh?

As he got older, he realised that you are the same person, just with something new called responsibilities. And the only difference is that when you were a boy, your dad worried about the responsibilities and made you feel safe.

But now that you are big and your dad is gone, everything comes down to you and in a crisis, we all have to take responsibility. This means taking risks and replacing mantras with hard thinking.

The little boy on the bike, racing to school with his dad behind him, realised that's what being big is all about.

| LENIHAN AND ME

On Wednesday, 17 September at 10.20 in the evening there was a knock on our front door. Our bell was broken, so the visitor had to knock loudly. I hoped he wouldn't wake the children who had woken as I'd gone out to Centra for milk and biscuits 40 minutes earlier. It was late and it was a school night.

The phone had rung about an hour earlier, so I was expecting him. Even so, as we'd never had a politician in our house, never mind a Minister for Finance, seeing the bulk of Brian Lenihan at the door came as a surprise.

In fact, I had only once met the Minister before and that had been in an RTÉ radio studio for 'Saturday View' less than two weeks before, on 6 September. That day he was confident and calm.

The man who appeared at my door was a different character. There was still the confidence and yet he was nervous and fidgety. His suit looked as if he'd slept in it. He had heavy bags under his eyes, his tie was undone and he held a copy of that day's *Irish Independent.*

Days before this late-night visit, Lehman Brothers had gone bust. That was on Saturday, 13 September. Merrill Lynch went on Sunday, 14th and AIG—the world's largest insurer—went bang on Tuesday, 16th. The financial world was collapsing and the Irish banks were worth pennies, not pounds; cents not euros.

The banks were running out of money. Ordinary people were beginning to panic. We were starting to twig that we had been lied to. My mother had called me earlier in the day to ask whether she should take her life's savings out of Bank of Ireland. I told her that the risk was now too great and there was only one thing that could be done: take your savings out and put them in a continental bank trading here. After all, the morons who got us, and their banks, into this mess wouldn't shed a tear for her, so why should she worry about them?

If something radical was not done and done quickly, it was crystal clear to me that the Irish banks would experience a traditional run, with depositors taking out their savings, and the banks would go bust. That one thing, at least, was certain.

The Minister walked straight through the hall and headed directly into the kitchen as if he knew where he was going. Jaded, he sat down and turned off his phone.

Our dog Sasha—a Labrador puppy—got very excited about a visitor coming in the dead of night, way after the children had gone to sleep. She slobbered all over the Minister's suit and tried to make off with his left trouser leg. At least she broke the ice. He laughed and went off on a tangent about dogs, kind of nervously. After a few minutes, Sasha settled down under the kitchen table, rested her head on his brogues and fell asleep. The Minister obviously preferred to let sleeping dogs lie. He was quite concerned about not wanting to wake the puppy from the pillow of his instep. But this meant that he sat awkwardly contorted, squashed in at the top of the table, the movement of his legs constrained by the snoozing Labrador.

Taking note of his 12 o'clock shadow and red eyes, I suggested that he should catch a kip too. He said he'd doze off in the car on the way home.

Then he pulled a bulb of garlic out of his pocket and started to peel it. It was one of the odd moments in a long night of odd moments. In subsequent meetings, the raw garlic was produced and squashed into bowls of soup. This time he just peeled a clove and left it on the table.

He explained to me that the garlic gave him strength and kept him healthy and alert. I had no reason to doubt him. He went on to say that he had been chomping raw garlic all summer, since he'd got the finance job. I didn't know what to think but when you have the Minister for Finance of a country that is going down the tubes sitting opposite you at your kitchen table, about to wolf down raw garlic, you have to suspend your disbelief.

I made him a cup of tea. That was to be the first of many that night. We asked the driver would he like a cup of tea too. He said no. Had he known how long we were to talk, he'd probably have asked for a camp bed.

I felt sorry for Brian Lenihan that night. He looked exhausted. He had been working day and night and he was trying to understand everything. This must have been very difficult for a man who had spent all his life in the law. I thought to myself that this would be like me being thrown in as Attorney General in the middle of the country's worst constitutional crisis. I wouldn't know where to start.

He told me he'd been breaking himself into the job and economics by reading Alan Greenspan's biography. *Sweet Jesus!* I thought. That was the worst place to start. That epoch was over. It was like a Minister for Transport a hundred years ago trying to learn about cars by reading a book about fast horses. Greenspan's nonsense caused this mess and I told the Minister as much. With that out of the way, I got a pencil and paper and we started scribbling. This was the way I'd learned economics years ago, always joining the dots as if you are piecing together a big puzzle. If that is related to this, then this will happen and if that happens, this is likely to move and so on and so on.

He gave me the impression that he was quite isolated from his officials. He repeated again and again, 'They just don't get it, we don't have much time.'

He was confused but was getting to grips with things. I offered him a glass of wine. He told me he wasn't boozing until after the Budget. I said the Budget was the least of his worries.

That night, even after a few minutes, it was clear that here was a man who could pick things up quickly. But we were starting pretty much from scratch. It was also obvious that he was at best sceptical about the advice he was getting. Given the spin that was coming out of the government, I wasn't too surprised and I was quite relieved that he doubted the Regulator and the Governor of the Central Bank when they continued to parrot platitudes about the banks being fine and being stress tested.

He kicked off by saying if his officials knew he was here in my house, there'd be war. They thought I was a maverick. I took it as a compliment.

He got to the point quickly. He was sitting opposite me and he had a habit of looking around rather than catching my eye as if he expected someone to join us at any minute. I told him we were on our own, just the pair of us and the puppy.

He leaned over and, in a hoarse voice, almost whispering, he said, 'What would you do?'

He asked me my opinion, so I gave it.

'SATURDAY VIEW'

The true extent of the mess our banks were in seemed to have suddenly dawned on him over the previous 24 hours, and the options the civil servants were outlining to him struck me as unrealistic given what we were facing.

The banks were having a financing crisis. Their pathetic loan books were not the immediate problem. The problem that evening was that they were running out of money and any action that didn't solve this immediate crisis would not be particularly helpful.

The reason I say Brian Lenihan 'suddenly' came to this realisation was because this strange story of Brian and me began less than two weeks earlier in an RTÉ studio. I had never met Brian Lenihan. I had no reason to. But this first encounter prompted a series of events in which the Minister began by peeling garlic and drinking tea in our kitchen and ended with the announcement of the bank guarantee less than two weeks later.

On 6 September, on 'Saturday View'—the RTÉ radio show—the Minister for Finance and the Opposition spokesperson on Finance, Richard Bruton, discussed the then faltering economy. There were two commentators on the panel. I was one of them and my colleague in the *Irish Independent* Brendan Keenan was the other.

During the interview, the presenter asked the Minister about the slump in house prices and tax revenue. The Minister claimed that there was little he could do because 'the Irish people decided collectively to have a housing boom' and therefore everyone in general, and by extension nobody in particular, was ultimately to blame.

This is the spin that was and still is being put out from the top. He batted well, making the narrow but legitimate point to Richard Bruton that the opposition parties had not seen the collapse of the economy coming either.

The discussion was about to get down to the dull and uninformative IBEC *v.* ICTU set piece when I interjected and said that the whole discussion on the economy was missing the single most important fact: we would definitely have a banking crisis in the coming months and one of our banks would be bust by Christmas.

My reason for saying this was not scaremongering but, having worked on both sides of the fence—as a central banker and as an investment banker—in previous crises in various parts of the world, I'd seen what happens. It's always the same.

The Minister—maybe because he was new to the job and had never seen this before—narrowed his eyes, leaned over and gravely warned that that was 'dangerous talk'. I had heard this 'dangerous talk' put-down before.

He went on to say that he wanted 'to reassure your listeners' that there was no problem with the Irish banks. He said that the Financial Regulator had stress tested the banks and they were fine. He said that the Governor of the Central Bank had reassured a parliamentary committee that there were no problems in the banks. He finally—and with hindsight laughably—suggested that 'those analysts and agencies who look at banks' were happy with the Irish banks, referring to completely discredited outfits like Standard & Poor's.

Richard Bruton agreed with the Minister, as did Brendan Keenan: this talk was unhelpful and highly dangerous. The discussion ended and it became clear to me that either the Minister deemed it better to dupe the people and risk their savings being plundered by a bunch of incompetents than to tell them the truth or he wasn't being made aware of how serious the situation was.

In fairness to Minister Lenihan, even if he was worried about the banks back then, he couldn't have said it publicly, but I know now that he wasn't concerned because he wasn't being told the truth. The Central Bank and the Regulators as well as his top officials at the Department of Finance either didn't know what was going on or, if they did, they sought to protect their own patch, their own little fiefdom, rather than do what was best for the country. My hunch at the time was the latter.

I had seen this type of protective behaviour at the Central Bank during my time there. Often it seemed that the number one concern at the top of the Civil Service was personal survival rather than the national interest.

My hunch was later confirmed. While the Minister was on radio busy reassuring us that the banks were fine, the National Treasury Management Agency—effectively a branch of the Department of Finance—was busy pulling its deposits out of Anglo Irish Bank because it felt the bank was too risky, and it didn't tell him!

In the next few days, he would change his mind on the banks' position because events were overtaking him and everyone else.

THE BULLSHIT DIET

During the following week, the Establishment wheeled out expert after expert to reassure the people that the banking system was fine. They told us the Irish banks were 'well capitalised' and they had been 'stress tested'. They had no subprime problems, so we were told.

Yet it was obvious to anyone who had worked in similar crises in the past, that we were within days of a run on Irish banks that would have left the average person, who trusted the banks, their good name and the credibility of the institutions, with no money. I had seen this happen before in places where I had worked in Argentina, Uruguay, Russia and Serbia. The big boys always get out first. And, as has happened in Ireland on numerous occasions, the 'little' people would pay.

As we walked out of the RTÉ studio, following the radio interview, the Minister jovially suggested that I come in and chat to him about the banks. He joked, as is his way, that everyone else was advising him so why shouldn't I?

Money continued to flood out of Ireland and our banks over the following week and, as the mid-weekend of September approached, the markets began to freeze. No one would lend money to anyone and a number of the big investment banks looked as if they would go under. Lehman Brothers, which had just survived the Bear Stearns collapse of St Patrick's Day 2008, was extremely vulnerable. Few thought the US authorities would let it go under.

Our banks, which had created their own ludicrous model of borrowing most of the money they needed from the international money markets on a very short-term basis, were weeks from bankruptcy. If this market froze, they were gone. They could not borrow more from anywhere. Many banks—and Irish banks in particular with their huge property portfolios and their made up business model of borrowing overnight to fund mortgages—were dead ducks.

But still the Establishment lied to the Irish people and said everything was fine. No, we have not hit an iceberg. No, that is not a sinking feeling you are experiencing. Any talk of drowning and making plans to save yourself is dangerous.

Early that week, Joe Duffy picked up on my comments on the 'Saturday View' interview on 'Liveline', and the 'Liveline' effect ran its course. I received a number of calls from senior bankers in Dublin accusing me of causing panic and being irresponsible.

But the people who were being properly irresponsible were those bleating that all was fine in the Irish banks because they were endangering the ordinary person's savings by not making the man on the street aware that the big corporations were taking money out of the Irish banks. If the little guy left his savings in there, when the big guy had taken the savings out, the bank would collapse and the little guy would lose everything.

THE VORTEX

On Tuesday, 16 September—the day AIG went bust—I got a call from a researcher at 'Prime Time' to ask whether I'd appear that evening and clarify what I thought was going on. At this stage the situation was critical.

I went on 'Prime Time' with the head of the Irish Banking Federation, whose last job, incidentally, was Secretary General of the Fianna Fáil party. This time, the 'dangerous talk' had turned to 'loose talk'. I was accused of 'loose talk'. Anyone who doubted the robustness of the Irish banks was engaging in 'loose talk'. Again the Establishment—not just the politicians, but something deeper in our country, the system—was rallying to hunt out the doubters and defend itself.

The same old mantra of stress testing and the banks being adequately capitalised was being spouted. And every time this line was spun and every time somebody at home was reassured by this line, that person's savings were being put at greater and greater risk.

We were witness to the Establishment—the insiders in Ireland (the senior bankers, the top civil servants, the lawyers and accountants who service the big firms, etc.)—defending itself to the last, denying that there was any issue.

On 'Prime Time' I repeated that the Irish banking system would implode if we didn't do something quickly. The problem wouldn't go away; it would get worse. But that evening driving home from RTÉ, I knew I had to do something else. The Establishment, in a last gasp effort to save itself, would drive the whole country over the edge without a thought.

I decided to do something I'd never done in my life. I decided to take up the Minister on his 6 September offer to talk about economics. It would probably have been easier not to have made the call, but I had worked in the Central Bank during the 1992/1993 currency crisis and I knew from experience that the mandarins wouldn't do anything out of the ordinary.

Also, having worked in two of Europe's largest investment banks in similar banking crises in Russia, Asia and Argentina, I knew that doing something out of the ordinary was exactly what was demanded. The financial markets often take huge risks when they smell blood. Counter-intuitively, they are at their most vulnerable just when they think they are invincible and, therefore, they underestimate the power of sovereign governments. Resolute action can stop them dead in their tracks but it has to be unexpected and unprecedented.

I picked up the phone and called the Minister for Finance.

The following evening my phone rang. Shortly afterwards I got a knock on the door.

We sat and drank tea. I asked him how bad the situation was. He was guarded, as I expected him to be. He was the Minister for Finance and I was an economic commentator, after all. But it soon became clear, as he revealed, 'The situation is worse that even you think and we all know what you think!'

I took this to mean not only that the banks could not roll over their debts, but that he had only just been told this truth. We had weeks at best, days at worst. My own reckoning was that the banks had a few weeks' financing. The Minister indicated that the problem was more acute. The most revealing thing about our conversation was that it was AIB not Anglo Irish that had the most severe funding problems. Ireland's biggest bank was actually our biggest problem. I was aware that the Irish banks could no longer finance themselves and were borrowing in the very short-term and rolling over. This is why I'd warned on 6 September on 'Saturday View' that we would have a banking crisis. What I didn't know was the bank that was pretending to be the most prudent was possibly the most delinquent. We were on the precipice.

On the table from the Department of Finance was a plan for the two big banks to take over the smaller and out of control Anglo Irish Bank and Irish Nationwide. This was the big banks' ploy, which was to hold their nose and suggest that they were fine but the two smaller ones were basket cases. I reminded the Minister that they were all at the same game and merging them wouldn't ease the liquidity crisis. In fact, if the financial markets weren't willing to lend, for example, to Bank of

Ireland because they were worried about its balance sheet, they'd be much less willing to lend to Bank of Ireland with the Anglo Irish toxic balance sheet added to it. The department's blueprint made no sense, unless the intention was to deflect criticism from the two big banks for optic's sake. The big banks had run themselves up the same cul-de-sac and were stuck. Anything that tried to disguise that would be laughed at by the financial markets.

So we to-ed and fro-ed with what had been done before. I had worked for UBS (Union Bank of Switzerland) in Zurich in the years after Switzerland experienced a banking crisis in the early 1990s. The Swiss government guaranteed all liabilities of the banking system even though the banks' balance sheets were a number of times bigger than the country's GDP. A guarantee had worked there and the Swiss cantonal banks that had gone bust gradually recovered. During these years, I'd also worked in Sweden where I'd seen the Swedes guarantee all their deposits in the face of a banking crisis. I told the Minister it seemed to me that Sweden's reaction was an interesting place to start.

Of course, the aim of any action in Ireland in the last week of September 2008 was not to see the banks gradually recover, but to stop the immediate crisis. We could pick up the pieces afterwards, pick over the banks' balance sheets and start again. If some had to go bust when the guarantee had expired, well, so be it.

Above all, we needed to protect the ordinary savers, not bond or equity holders. They were playing a different game. They were in the business of gambling. But the savers, the ordinary people who had bank accounts, needed protection. The crux of the issue was that the problem had gone way beyond normal remedies. The Minister was aware of that. The officials in the department were also advocating a guarantee of people's deposits but only to a certain level, which was not unusual in these circumstances. However, I argued because the Irish banks' funding had become so unstable, if we didn't guarantee the funding as well as the deposits, the banks would come crashing down and you would have had to come up with the money immediately for people's deposits. The whole point of a guarantee is that you want to avoid paying out right away.

Now, on 17 September, we were stuck and only the nuclear option would work.

Over tea and digestive biscuits, to the background noise of the gentle snoring of an eight-month-old puppy, the Minister naturally worried about pushing the button.

I showed him an article I had written earlier that evening for my regular column in the *Sunday Business Post* which outlined the bank guarantee plan. I had wanted to get the idea down on paper so that I was clear. Because we were all groping in the dark. This was economic policy-making formulated in a kitchen and made up on the spot.

I told him that the article would be published on Sunday and high-lighted on the front page. He was worried that this guarantee idea was too radical. And I could understand this because he was the man who had to make the decision, not me. I was only a commentator scribbling away; he was the Minister. I could sympathise with him. In fact, I did.

I told him I thought we were in the vortex or at least might end up there. He simply had to guarantee everything for a limited period to make sure that an illiquid dilemma didn't lead to an insolvency catastrophe.

But, he argued, warming to the idea, what if we got the insolvencies? We could never afford to cover all the liabilities. This was the risk, a huge risk, but one that could be reduced if the guarantee was not extended beyond a fixed period. I argued that over the two years of the guarantee, the true extent of the bad debts would become apparent as would the depth of the recession and, armed with this knowledge, he could then choose which banks to save, or not, in an orderly fashion. If banks can't finance themselves after two years, well, they have no reason to be in business.

I said that this was not the perfect solution but we were in a crisis and anything we did now was from a position of weakness. The US had let Lehman go and it had prompted the market to freeze up. It had written a huge cheque for its banking system's toxic debt; we didn't have the money to do this so couldn't. There was simply no alternative. We had to do something that cost nothing in the immediate term but might stop the money flowing out of the economy. Otherwise the system would break and with it would go the savings of thousands of ordinary people.

We both agreed that this would mean saving banks that probably didn't deserve to be saved but I contended that we didn't have time to disentangle the good from the bad. The bad would simply drag the good over the cliff with them and we'd all end up in the abyss. This way, if the plan worked, he and his officials would have time to unpick the mess.

Meanwhile it would be essential to make the guarantee conditional so that the Minister would be in control and the banks would be working for him, not him working for the banks.

The logic of the guarantee was to give the banks time to sort out their balance sheet problems. If this could not be done, then the banks would be wound down after the guarantee. A new bank would emerge because it always does in this situation. The old banks' depositors are guaranteed and moved to the new bank and the assets of the old bank are sold off in an organised fashion as would be the case in any receivership situation. The creditors of the bank lose out and we start all over again.

That night, it never struck me that the banks would be allowed to get away with what they did in subsequent months. I never thought the terms of the guarantee would be so loose and so all-encompassing. Nor did I think the subsequent legislation which was to follow the announcement would be introduced with so few conditions on the banks who were ultimately saved by it.

We outlined how the plan might work on a piece of paper. It was well past one in the morning when we decided to call it a day. He stuffed the paper in his pocket and was about to go when he said he'd have another cup of tea.

He suggested that this wasn't a Fianna Fáil house. I don't know how he could tell from the kitchen. In fact, it was a nothing house, but he spoke to my wife about the North for some time. My wife is from a part of the North where even the SDLP wouldn't dare run a candidate—they'd lose their deposit. So it was odd for her to be chatting to the Irish grandson of a Republican freedom fighter, as she was the Irish granddaughter of someone who was offered an OBE from the Queen for services to the Empire. They chatted for a while and it was clear that Lenihan was a Northern politics addict—which I suppose is not surprising. For people like me, from a Dublin suburb and with no real leanings either way, the North was always a foreign place. I suppose that's what happens. It's people like me who end up marrying Northerners and understanding the place possibly better than those who took an interest in its politics from the beginning.

The chat ebbed and flowed and there was more tea. I felt like Mrs

Doyle by this stage. He wouldn't take a drink and, by the time we finished up, it was nearing two and we were all wrecked.

I walked him out to his car and he reiterated the fact that his officials would explode if they knew he was there.

BEIJING

The Minister called me the next day, and again on Friday, 19th when he rang to say they were contemplating a partial guarantee. My view was that a partial guarantee would just alert the world—those who were asleep—to the extent of the problem and would accelerate capital flight not avert it. From then on we spoke on a daily basis, but he still wasn't convinced and, from what I could gather, his officials in the department were dead set against a full guarantee. But they didn't seem to be coming up with an alternative that had any hope of stopping the crisis.

I told him I was flying to China on Tuesday, 23 September for the World Economic Forum in Beijing, but that the phone would be on.

To keep up with events, I kept in constant contact with old friends in the financial markets in Switzerland who told me that the situation in Ireland was deteriorating on an hourly basis. You can't talk to anyone in Dublin about these things because everyone is compromised and everyone lies.

I decided to use my articles in the *Sunday Business Post* and the *Irish Independent* to outline the plan and how it would work. Over the following week, three different articles appeared advocating the guarantee as the only option: on 21 September in the *Sunday Business Post*, on 24 September in the *Irish Independent* and finally on 28 September in the *Sunday Business Post*—the day before it was announced.

The purpose of the articles was to keep the pressure on the Minister to remain open to the idea of a full guarantee and they could also serve to ventilate a new idea to a wider audience.

Throughout the week, the Minister was on the phone but it seemed to me that the guarantee would not be introduced as the officials still thought the merger of the bigger and smaller banks was the right way to go. On Saturday, 27 September, I decided to go for a traditional Chinese foot massage in the early afternoon. I didn't expect anyone to call because of the time difference, Beijing being eight hours ahead of Dublin. On that day the Cabinet was meeting for an all-day session on the crisis, the Minister had told me the day before. So, as a young Chinese girl was slapping the bejaysus out of my feet and shins, the phone rang beside me. It was the Minister.

'Where the hell are you?'

'You don't want to know!'

We chatted and I told him that from what I was hearing in international markets, and the World Economic Forum meeting which was full of bankers and policy makers, the news from Ireland was bad. I had heard that the banks were done for and it was only a matter of hours now.

He hesitated, which is absolutely normal and I could understand it. Clearly he was talking to others as well and had to make his mind up. This was an impossible position. I could sense down the phone a man with the weight of the world on his shoulders.

He said to me, 'Are you sure about this, David?'

I remember thinking how bizarre and yet catastrophic the situation had become, as I looked down, trousers pulled up to the knee, my naked feet in a red plastic bucket, getting pulverised by a migrant girl from the Chinese provinces. I caught her eye and she giggled in that Chinese way, covering her mouth.

'No, Brian. I'm not sure it will work. But I am sure of one thing: we have no alternative.'

He phoned again on Sunday, 28 September. I had written an unequivocal article in the *Sunday Business Post* which turned out to be the final article before the decision. It had been picked up by the morning radio shows, particularly the 'Marian Finucane Show' which politicians and their media handlers listen to religiously.

When I spoke to the Minister that evening, he was like a different person. I had no idea what had changed or whether he had made a decision either way. He was joking and in good spirits and he seemed to be relieved. I couldn't figure it out. He asked about Beijing and what it was like.

I wished him luck in the week ahead. He chuckled and said he might need it. I heard him laughing as he hung up.

As I touched down in Munich on Tuesday morning on an overnight flight from Shanghai, my phone rang: RTÉ radio asking for an interview on 'News at One'. At that stage I had no idea what had happened in Dublin during the night; I didn't know that the guarantee had been adopted.

Sean O'Rourke, a combative host at the best of times, reading from the *Sunday Business Post* article of two days before, demanded to know how the guarantee would work. The article, together with the two previous ones, comprised, according to him, the only blueprint out there. He asked me if I spoke to the Minister before the decision. I denied it as I had assured Lenihan I would, if asked.

I told O'Rourke that, as far as I understood, the guarantee was the first in a number of complementary stages which would involve a clearing out of the banks' top brass and now 'the bankers will be working for Mr Lenihan, rather than him working for them'. My assumption was always that if some banks were complete basket cases, then they would be wound up in an orderly fashion after the guarantee had lapsed. This would take the form of a normal receivership or a new bank might pick up the assets, such as the branch network, of one of the fallen banks. We had bought time—time to do the right thing.

A little later the Minister called me. He was euphoric. He guffawed, 'The Brits are furious, so we must be doing something right'. The dyed-in-the-wool Republican who was on display in our kitchen two weeks before was still there.

Things had stabilised, he said. The Germans were being a bit tricky but that would pass. We were back from the brink and the financial markets loved the move.

I suggested he should really go for it and clean up the whole system. He was the boss now. He could orchestrate a clean sweep of the old regime and put the economy back on track. We'd meet up over the weekend. He had to go to Brussels so we arranged to meet discretely at Bewleys in Leopardstown on Saturday morning.

I put the phone down, thinking we were now in a position of strength and hard decisions would flow from this, and that the people who had brought the country to its knees would be brought to theirs. I expected our most delinquent banks would eventually go to the wall, with the Irish State acting as broker, not principal, in negotiations between the bankrupt Irish banks and their creditors.

How wrong could I have been?

Chapter 3 ~

| STEAK AND CHIPS

IRELAND'S SERENGETI

If you want to visualise what is now happening in the economy, think about the great plains of Africa. Have you ever seen the wonderful image of the rains flooding the savannah of the Serengeti? The cameramen on David Attenborough's fantastic series 'Life on Earth' mounted a camera on a helicopter and for weeks on end filmed the migration of animals and the gradual rehydration of the Serengeti plains. It is one of the most memorable sequences of photography in a series of exceptional imagery.

Once a year, between October and November, the arid, sun-parched plain undergoes an extraordinary transformation as the rains bring life and abundance. Flowers and vegetation bloom, and animals and insects return to the lush pasture to graze, mate and generally do their thing. At the height of the rainy season, the Serengeti is a fertile arcadia of wildebeest, crocodiles and zebra. All God's creatures are swanning around, revelling in the extraordinary transforming power of water.

Then, as the seasons change, the waters recede. Water disappears, first from the extremities and then progressively retreats until the last remaining verdant area is a small knot around an almost dried up river. All the animals migrate, the vegetation dies and the sun scorches the earth. Where once there was abundance and plenty, there is now only dust and barrenness. The burnt earth can't sustain any life.

One way to think about why you can't get an overdraft any more, why your bank is cutting back on your working capital or why, despite wanting to trade in your car, you can't get car finance anywhere, is to compare the flow of credit all around our country to the flow of water in the Serengeti. For years, Ireland was starved of credit. We were the financial equivalent of the Serengeti in the dry season. Credit, where it did exist, was the preserve of a small well-connected elite, and the hand on the money tap, turning it on and off, deciding who got it and who didn't, belonged to the local bank manager.

Hundreds of thousands of ordinary people could not get any credit. What's worse is we had a young population who wanted to spend and needed jobs. These young people were full of ambition and energy, but their ideas always bounced off the 'no connections = no credit' glass ceiling. Without credit, we couldn't finance lots of things we wanted to do, so many of us chose to emigrate rather than stay here unemployed. For most of the history of our State, Ireland failed economically neither from a lack of brains nor from drive but from a lack of credit.

This is what makes our present predicament so unforgiveable, because the moment credit became available to us, we didn't spend it wisely, acknowledging its preciousness. In contrast, our banks blew it by inflating our property bubble, spending other people's money like a drunk, bragging gobshite at a stag night and, in so doing, sent a signal to the rest of the world that we are not a serious nation when it comes to finance. We have reverted to type: good fun, great company but just not serious.

But let's go back to our Serengeti image. We were parched and then, suddenly, when we joined the euro, money flowed in. The rains came.

In practical terms, we were given the pin number for the ATMs of old German savers. We took that cash willingly and with gusto. The typical Gunter is old and saves a lot and the typical Paddy is young and hasn't the arse in his trousers. So the banks borrowed all the cash they could.

But for all its faults, credit, like water, is absolutely essential for society to thrive and function. It's a question of getting the balance right. Credit allows us to finance and make concrete plans for the future that would otherwise remain pipe dreams. In Ireland, unfortunately, we got the balance wrong, so instead of bathing in sufficient credit we ended up drowning in the stuff.

When credit recedes, so too does economic life. Like the water cycle in the Serengeti, credit follows a pattern. Initially it is only plentiful around the river, but then, with the rains, it cascades into remote regions of the plain. These outer reaches only experience life for a few weeks of the year, when they are joyfully submerged before they are choked off again.

The global financial system operates in the same way. When credit is plentiful and investors aren't too worried about risk, money flows into every nook and cranny of the system.

Internationally, credit rating agencies are prepared to give the thumbs up to almost any country or company and what follows is nothing less than a deluge of free—or at least cheap—money. Other people's cash is available everywhere to everyone.

So in the case of the Irish boom, no ambition was too overblown to get finance. All over the country, housing estates with no economic or demographic logic were financed. During the boom, less than half of our new houses were being bought by people who actually wanted to live in them, and yet more and more estates were built. Many of these are now 'ghost estates' which lie empty. They are the economic equivalent of the nether regions of the Serengeti, which experience water once a year and are buzzing for a few weeks. Then when the rain recedes, it is hard to believe that anything ever lived there.

In Ireland, we were offered car loans, holiday loans and interest-free mortgages. Banks' coffers overflowed and they lent and lent and lent. And then when they should have been worried about the solvency of projects, they simply lent more to paper over the cashflow problems. In fact, some of the commentators who are now prominently criticising the banks were, as late as 2007, advocating the creation of a subprime market in Ireland into which the banks could have lent more and more money!

But unlike the animals in the Serengeti, who are conditioned to understand the limitations of the natural water cycle, most of us (including the very people who were lending the cash) have no appreciation of the economic cycle. And humans, for all our sophistication, have a clear blind spot when it comes to learning from economic history. We are optimists. Most of us are willing to believe that this time it's different. We allow ourselves to forget that things can change quite quickly.

Suddenly, in a matter of weeks, like a change in the seasons on the great African plains, Ireland changed from an economy with loads of credit to one of none at all.

Most people find this hard to understand. How can we go from being 'apparently' the second richest people in Europe to flirting with default? How could it have happened so quickly? And who is to blame?

THE STEAK AND CHIPS INDEX

Over the course of the last year, the questions I am asked most frequently on the street, on the train, in cafes and bars by complete strangers who are perplexed and more than a little bit worried are: Where did all the money go? Weren't we supposed to be a Tiger economy?

A good place to start unpicking this dilemma is with the Irish banks. They will recur again and again in our story. Let's try to piece together this puzzle.

When you cut through all the nonsense and spin that is being put out now, largely in an effort to protect political, institutional or individual reputations, one piece of evidence stands out.

Ireland was unique. No other euro country abused the currency like we did. Yes, some German banks are in trouble, but the trouble is restricted to certain banks and specifically certain departments in certain banks. Yes, Spain had a property boom but no country experienced the financial madness that we did and no country is in the same mess that we are. This is important to appreciate because it means that something was going on in Ireland that did not happen elsewhere. It wasn't so much euro membership itself that caused the problem, but how the Irish banks alone used and abused that membership for their own ends.

Why did Ireland experience financial madness after adopting the euro on a scale unmatched by other European countries? Think about Portugal, Greece, Belgium, the Netherlands, Italy and France—all these countries could, like Ireland, have used the euro as an excuse to borrow from the richer countries, mainly Germany. But they didn't.

To help understand why we borrowed like crazy and no one else in the euro zone did and what it did to us, we can examine the highly sensitive 'steak and chips' index.

Picture the scene. You have landed from your holliers in Spain or somewhere else warm on the Continent. You are a bit hassled. The kids have been a nightmare on the flight, and the lads drinking the last of the Sangria in the row in front got a bit out of order, in the way strangers drinking through a hangover always do, making you nervous. You know their 'happy drunk' faces have been left behind in Spain.

All told, you just want to get home and flop into bed for a good sleep before you have to face work tomorrow.

The taxi pulls up. You can already sense that this will be a lippy one by the way he saunters around to pop the boot. The way he is poured into his Dubs jersey gives him the appearance of a man who thinks that blue bubblewrap is a good look. He makes no effort at all to help you with the bags despite seeing the screaming kids hanging out of you, hitting each other.

The small tricolour on the back window should have warned you. It's a new thing—there to make sure you don't mistake him for a Nigerian, apparently.

He eyes you in the mirror, looks you up and down, nonchalantly spits out the window and then, unsolicited, launches into a vicious tirade against the country.

You are impaled, speechless, but more than anything else you are shocked by the pitch of his voice. It is so comically high. You were expecting a gravelly Ronnie Drew after lowering 10 pints and you get a camp, breathless Vincent Browne after a mouthful of helium. He sounds like one of 98 FM's Toll Trolls.

'It's a fuckin' kip, love.'

He screeches as he swerves around an abandoned traffic cone, one of 20 someone has just knocked over 'for the craic'.

'And he's worser'—pointing to Brian Cowen in a shiny blue suit on the front of the *Herald*, which makes our dear leader look like an obese bus driver.

'Hasn't a clue.'

He taps the side of his head.

'It's all the wan—none of dem has a bleedin' rashers.'

You've heard it all before. You try to drift off, wondering whether to stop for milk and bread on the way home.

'Dat wan, Harney' is mentioned a few times in less than flattering terms before you are out of the airport. Respectfully, she's always given her full title of 'dat wan, Harney'.

'String dem up, all of dem—every last wan of de fuckin' eejits.'

He rearranges his arse in the hollow, the way taxi drivers do when they are on a roll. The highly inflammable Dubs jersey is sticking to the plastic seat. Man-made fibres attract, obviously.

'Oh Jaysus, sorry, love, sorry, de language an' all. Didn't see de chisellers der.'

How could he miss them? He calms down and just when you think it's all over as he punches the dial away from 'The Last Word' he changes tack.

The inevitable 'steak and chips' index is flagged.

'Alicante, it was, last month. The brudder has a gaff der. In a fuckin' beau-ti-ful complex. Top of the range, no toerags, the crème de menthe of developments. Me, me mot, his mot and his mot's ma.'

You are trying to picture it, the five of them scalded with the sunburn on the balcony, screaming at other dandies down at the pool.

'Me and her went out for a meal.'

You are trying to picture 'her'.

'I goh steak, chips. She goh some class of fish an' a bottle of red, two cappuccinos and a sweet and a Baileys for her and a pint for me for finisher, offers an' all.'

'How much?'

'Guess?'

You, warming to this, are about to offer a high bid to keep him in a state of apoplectic indignation.

'Swear on me mudder's life'—as he touches the Virgin Mary on the dashboard—'twenty fi-ev Jaysus Yo Yos for de boat of us! Ye wouldn't get Burdocks for dat bleedin' price.

'And four litre bottles of Smear-noff!'

He pauses for dramatic effect.

'Four Jaysus bottles of Smear-fuckin-noff, for a bleedin' score!'

His eyes are nearly popping out of his head.

'Don't get me fuckin' talkin' an' all. Tings is all ourra whack here, man!'

What the taxi driver was summing up, much more comprehensively than many economists you hear spouting on the telly, was the state of Ireland's competitiveness vis-à-vis our euro partners and how our borrowing binge has made us ridiculously expensive.

In economics, the price of all things should be more or less the same across a monetary union such as we have in Europe. If there are persistent differences between one country and the rest, then things are considerably out of synch in that country.

As we all know from the 'steak and chips' index, Ireland is way out of line with other countries. We are twice or three times more expensive.

Now how did that happen in less than five years?

FROM STEAK AND CHIPS TO FOIE GRAS

Usually a country can only spend as much as its people save. When a country starts spending more than its people save, it has to borrow from abroad. This is called a current account deficit. And this figure gives investors an idea of the sustainability of the country and, in particular, the ability of the country to pay back its debts.

As a result, modern economics has developed all sorts of ratios and measurements that act as warning signs, not unlike traffic lights. When the current account deficit gets too big, the lights flash amber. This system works reasonably well for countries that have their own currencies.

But when a country joins a monetary union with bigger countries and it gives up its independent currency, the financial traffic lights stop working. No one cares about the warning signs because the little country is tied to the bigger countries by a single currency and that means there is no currency risk for investors. But this does not mean there is no risk; there is just a different kind of risk which is masked by the single currency.

Once a country joins a single currency, all that is left to police the economy is the integrity and foresight of that country's banks, regulators and government. These people's abilities and motives become essential for the health of the economy.

Now getting back to the 'steak and chips' index, our overinflated prices were created because our banks used the safety of the euro to borrow as much as they feasibly could to inflate our economy. The 'safety of the euro' refers to the fact that if we had our own currency—the punt—and we went on a binge, the traffic lights would have worked. The financial markets would be concerned about the current account deficit and would have worried that the whole thing could come crumbling down around our ears, as is happening now. But with our own currency, they would have started to worry some time ago after using basic economic indicators like inflation, wage increases or our deteriorating balance of payments deficit as warning signs. This would have meant that, internationally, Ireland would have been seen as risky as we binged away, and the foreign investors who finance us would have demanded a higher interest rate to cover them for the higher risk.

This higher interest rate would in turn have made it more expensive for the banks to borrow abroad, and for us in turn to borrow from the banks. In addition, the currency—the punt if we had it—would have risen as money flowed into the country. The rising punt would have put pressure on those companies in Ireland that export, resulting in people losing their jobs.

So gradually, with these brakes on, we'd have had less borrowing and higher unemployment and the boom would have been choked off before the crash. But that didn't happen because when you are in the euro you don't have these signals. The banks thought that they could borrow as much as they wanted, indefinitely, and that's what they tried to do.

Therefore, when we ran out of our own savings, we borrowed other peoples' money, and when we ran out of our own workers, we borrowed other countries' workers.

In the past five years, Irish people got into debt 15 times faster than the average European.[1] All this money had to go somewhere. It cascaded into the country and seeped into everything. First it went into houses, then into wages, then into the price of cars, services, food and all across the board. The new cash simply shunted on from one thing to another, pushing up the price of everything.

Where did all this money come from in the first place?

In *The Pope's Children*—written in 2005—I introduced the reader to an elderly German character called Udo Lindenburg. Udo lived then and still does in Stuttgart (not far from where Ray Houghton lobbed an agonizingly slow header over the gambling-mad English keeper Peter Shilton).

Udo, like many millions of Germans, is a fastidious type and in the immortal words of the former Dublin City manager John Redmond, he could be accurately described as a 'heavy saver'. Apart from a nudist holiday once a year in Dalmatia where scores of geriatric Germans swan around with their tackle out—not a good look, by the way—Udo, in the vernacular, wouldn't spend Christmas.

He is not alone. The rest of his generation of Germans are equally watching their pfennigs. They rebuilt the country after the war and they aren't about to blow it. So they put all their reddies on deposit in Germany.

In 2005, when we last saw Udo, sprinkling his well-tended garden plot, Germans were saving a phenomenal €130 billion more every year than they were spending.[2] Today that figure has risen to €250 billion.[3] So where does all their cash go?

Well, they lend it to other people.

Now look at the balance sheet of the Irish banks and we will see not only where the Irish money came from, but how it blew a hole in the Irish banking system, which forced the government to bail it out last September.

At the end of 2004—when I first met Udo—the Irish banks' total lending was €256 billion.[4] By the end of 2008, that had risen to an astounding €591 billion. The Irish banks had increased lending by €335 billion or 130 per cent.[5] It took the Irish banks over 100 years to build up the lending book of €256 billion, but in less than four years they had more than doubled that!

So all the money came from savers around the world but largely from those Germans. The Irish banks—driven by short-term greed—decided to inflate the property bubble. When they ran out of our savings, they used EMU to borrow other peoples' savings. So, from 2004 onwards, they borrowed billions from abroad and, like foie gras farmers fattening up the poor bloated goose, the Irish banks stuffed this money into every orifice of the economy until the economy simply couldn't take any more.

By this time last year, the situation was so desperate that the banks owed over €200 billion to foreign investors. That is considerably more than our total income.[6]

To see why this is important and to understand why the credit evaporated so quickly, let's fill in the next part of the jigsaw.

THE LONG AND SHORT OF IT

Banks borrow in the short term and lend in the long term. This is how they make money. They borrow for, let's say, 4 per cent and they lend for 8 per cent. The difference is profit. The more money they lend, the more profits they make, so there is always an inbuilt weakness to lend too much to the wrong type of person. As the banks lend more and more, the quality of the collateral they receive as security must fall. You'd expect banks to be aware of that. Unfortunately, in Ireland the lunatics took over the asylum and instead of worrying about the collateral they were receiving, the banks—in a bid for profits—actively debased the collateral and ended up buying worthless stuff with real money.

So an Irish bank, let's say Irish Life and Permanent, that is offering a 100 per cent mortgage needs to get the cash from somewhere. Irish Life is particularly delinquent in this regard so it is probably a good example. In December 2007, I bumped into the former chief executive of the bank at an official dinner in Áras an Uachtaráin of all places. As we listened to the President talking about the uniqueness of the Irish spirit, it was hard to avoid the conclusion that she didn't quite grasp just how unique and out of line we actually were!

When it was suggested to the banker that maybe the banks—and his own in particular—were borrowing too much abroad to finance first-time buyers at home, he assured me with glassy eyes—as if talking to a genial but misguided halfwit—that there was nothing to worry about and wished me a Happy Christmas. No wonder he was in good form. He was about to trouser a bonus of over €1 million.

So the Irish Life crowd was issuing IOUs to the German pension funds saying they'd pay them above German government bonds per year for money. Given that the Irish banks had been awarded AAA ratings by the rating agencies—for which the banks paid handsomely and why wouldn't they?—the Germans were happy. The banks then borrowed on a monthly basis to keep the cost down and rolled over these loans all the time. The reason they borrow in the short term is that it's cheaper.

Think about it. If I borrow €1,000 from you and tell you I'll give it back to you next week, all you have to worry about is what happens to me for the next seven days and what else, in the next seven days, you could have done with the cash. The risk is low, so the interest rate I need to pay you for taking that risk is correspondingly low.

If, on the other hand, I borrow €1,000 from you and tell you I will give it back to you in 20 years' time, you have to worry if you will ever see me again and think about all the other investments you could have made over the 20-year period. The risk to you is considerably higher, so you need to be paid extra interest to take on that risk. That is why money borrowed for a short time costs the borrower less than money borrowed for a long time.

The banks sit in the middle, borrowing in the short term and charging more to lend in the long term. That's the long and the short of banking. When things are going well, the banks make a fortune; when things go belly up, they are screwed, particularly if things go so belly up that the people who lend them money refuse to lend them any more. Then the banks run out of money and face going bust. This is what happened to the Irish banks in September 2008.

But before we get there, let's follow the money a bit. When this cash came into Irish Life, it would then lend it out to a first-time buyer in Stamullen through, possibly, First Active, which usually had a tie-up with the estate agent. The difference between the cost of borrowing and lending was Irish Life's profit. Not surprisingly, profits soared. The fact that it never had enough deposits to cover the loans didn't matter as long as the Germans were continuing to lend to it. But this made its financing position very precarious. When the crash came, Irish Life was the most unstable bank in the system, lending out €26 for every €10 deposit it had.[7] In short, it was making an enormous bet on Germany remaining docile and the Irish property market remaining wildly overvalued. This is hardly any way to run a bank.

But for our purposes, it is now easy to see where all the money was coming from. It was not ours. It was Udo's, not Paddy's. Ireland became nothing more than a recycling machine for the Irish banks, making them a fortune for their shareholders and turning us into the most indebted country on earth. Ireland was turned or turned itself, depending on what you think, into one of the world's largest hedge funds, borrowing other people's money to make a monumental bet on property, both here and—increasingly towards the end—all around the world.

WHERE DID ALL THE MONEY GO?

Even without a global credit crunch, the position of the country was perilous. Do not believe the nonsense that is now being spun about the fact that we were caught in the eye of an international storm. This is an insult to our intelligence.

When lenders stop lending to a country like Ireland, the entire credit market freezes. But if we hadn't become so dependent on them, the situation would have been difficult but manageable.

To get a handle on how precarious our position is, consider that six euros in every 10 that was borrowed at the top of the market was being supplied not from savings of Irish people but from people like Udo.[8] When he stops lending to us, imagine the contraction of credit. This contraction of credit—when you have to go from a position of being able to borrow what you like to where you can spend only what you earn—is called, in one of these yucky terms that only economists can come up with, deleveraging.

Had our banks not behaved like children, none of this would have happened.

THE DOWNWARD SPIRAL

Think about deleveraging like buying rounds in a bar. You are going to the pub every evening and you are buying drinks for your friends. But over time you run out of cash and start borrowing to buy the rounds. If the bloke lending to you to do this stops giving you cash, there are no more extra rounds. It means you just have to slash your pint buying right back to the number of pints you can afford out of your own pay packet. Depending on how much extra you were borrowing, this could be a seriously sobering occasion.

Now think of the other money we borrowed, not to finance having a laugh, living the life and loving the music but to buy assets, particularly property. Most of our money went into property. In 2006, 87 per cent of all the money borrowed in the country went into property of some shape or form.[9]

When property prices are rising, the balance sheet looks impressive. You borrowed €100,000. The property is now worth €150,000. You are €50,000 richer on paper.

Now consider what happens to the balance sheet when the property's price falls to €70,000. Your asset is now worth €30,000 less than your borrowings. So you are in a bind. But what happens next turns the screw even tighter. The bank sees that you are in negative equity and it gets nervous, even if it has money to lend. So it calls in the loan rather than extend credit and we get a double whammy. The original price of the house, we can now see, was not maintained by supply and demand which was the shallow spin of the boom, but by the huge amount of other people's money in our system.

When that money evaporates, the price of houses collapses and that very collapse frightens the investors even more and yet more money flees the country.

The first thing to suffer is banks' share prices, which start to fall dramatically, and this in turn makes it harder for the banks to borrow because they were using their shares as collateral in the boom. Now no one wants the shares as security on the simple basis that they are not secure! Suddenly what was a manageable credit problem becomes a major systemic problem.

Credit is the lifeblood of the economy. Without it, normal business chokes. It is the working capital that allows businesses the time to sell products before paying back the supplier that originally supplied them. If there is no working capital, there is no time to sell and if there is no time, there is no business.

So now we get a third negative shock to the system. The sellers go out of business, unemployment rises and tax revenue falls. This forces the State to pay more social welfare but, without the tax revenue, the budget deficit explodes. Therefore a country that had a healthy budget position in the boom starts to run huge deficits just to keep the system afloat.

As the government deficit swells, two other things happen. First, the government has to borrow. But with the economy in freefall, the financial markets begin to doubt the country's ability to pay—which is, after all, just the accumulation of all the people's ability to pay. This forces up the interest rate on the government's debt. Second, the people get nervous and start to postpone spending.

By postponing spending, the average person takes yet more money out of the system and hoards it. This causes prices to fall, and a situation of inflation (with prices rising) can turn around very easily and end up a situation of deflation (where prices are falling).

But if prices are falling, then surely you would be mad to buy something today that you didn't absolutely need because you will get a bargain by buying it tomorrow. So we hold off spending. This clatters those sellers who managed to stay in business and we get another downward round of redundancies, less tax revenue, falling prices and a withdrawal of more cash. At this stage, the economy is in real and present danger. And defaults on one property trigger defaults in other ones.

A helpful way of imagining how the system is so interlinked is to think of rush hour traffic in your city. I'll use Dublin because I know it, but the same applies all over the country. Do you ever wonder how a crash, let's say in Pearse Street in Dublin 2, can have a massive knock-on effect on traffic all over the city? The reason is simple. We have no idea of how interconnected the whole city is and how we are crucially dependent on everything flowing. Without that fluidity, the exits and intersections become chaotic and clogged and then all the slip roads onto them get clogged too. Then all the side streets get jammed and the lights don't work effectively because everyone is so fed up by the time they get to the lights, having sat in the car fuming for ages, that they nudge into the yellow box when the lights go amber, and the intersection gets bunged up.

So we can see how a crash in one area causes chaos throughout the system. Now think about an economy that was based on a huge number of loans that were personally guaranteed, cross-collateralised and in many cases pledged against all sorts of income. This type of opaque economy, where one thread leads to another and another, is ripe for a collapse when lending to it stops.

Initially, the outlying assets get hammered, then the better ones and then the better again—all the way up to the finest triple A assets. Money simply disappears, gets hoarded or retreats to the foreign countries which it came from in the first place.

This is how the system seizes up and in no time the place that had abundant credit, like the Serengeti in the rain, becomes parched, dry and lifeless.

Chapter 4 ᔓ

| THE FALLOUT

FROM EAST TO WEST

For many of us, the crisis began with the announcement of the government guarantee for the banks when, out of the blue, the seriousness was brought home. Before then, the airwaves were filled with 'maybe's', 'might's' and 'what-if's'. The big guns were blasting in the distance, but we were safe in our houses until 30 September 2008, when the guns were right over our heads and we discovered we were at the centre of a massive financial explosion.

So, what sort of country was this financial artillery raining down on? We weren't the country that muddled through the 80s any more. Nor were we the hopeful nation on the cusp of the Tiger years. Did we have anywhere safe to hide?

During the bonanza we moved house as no other time in our history. We traded up, down, escaped to the country or fled back to the city. We built new suburbs and gentrified old ones. We queued for pokey city centre apartments where you couldn't swing a mouse, never mind a cat. We bid millions on Malahide McMansions that could comfortably house Dublin Zoo's African Plains.

We foresaw huge population movements, but we didn't plan for them. We dotted the landscape with estates and one-off houses, refurbished old places, tore down even more. We rezoned like it was going out of fashion, which it has—Ennis has zoning for a population of 100,000 but only 27,000 residents.

In all, a staggering 375,000 houses changed hands in the three years between 2005 and 2008. That's a lot of people on the move. Just over one in four houses that have ever been built in Ireland changed hands during that time.

If we couldn't or wouldn't move, we improved. In our renovation boom, we chased the dream of added value, worshipping at the Church of Homebase, egged on by crews of celebrity gardeners and architects who saw Frank Lloyd Wright in the mirror.

Half a million new houses were built since 2001, almost doubling the number of houses in the country, with thousands more planned for the years ahead.

Behind all of it was the unspoken motto: Everything is temporary. We'll pause for a few years and then move on to the next bigger and better thing. Until, one day, everything stopped and, like a giant game of musical chairs, many of us were caught out and discovered we were stuck. We are shackled by fear and finance to the places we bought.

The housing market will not recover soon. With 720,000 houses now valued at much less than they were bought for, only the desperate will sell now. Many will cross their fingers and try to wait it out rather than realise their losses. The banks are in no mood to throw mortgages around—even if they had the cash—and people who have been burned are unlikely to want to take another risk when all the signals are that house prices are now on a long-term slide.

It is important to see the different repercussions across the nation, not only for geographical reasons but also to assess the financial and political implications of what is happening to us.

We're going to drive across the country, from east to west, to see where we landed when the music stopped. Starting in Dublin's Docklands we will travel west to the Atlantic coast ending up in Co. Clare because Clare went from being the least indebted county in Ireland to the most indebted in the alarmingly short timeframe of four years.

Along the way we might also find out something about ourselves. What sort of nation did we become?

THE FIRESTORM

If I told you that a bomb was about to go off and asked 'Where's the best place to stand?', you'd probably say 'As far away as possible.' But in Hiroshima in 1945, the people at the epicentre of the explosion miraculously survived, while those farther out experienced the highest mortality rate and the most destruction. Similar patterns are seen with earthquakes. It's not much fun at the epicentre, but the carnage gets exponentially worse as you move outwards.

In Ireland we are seeing a similar firestorm from what we might call the FIRE—Finance, Insurance and Real Estate—economy. The FIRE economy is based on the cheap fuel of easy money.

We start our drive at the epicentre—the gleaming IFSC in Dublin's Docklands. This new city of steel and glass hosted the banks' headquarters and it was here that the deals were done. Somewhere amid this financial Utopia the treasuries of our main banks made more and more cheap money available to their sales forces all around the country.

Other big players in the IFSC were the facilitators, our corporate lawyers. They dotted the 'i's and crossed the 't's on paperwork that will keep our banks and now us in hock. They were well paid for their services and their fingerprints are everywhere.

After the facilitators come the enablers, our major accountancy firms, the backbone of the financial world. They signed off on the dodgy accounts of the banks with not so much as a question mark over the viability of the business nor the financial efficacy of what they were seeing. Why not? They were creaming it in fees, a significant proportion of which came from their banking business.

PricewaterhouseCoopers, one of the biggest lions on the block, advised the government in November 2008 that the bank bailout would be limited to €11 billion. It is now likely to cost €90 billion—for practically worthless assets. Such foresight helped their fee income jump from €151 million in 2004 to €355 million in 2008.

Ernst & Young, Anglo's auditors, earned €148 million in fees in 2008, up from €93 million in 2004. In total, the big four accountancy firms saw their total fees double from €490 million in 2004 to €976 million four years later. These were their salad days, make no mistake.

Over the river, eating lunch at the same Italian restaurant as the others, are the stockbrokers. These guys were the cheerleaders for the boom. They made their commission by placing huge blocks of Irish bank shares with international investors so the banks could make more money selling mortgages to first-time buyers in places like Ballincollig.

They coaxed pensioners into investments in the banks. They wined and dined pension fund managers, who, in return for some foie gras and a bottle of vintage Meursault, signed away our cash for positions in the Irish banks that were hopelessly overextended.

The IFSC was the daisy chain of Irish financial power.

Today, the IFSC is quiet. Huddles of pinstripe suits pull on their last drag, their backs to the wind. This architectural ode to finance doesn't do windbreaks, so the mid-May gale is funnelled through the streets.

The periodic circles of used fag ends are the only hint of the frustrations of the hardened IFSC smoker.

When you cut through all the spin, the reason money came to Ireland is simple. We allowed foreign banks to do things with cash that they wouldn't be allowed to do at home. The IFSC was the red light district of the international financial markets. It catered for every fetish and sought to service every need, the more profitable the better.

This was the classic FIRE economy model. The Docklands attracted half of the world's top 50 banks and half of the world's top 20 insurance companies. It was easy money and generated €700 million in tax revenue and over 10,000 new jobs. Today, this model is broken.

The foot soldiers of the IFSC are the same as in any business park anywhere in Ireland. Navy suits—with high heels for the ladies, pointy toes for the fellas—travel the streets by day, the all-important ID pass swinging from their neck like corporate rosary beads.

It's lunchtime and the shops are quiet. Who buys furniture on their break? This is takeaway coffee land. Travel outfits optimistically offer golfing holidays, but no one's buying.

A giant hoarding displays an artist's vision of what the Docklands might have been. Mums with buggies, kids on skateboards and bikes, a fire eater. There's an Elvis impersonator too, eating an ice-pop for some reason. It's a little heavy-handed, but the intent is clear—the IFSC would be a community, a new place to live in modern, sophisticated Ireland. A little bit of Manhattan off Moore Street, if you will.

Architecturally, Docklands all over the world look exactly the same. This is because land was comparatively cheap in these areas and planning restrictions were virtually non-existent. Little attention was paid to locals, since no one expected them to be part of the new city. This is as true in the IFSC as anywhere else. All you have to do is walk five minutes from chq into the heart of East Wall and, if you ignore the satellite dishes and the odd lonely gentrified artisan cottage, nothing has changed since the 1980s.

Here's the rub: although the prices of apartments have held up in the docks relative to other places, they are now 40 per cent below where they were three years ago. Even here, where Ireland's future was meant to take wing, the spectre of negative equity is pulling us down. The people here are going nowhere fast and if the global financial industry remains strapped for cash, there won't be the demand here to maintain values.

Drive down the docks a bit, towards town and past the echoey waste ground that was supposed to be the headquarters of Anglo Irish Bank. This was to have been the crowning glory for former Anglo chairman Sean Fitzpatrick, a director of the Dublin Docklands Development Authority. With a pleasing symmetry, the former chairman of the Dublin Docklands Development Authority, Lar Bradshaw, was also a board director at Anglo. Now the building is half-built and the crane is a solitary skeletal mourner and a remnant of the good aul' times.

THE PIONEERS AND INNER CITY CHIC

The IFSC is like a medieval castle. The big house is walled in, with all but a few peasants on the other side. When an attack comes, the peasants' houses are the first to fall. When you drive out of the IFSC, looking for the M50, you hit Ireland's first outsiders, in East Wall and North Strand.

During the boom, if you were a young couple looking to buy, you had to choose between the farthest suburbs or, in estate agent parlance, an 'up and coming' area. Adventurous couples chose the latter, betting that prices would rise and allow them to move on to a more picturesque area. These Pioneers didn't intend to stay, but many liked to imagine that they were having an eye-opening social education. For many dinner party intellectuals, this was to be the Irish Cultural Revolution. It was only too bad that no one read as far as Tiananmen Square.

The craze for artisan cottages was fuelled by our old friend Breakfast Roll Man, as well as these young couples who couldn't face life in Portarlington and mammies and daddies figuring it was cheaper in the long run to buy Fiachra his own place for college rather than throw money at a landlord.

Like all crazes, the first in—Breakfast Roll Man, usually—made a fortune, flipping a two-bed terraced cottage into a 'sensitively restored artisan property perfect for modern urban life'. This helped push up the prices, because the only thing better than a traditional cottage is one with working plumbing.

It's easy to spot the Pioneer houses as we drive past. They're the ones that have unpainted brick walls—and a locked front door, because those mortgages aren't going to pay themselves.

Let's keep going, zooming past the Korean restaurants, Chinese massage parlours and the internet cafes, and up the property ladder. Look up at all the new apartment blocks. Who's living there? Our inner cities have seen huge demographic change in the last five years. Now they are home to students, young workers and foreigners who live in the thousands of apartments built in the past decade. The 'aul' Dub' isn't with O'Leary in the grave, but he's pretty well fenced in. Most of his family already live up in Ongar and beyond.

THE GREEN BELT

Let's put our foot down and head towards the older inner suburbs where the Green Party gets most of its dwindling votes.

It's all redbrick and upmarket around here. Back in 2005, when I wrote *The Pope's Children,* this was one of the cherished destinations of our intelligentsia. From the outside, it still looks perfect. The food shops sell organic, the supermarket bulletin boards advertise yoga and Filipina au pairs, and you can't walk five minutes without falling over a coffee shop.

But this leafy, green arcadia is getting hammered in the crunch. Most people here are in the FIRE economy or derivatives of it. Advertisers, marketers, interior designers, solicitors, wine merchants, small-time publishers, pre-silk barristers on the way up, luxury retailers—all are floating on the froth and flotsam of too much credit. When that credit dries up, they don't get paid. From these heights, it's a long way down.

Let's drive further into the old suburbs with their gravel drives, cherry blossoms and mounting school fees.

THE CLOBBERED CLASS

Recently it was reported that a student in Alexandra College in Dublin had run up a bill of some €20,000 in unpaid fees. The fee issue is bubbling away, not just in Alexandra College but all over Dublin's southside as the beginning of the meltdown hits home.

Until recently, the Dublin go-getting class was involved in a bidding war to get their children into the best fee-paying schools. This reached epidemic proportions, with children's names being put down on lists the week after they were born. When demand rises, prices go up. Fees increased significantly in the boom, and if you wanted little Setanta or Ella to be in the right school, you'd be paying for it.

From 2000 on, south Dublin experienced a cull of non-fee paying schools. In my own area, Dun Laoghaire, two boys' schools that had educated the fathers and sons in the borough for years closed down. But this pattern of closing free schools while the fee-paying schools couldn't charge enough has come to a sudden end. Well-founded rumours suggest that some of the best-known schools in the country are now facing significant defaults and arrears in fees for the first time ever. Blackrock College's 'Blue and White fund' for children whose parents are in financial trouble is apparently exhausted.

In Ross O'Carroll-Kelly's back garden, the best barometer for the recession is the number of transfers that the non-fee paying schools are receiving. A school in Stillorgan is getting 20 transfer requests a month. These are for children whose parents can't afford to pay the fees in the following term or are far behind. The Alexandra College episode is only the tip of the iceberg.

A bank manager friend of mine explained that up until September 2008, the bank was happy to finance loans to cover fees. But now, given the huge numbers of arrears on these loans, the banks have stopped rolling over the interest. Shocked parents repeat the plea 'but it's for our children's education' to no avail.

These used to be the areas that the car showroom could depend on. But since 2006 the sales of cars over €100,000 have fallen by 87 per cent. Take a drive up to any luxury car saleroom and have one look at the face of the bloke with the empty clipboard.

House prices are down here by 50 per cent and a significant amount of property is now in that state of limbo that estate agents euphemistically call 'quietly on the market', which is property people's way of saying up the creek. Nothing is moving. No one is spending. Even 'Mint'—a Michelin starred restaurant in redbrick Ranelagh featuring a trademark shouty chef—has closed.

In 2008 alone the wealth of Irish families fell from €139 billion to €81 billion and the way house prices have gone this year and are likely to go next year, this figure will slump again.

These professional areas experienced a type of mania at the tail end of the boom. In a part of the country where the aspiration of every mother is that her daughter marries either a doctor or Gordon D'Arcy, people don't take risks easily. They only do so when everyone else has taken a punt and, therefore, leave it too late. Behind the unruffled solidity of the black-lacquered hall doors and conservative bay trees, people are beginning to panic. People here got into 'property syndicates' late in the day.

Arguably, because most Irish professionals are risk averse and cru-cially 'late-comers' to every trend, whether it is Pilates, world music or Leinster Rugby, they are sitting ducks. They may have got to the top of their fields in law, medicine or retail banking, but because of their hubris they were in fact the most susceptible to the hype. They desperately wanted to be players. They are Ireland's worst investors, and were prey to the very last snake oil salesman to crawl out from under a stone, flogging 'hotel opportunities'.

These 'opportunities' often present themselves when the developer/ owner is a few weeks from bankruptcy and the cross-collateralised nature of his pyramid of debts means he has to get fresh cash in to plug the hole, pay some other creditor, buy some time and stay above water. The final victim is a surgeon or a solicitor who gets in at the end, dying to trade stories with someone at a dinner party. Everyone wanted to be Seanie Fitzpatrick.

If you doubt this just ask Breffni O'Brien, south Dublin's answer to Bernie Madoff. His professional mates couldn't give him enough cash even when he got so blasé as to quote the address of the Ritz in Paris as the site of a new development, which he was 'allegedly' financing. With that sort of due diligence, can an investor—no matter how shafted by a charlatan—honestly feel aggrieved?

But out here under the leafy willows, where proud, well-coiffed mothers agonise over their daughters' wedding notices in the *Irish Times*, lapsed Catholics hold baptism parties in the Four Seasons, 'new' Protestants prepare plum chutney for the school fête and portly fathers practise their 'air golf' swings in the back garden, position, status and perceived success are everything. When they suffer, they do so in silence.

Expect the school fee scandal to become more prevalent in 2010 as the now strapped middle class switch en masse back to the schools their parents went to. Expect echoes of Britain's 'catchment area inflation' as canny investors start looking to grab properties near the best state schools.

TOWARDS DECKLAND'S GHOST ESTATES

Let's drive past the 1940s and 1950s council estates where the first mass movement from the city to the suburbs occurred. These houses were built to last and these areas have seen a huge surge in wealth and stability since the 1990s. Gone are the Hiace vans on blocks in gardens,

Halloween bonfires and chippers and in their place are black SUVs owned by residents with steady incomes and holiday homes in Alicante.

This is where the ratio of televisions to people has exploded, in favour of the flat screen. This is a hire purchase, zero-rate finance economy. But there are some bright spots, particularly if you are selling takeaway food. For example, the Domino's Pizza in the Square in Tallaght sells more pizza than any Domino's Pizza outlet anywhere in the world—which is quite an achievement when you consider that Domino's Pizza has over 3,400 outlets in 55 countries outside of the USA!

But this is only the fringe of Deckland. As we drive further out, we enter a world that, at first glance, looks not dissimilar to the country of John Hinde's iconic postcards, where strawberries and eggs were available at every gate and a house wasn't a home unless it was whitewashed and covered in straw.

It's a popular image and, as we all know, it's done great things for tourism, but it's not quite that simple any more. Laois is commuterville. So too are Meath, Kildare, Offaly and every other county within sniffing distance of the Dublin road. And it is here that the problem with the tail end of the boom comes into focus. Easy credit pushed the concept of 'Dormitory Dublin'—where entire towns existed to force-feed the capital with workers—out farther and farther into the countryside.

Laois was the third fastest growing county in Ireland in the past five years, with the second highest proportion of children under 14. This is Ireland's babybelt, where one of the few businesses keeping its head above water is the giant children's indoor play-zone called Manic Monsters. Here, birthday parties and communions come to blows over which group—the child brides with parasols or the miniature Liverpool FC first 11—is next at Quasar. Scores of abandoned kids hurtle around, like freckly extras from *Slumdog Millionaire*, as hungover parents try to keep a semblance of control, doing penance for their night on the tiles.

This is the outer limit of Deckland, a place where people moved to in 2005, not intending to stay. Now they are trapped. They are the real victims, hidden behind pleading auctioneers' hoardings in the ghost estates. House prices are plummeting, not that it makes any difference since no one is buying at any price. Unemployment is rocketing and what was once a difficult but doable commute has now turned into an isolation ward. No one is getting out. Each mortgage is a life sentence.

The road to Limerick narrows to two grotty lanes made filthy by the endless trucks. Then you screech to a shuddering halt. A bored-looking construction worker leans against a 'stop' sign, holding up traffic while his compadres do a bit of ditch-cutting. The packet of Tayto Cheese & Onion sticking out of his jacket and the can of Lilt that he swigs as he considers the traffic is hard to square with the image we remember from the razzmatazz at the launch of Transport 21: our promised motorways and bullet trains.

Eventually the traffic starts moving again. On the left you pass an ad for Ossory Court: 'Bargain! Prices slashed! €185,000! Only five units remaining,' screams the sign. Here's the spiel for this ghost estate as relayed in the sales pitch.

> Borris in Ossory (Buiríos Mór Osraí in Irish) is a flourishing town in the heart of the Midlands.
>
> Strategically located along the N7, the town offers commuters peaceful rural living with close proximity to busy surrounding towns and easy access to the capital. Travel time to Dublin is 1 hour & 10 minutes and Limerick is less than 1 hour.

Only two years ago, Decklanders were clambering over each other's 100 per cent mortgages.

The sales spiel was nostalgia fused with opportunity, conceived in the marketing department off Baggot Street. The dream was of freshly cut grass, brambly lanes and blackberries. You, the buyer, were led to believe that Borris was a place of savant farmers, fresh air and wholesome living. Everything in this rural arcadia suggested home, contentment and long summery nights where children would run free in short pants playing 'roley poley' down soft hills like De Valera's version of the von Trapp family. Your wife would look beautiful with the last gentle light of the evening on her face as she called in the children, from over the back wall, for a bedtime snack of Club Milks before tucking them in. You were doing the right thing; country living could only be good for the kids. Your commute would be your sacrifice for them.

After all, you were not just buying a house 'fairly priced' at €260,000 with the bank giving you a 100 per cent mortgage and more if you needed to buy your big screen TV and a sofa to watch it from. You were buying a place in a rooted community. Even if that community was only a few months old. You were buying a mirage of 1960s Ireland, only now it was wired for broadband.

But the reality today is different. In Ossory Court and hundreds of estates like it all over our country we get a glimpse of a future that few of us dared to contemplate only a year or two ago.

From first impressions, you would think Ossory Court is well-kept, respectable and inhabited by people who care about each other. You can feel the local under-10 GAA team taking root. The first few houses (the first sold) are occupied, with well-tended lawns, themed doorbell tunes and '05 Daihatsus parked neatly. Go a little farther and the scene changes. Behind the row of showhouses, lawns have not been cut in over a year and are choking in weeds.

Every other window is smashed and the front doors of unsold houses are boarded up. Building materials are still scattered everywhere like gravestones. As you go deeper into the estate, the place gets considerably worse, and emptier. There is rubbish everywhere. This development was only completed last year, yet three-quarters of it is abandoned.

We could well see the commuter towns being redefined as there are no jobs to commute to. Unemployment in Laois has tripled since last year. Ghettos are emerging.

The 'broken windows theory' explains why areas go bad quickly. It argues that an area turns bad because the little things are not fixed. It is the accumulation of ignored 'little things' that makes the 'big thing' degenerate. If the locals allow small things, like a broken windowpane, to go unfixed it sends out all the wrong signals. The people who smashed the window will then conclude that no one cares and will smash more with impunity. Respectable people will not move into an area like this. And those who already live there will try to move out, ceding the ground to the hoodies. Over time the area goes downhill. Initially this is a slow, rather hesitant process but then it becomes a stampede.

Could this happen in Ireland's commuter towns? Most definitely. In fact, reasonably smart money would give narrow odds that in five years' time these places will be no-go areas—a blight on local towns—which the cops will have marked down as trouble. It's difficult to imagine now, but trends in the US bear this out. These estates, deep in what was once called 'rural Ireland', are the semi-urban ghettos of the future.

The process of degeneration is already beginning in Borris and all over the country where these 'ghost estates' have been built. Whether it is Borris in Laois, Stamullin in Meath, Gorey in Wexford, Rathangan in Kildare, the story is the same. Drive around your local town and see them for yourself.

At this stage it might be worth considering the financial implications of these ghost estates. When developers go bust, leaving huge debts to the bank, what happens? The State has decided to pick up the tab in our name. The bank will put this estate into NAMA and we—the taxpayers—will have to buy it. But the problem with a place like Borris is that property depreciates if it is left empty. Once this place becomes a ghetto, its value will never recover. So we will be left owning something that will be worthless. So why should we be buying this stuff at all?

THE EMPTY TOWN

Let's leave this desolation and keep going to Nenagh in North Tipperary, where the most swanky edifice is the new state-of-the-art County Council building. Is this petite version of government buildings—out of which you could happily run a small empire—really necessary to run half a county?

Here again, you see the sordid imprint of the last phase of the boom, out on the Limerick road: Springfort Retail Park. For some reason, in the past five years, every townland and parish in Ireland seemed to think it needed an out-of-town retail park with Currys, Tesco and Toys R Us. If these brands are the A-list celebrities of the retail park world, Springfort is firmly Z-list. It has Expert Electrical, Supervalu and the Wonder World of Babies instead.

Reflecting the fall-off in spending, many units are boarded up. The Tile Market is advertising everything at 'Northern prices', revealing that the long arm of sterling and the B&Q in Newry reaches down here, to the heart of Munster.

The car park has 600 spaces—testament to the optimism of better times when we were buying more cars per head than any other country in Europe. This morning, there are only 12 vehicles in the entire place. As eight are owned by people working here, you are not talking about the 'heavy footfall' the ebullient auctioneers were fond of gushing about in the boom. Today, it's less footfall, more echo.

The only thing that is full is the trolley area. Thousands of trolleys are concertinaed together, waiting expectantly for customers. The forlorn, unwanted trolley queue is the best indicator of what might have been. If hundreds of trolleys are jammed together, you know the rent on these units won't be paid in the next few months.

Just when you think all the cars in the Irish boom have been beamed up by Scotty to the *Starship Hibernius* for another part of the solar system, they re-emerge, stationary, glinting in the sunlight. Cars that should have been spilling out eager shoppers, overflowing with decking, barbeques and flat screens, are lined up, unsold, in the chrome and glass car distributor across the road. Think of the leather-upholstered debt sitting on those forecourts.

There isn't a sinner around, except for four workmen in overalls looking at the skeletal structure of an office park, which is just about to be completed beside the other new but empty office park. Who is going to use these buildings and when?

INTO THE WEST

Let's drive on towards the Atlantic in our east to west traverse of the country. Is any place safe from the financial tremors?

One might think that somewhere like Co. Clare might have been spared. After all, it's almost as far from the IFSC as you can go and still be on the mainland. But this idyll has had a more turbulent history than many realise. Over the years, it has been fought over by all comers. The rich land of hillocks and open fields is well supplied with water and is perfect for farming. However, that beautiful landscape has not escaped the aftershock.

Motor on towards Shannon New town—the great hope of a different age—and then to Bunratty Castle, where our Irish-American cousins get their first taste of Irish hospitality (and prices).

The 'Banner' is as far away from Dublin as you can get. Ennis is the capital of Clare and ranks as one of the spiritual homes of Irish nationalism. Both the Liberator, Daniel O'Connell, and the Long Fellow himself, Eamon de Valera, represented Ennis and Co. Clare. Ten years ago, Ennis was named Ireland's first 'information age town'; it would lead the way in the new digital era.

Drive over the Ennis bypass, probably the most expensive piece of road in the country. The land upon which it was built was bought by the County Council for the madly inflated price of €37 million before someone noticed that it was a swamp. It had hardly any agricultural value.

The bypass was opened before the last election. Although it seems like aeons ago, this was the election that Bertie and Fianna Fáil fought and—strange as it might seem now—won on their handling of the economy. In an episode worthy of 'Father Ted', the Ennis bypass was opened before any of the slip roads were ready so it literally bypassed Ennis and all other routes in the area. Once you were on it you couldn't get off and were deposited halfway to Gort. It didn't so much bypass the town as cut it off completely. 'A lot done, more to do'—as the man said.

Ennis is wonderfully pretty. On a sunny day, it is like a miniature Galway or a bigger, more robust version of Westport or Kenmare. It has a laidback, almost hippy feel to it.

In the glass reflection of Sacred Earth on Market Street, which sells 'holistic gifts' and advertises meditation classes, you see Scéail Eile, an upmarket bookshop. It is selling a classic Russian literature set. No *Heat* or *Grazia* magazine flogged in there.

The town of 27,000 is the eleventh biggest in Ireland, but it doesn't feel like it. It feels small, intimate and friendly, with a preponderance of Irish language shop fronts, which is reassuring. Like the nostalgic advertising hoardings for Borris in Ossory, they conjure up a world we never really knew, but like to imagine. The more colourful the shop fronts and the more cosmetically *Gaeilge* the town, the more we come and spend our easy credit.

The cafes are full, as are the organic butcher, the bookshops and the Saigon designer boutique which today displays leaflets asking people to support the Rossport 5. Who said shopping wasn't political? Even the local auctioneer is sophisticated. His sign reads 'Brian McMahon and Daughters'.

As this is Ireland's first 'information age town', it must be paperless, green and eco-friendly. What's more, it has deep culture and possibly the finest musical tradition in the country. The 'Celtic Rest' sculpture outside the Glor arts centre signals a people who know where they come from and what is important—even if the busker in the lane outside the Aroma cafe lowers the tone by blasting out a cover of 'Highway to Hell'. You can't have everything.

Just for a brief minute as you move up O'Connell Street you think maybe, just maybe, we are in a place that is so far from Dublin and the headquarters of Ireland's corrupt financial elite that it has escaped the madness. Could the financial ripple effect—which has wrought such damage and devastated much of the country we have driven through—be fading?

The O'Connell monument in the square stands proud, guarding the high ground over the centre of the town. But as you get closer, your heart sinks. There, trying to swamp our national hero, are the gombeen men of the twenty-first century. He is outnumbered and besieged by them. They have surrounded him.

First there is National Irish Bank eyeing the hero from one corner of the square, then Ulster Bank, First Active and Irish Nationwide. To the left are Hibernian, Halifax and National Irish Bank—and this is without mentioning the big two. This is Ennis's Wall Street.

Yes, here are the agents of destruction, lined up around O'Connell. Recent bitter experience indicates that with so many banks close at hand, carnage can't be far away. It is time, once again, to follow the money. To locate the financial massacre, go no further than the local Sherry FitzGerald, which is tied to the First Active. Let's check out the window.

These days, an estate agent's window is akin to a crime scene, offering clues and tips for the investigators. On the board, which still shamelessly urges people to buy despite the fact that we have no money, all roads appear to lead to a development on the outskirts of town: here is another ghost estate.

A bored security guard, Maori tattoos wrapped all round his forearms, guards the abandoned Acha Bhille estate just in case the showhouse is ransacked. Only 50 of the 200 houses and apartments have been sold. The builder is bust and the banks have taken a €40 million bath. The weeds are beginning to appear and although the poster announces that there is going to be a relaunch soon, you can almost hear the death rattle as you drive in.

Someone lost money here. An awful lot of it.

FAMINE ECHOES
Off to the far west is the Atlantic, then the Aran Islands and beyond to the USA, the only hope for thousands of Clare people and millions of us over the years. You can feel that history in Clare as you go towards Ennistymon and Lahinch to the sea. The first ever Famine memorial in Ireland is here. This bleak, harrowing piece of rural desolation, erected in 1995 to mark the 150th anniversary of the 'Great Hunger', was financed by an Irish-American group—the Ancient Order of

Hibernians. We—the descendents of the Irish who stayed at home—don't seem to have been moved to do it, so we left it to our Yank cousins to put up a monument to the millions who died or left.

The Famine occurred in an Ireland with strong demographics and a seemingly stable source of economic growth. The parallels between our obsession with land and cheap credit and our ancestors' obsession with land and cheap food—the potato—are instructive. Let's not stretch the metaphor, but it's worth noting, particularly as we survey the financial wreckage. In the 1830s and 1840s, people cited the strong population growth as justification for the increase in land prices and the reason to remain optimistic about Ireland's economic future. In 1821, the population of Clare, like much of the country, had doubled in two decades. It stood at 208,000. And this rural population explosion continued until the Great Famine in 1845.

It was the result of an innovation that saw huge tracts of land reclaimed. The potato was capable of feeding thousands and people felt it would never fail. Feeding the Napoleonic Wars greatly inflated the price of crops, making subdividing the land possible. So large families sustained even larger families.

Now fast-forward to 2006, before the meltdown, and a similar, if not quite so appalling, vista emerges. We rezoned land in the same way as our ancestors subdivided land. Both were based on the false assumption that the price of land could go only one way. They bet on the potato, based on the catastrophic assumption that the crop would never fail; we bet on property based on the disastrous and false notion that it could only go up.

Interestingly, the people chose to forget the huge potato shock of 1821 when the crop had previously failed. They didn't learn their lesson or change their ways. They just assumed it was a freak event and wouldn't happen again. They got another warning in the early 1840s but ignored it. We similarly failed to heed warnings, failed to look at the other examples of property and financial market collapse and, in some cases, vilified those who warned publicly about the dangers. So when the big one came, it devastated all around it.

As the Famine memorial in west Clare says, the shock was enormous because, 'the people had no apprehension of poverty'.

The Famine analogy doesn't seem so far-fetched when you stand in the empty ghost estates that litter the countryside.

But there is more to the story. Someone built these pseudo-towns, someone who had all the cards back in the boom.

Chapter 5

THE MERCHANT OF ENNIS

'Great turnout. He'd be delighted,' whispered his mother, breaking the silence.

The hearse pulled up slowly, nudging its way almost self-consciously through the crowd. He gazed out the window, wedged between his sisters as he used to be when he was a boy. The grandchildren had pleaded to go in what they called the 'limo' but—unusually for this tight family—today wasn't focused on the small ones.

He stared blankly at the huddled crowd, most of whom he knew well. They were friends. They weren't only mourners; they were also his investors but that bombshell hadn't gone off yet.

It was an article of faith that the boom would last for ever. Hadn't Bertie told the sceptics to go commit suicide? How could it all come toppling down? At worst, there would be a soft landing given the strong fundamentals and the excellent demographics. Weren't the banks stress tested?

He sensed their compassionate looks as he walked slowly, carrying the coffin. The undertakers had perfected the slow funeral march. He took his cue from them.

'Sorry for your troubles.'

One of his 'investors'—the local school principal—clasped him.

He couldn't look him in the eye. This was the man who had taught him as a child.

'Investors'. Jesus, such a grandiose term.

But the country's language had changed. In the last few years, everyone became proficient in the language of success. An entire generation learned the imported lexicon of finance. The conversation in O'Neill's had moved away from tales of daring-do in the county finals of yesteryear, to sounding like the Horseshoe Bar in the Shelbourne after work on a Friday, alive with the excited Creole of

Lisney. We adopted this patois for the same reason and with the same enthusiasm as our ancestors adopted English: to get ahead.

We were all investors now. We were risk-taking—a race of natural entrepreneurs. We thought we knew our upside from our mezzanine finance, our leveraged loans from our subordinated debt. With a Black-Berry in one hand and a fist of borrowed cash in the other, we were the *Starship Enterprise* of finance, ready to boldly go where no man had gone before.

Fr O'Mahoney slowly arranged the Bible on the podium, flicking through the pages, looking down in that meticulous, officious way older priests do.

The Merchant of Ennis heard the constant shuffling of the elderly as the pews filled up behind. Just as Fr O'Mahoney stretched out his arms to address the throng, the Merchant caught his own reflection in the shiny handles of his father's coffin. He looked wrecked. He could sleep in the bags under his eyes.

The anxiety, the worried nights. How much longer could he cover it up, borrowing from here and there, tapping mates for a few more quid, forging signatures, using tomorrow's money to pay for yesterday? He wanted it to be over. He'd take it like a man, like he'd always done. Let the last night be the longest.

He knew the game was nearly up as he pressed the flesh of those who shuffled up the echoey church to pay their respects. There was one last chance for salvation. It was a long shot in Rialto up in Dublin. But he was in with one of the biggest names in the country. This could be it.

What if it failed?

The Merchant sat beside his mother, who stared straight ahead of her, avoiding looking at the coffin, which was now sinking under the weight of the Mass cards. Yet another way of selling dreams, those Mass cards! In fairness, at least he'd only tried to make money out of the living; the Church was still making it out of the dead.

Over the past few weeks, when the Merchant of Ennis realised that the numbers were not only not adding up but the money was missing, he comforted himself in comparisons. There was always a bigger chancer out there, spoofing to even bigger suckers.

He'd wanted to talk to his dad in the last weeks. He'd wanted to tell him he loved him and sit with him as the life drained from him. But he was always so busy now, making phone calls, meeting creditors, trying to keep the whole thing going. His father probably sensed something was wrong. He knew him inside out, his only son, and he knew when he was in trouble.

They'd always been so close, going to matches together when he was a child and going for a jar as he got older. He remembered his father explaining the business to him, telling him to be careful.

In the last days, he was up in Dublin and he never got the chance to say goodbye. They'd talked on the phone and he promised to be back home by the weekend. And then his dad was gone.

Now he just wanted to be left alone, to remember and take it all in. But he couldn't. They all wanted a piece of him.

And as the man of the house, he had to be big, particularly today. He had to be strong. All he wanted to do was cry and grieve but money wouldn't allow that.

Deep down, he also realised that in the swinging pendulum of Irish indignation, people like him had replaced sleazy priests as the enemy of the people. Complicit or not, the Irish needed their villains and these days there were few characters more despised, more base, than failed property developers. Particularly small-time ones who weren't big enough to bring down Anglo Irish Bank. He wasn't one of the 50 Irish people who today owe over €80 billion between them.

Yesterday, he'd spoken to Fr O'Mahoney as if his dad were still there, as if he'd just walk through the door at any minute, smiling and telling him not to worry. They'd sort it out together.

In all honesty, he hadn't taken much in since he heard his mother whimper down the phone, 'He's gone. Dad's gone, Kevin.'

No one else appeared shocked. It all seemed like second nature to people of a certain age. They just kicked into removal overdrive. Irish people did funerals well.

How could he tell them? Certainly not those three fellas four rows down, jowly-looking cowboys with their pantomime smiles, who were typically—but inappropriately—sitting far too close to the top of the church, in full view. He knew the local whiskey-faced politicians would be there to take over proceedings. Every funeral was a hustings to them. But they'd be going down with him.

'97 KEVIN

Kevin Rice was a hero. He was the man. Ever since he won the county final single-handedly in 1997. Hadn't they nicknamed him '97 Kevin after that performance, carrying him on their shoulders through the village? The first O'Toole Cup they'd ever won. The tattered bunting was still up over the Alamo chipper. They'd trusted him, like they trusted his dad. And as they lined up to commiserate with him on his loss, he couldn't face what he had done to them.

The older people focused on his mother, muttering soothing words, pulling that mawkish expression in the face of someone else's grief. The experienced ones knew that it was all in the eyes. If you could get the eyes to speak, you were a pro. They were a different generation. For all their faults, they didn't mortgage the country. Not like his shower.

The younger ones zoned in on him and his five sisters, saying the wrong things and giving little affectionate rubs and pinches. Everyone looked older, much older than he'd remembered. Most had left years ago; most couldn't wait to get out of here. He'd stayed to make something of the place and now this! He caught a brief word with his cousins from Galway for a while. They were always good fun and his dad liked them too, especially the twins.

'Very sorry.'

'Thanks for making the effort. See you back at the house.'

'Please God.'

Next up was the local doctor and with that, the Merchant of Ennis was brought back to the tattered balance sheet.

Last week, he'd done a quick back of the envelope calculation.

With the flats in Liverpool underwater and the golf club development going nowhere, the doctor's share brought the total debt he owed to the mourners to about €1.9 million. That was before he paid the 22 per cent he promised to the local pub syndicate for the planning 'flip' he'd expected in Wexford. No one would touch that stuff now.

'Sorry for your troubles,' mumbled the doctor.

Not as sorry as I am for yours, Doctor, he thought as he nodded appreciatively.

'There was nothing I could do for him at the end. It all happened so quickly.'

'Thanks, Doctor.'

How could he tell them?

THE DAY OUT

This time two years ago, it was so different, when Bertie Ahern cut the ribbon on the new out-of-town retail park, down by the river. All the locals knew it was a floodplain but the local chieftain, now sitting four pews back in the Hugo Boss overcoat, pushed the planning through, no questions. Too much at stake.

They were getting Currys and PC World. They'd got Tesco and Toys R Us for the great Irish baby boom of the first decade of the new century. They'd got 2,000 new car parking spaces, a Costa Coffee and some place called 55 Degrees North which sold all-weather glacier climbing gear from New Zealand, absolutely essential in the flat Irish countryside.

All the locals dived in for 'the flip' of the new apartments grafted onto the side of the giant Woodies. Sure they'd all sell on to some eejit from Dublin looking for that 'dream home by the water'.

Everyone was ecstatic that afternoon. The local estate agent, the one who still wore his mobile phone hanging from his belt holster, beamed enthusiastically. He was on the up. His clipboard was filling up and he was taking deposits as if doing the half-eleven Mass collection. Only amadáns spurned a chance like this.

Brushing dandruff off his collar, he confidentially projected 'thirty per cent on the conservative side, ye know'.

The synchronised glint off the silver Mercs gave a Nuremberg Rally feel to the day. Everyone was certainly singing from the same hymn sheet. The local radio station, owned by the same lad who sold the land in the first place, was doing vox pops to be aired between the property ads on drivetime.

The sun shone and the men sweated uncomfortably in their new Louis Copelands. With so many overweight mammals hovering around the finger food, it looked like the seal pen in the zoo at feeding time.

The persistent wasp-like photographers buzzed about, always on the lookout for the 'money shot'. They summed up the indignity of low-rent fame, as they pushed, shoved and manhandled local dignitaries.

'Just one beside the logo, Tom!'

'Squeeze Mary in beside you, like a good man, Michael.'

An expensive Karen Millen arse, the size of a small housing estate, reverses into a space between the Caterpillar plant hire sponsors. It could do with those little reverse bleepers that are standard in most cars these days. Three inches, two, one, whoops, there go the sausage rolls.

Paper doilies everywhere, slow-motion chaos. Say cheese. They're always front-page material, those developers' wives.

HOW DID HE GET HERE?

The Merchant of Ennis just found himself in the middle. One deal led to the next and before he knew it, he was the lynchpin of a property empire, selling, flipping, investing, building, buying and selling on again. Every deal was bigger than the last one. He had no reason to believe it would ever end. He didn't know any better and neither did the investors.

Financing wasn't a problem. They queued up like communist housewives at a full bakery. He was a GAA hero and that was enough. He was from a good family. His father was a decent man. He'd never screw you, and he didn't intend to. He'd never intended to. He wanted to make them rich and they wanted to believe him. It seemed so easy. The bigger the deals were, the less work he had to do. A phone call here, a few pints there. A nod, a wink and Bob's your uncle.

And when he had to go out to raise money, 90 per cent of his sales pitch centred on Sunday's game. Pat Spillane was either an unmerciful bollix or an unmitigated genius depending on where in the country he found himself.

But building was only the half of it. He had morphed into an 'advisor'. Nothing was too remote or complicated. What about the holiday villas in Bulgaria, the syndicate in Waterford with the student flats and the development site out past St Enda's on the new link road?

He was on his way. But what would you expect from a man who'd led the troops? The banks in the town, up beside the statue of the Liberator, were falling over him.

He tried to focus, to sort himself out, but his mind was racing, trying to take in the enormity of what had happened and trying to prepare himself for what was about to happen.

He could just make out the Latin inscription at the perfect sculpted feet of the Blessed Virgin.

He was drifting off into his own world, but now was not the time. *Concentrate, Kevin, for fuck's sake! It's your father's funeral!*

Initially the words were indistinct but eventually they became clear. *'Fides et Credes.'*

Faith and belief.

Jesus, that was what the red-headed eejit was going on about in Wednesday's *Independent*.

The Merchant had read that the word 'credit' came from the same Latin source as 'creed'. The Creed comes from the Latin verb *credo*, which means 'I believe' or 'I trust'. This is what we believe; this is what we find credible. He'd never made the connection before.

The jackeen in the paper said that *credo* was also the root of the modern financial term 'credit'. To accept credit meant that you trusted the person you were dealing with. What's more, the word 'fiduciary'— a word the Merchant was newly familiar with, as he was constantly signing loan documents about his 'fiduciary responsibility', also came from Latin, from *fides*, 'to have faith'.

How did they ever believe in him? That was the thing, though. Like religion, it was all based on trust. As long as people trusted you, you could sell them anything. And like the Church, once you constructed rituals around it, like weekly texts, newsletters and golfing away days, you were made. They were the financial equivalent of Mass, confession and the novena.

At the end, it was almost cultish. He shone with a halo, powered by greed, fuelled by other people's money and the promise of riches on this earth.

His mother bent down to hear a few words from one of the ancient nuns from the convent—the ones who never seemed to die but who would just shrink into themselves, as if sucked from within. A few older men, friends of his dad from way back in national school, shook his hand. How could they have such firm handshakes when they hardly seemed to breathe?

How did the investors not see that by guaranteeing them rent for three years with fictitious Lithuanian tenants, all he was doing was giving them a little bit of their money back, while taking the rest? And they thanked him for it!

He remembered the conversations.

Great deal, Kevin, thanks for thinking of us.

I wouldn't have done anything else.

We're in on the foreign one too, aren't we, Kevin?

You know you're always on the list.

June '09, you say. Sure, take the deposit now. It's only sitting there, wasting in the bank.

Grand so. I'll send you the forms.

Imagine what his dad's generation, the quiet old men at the back of the church, would make of that class of carry-on? Not a second house between them. They didn't turn the country into a nation of clawing absentee landlords.

He thought of his father and the shame he was about to bring on the family, their good name and the business. His dad had been the local auctioneer. When the Merchant started out, his father had warned him, that day in the back of O'Neills, 'Son, never slight anyone in the town even if you think he deserves it. These are our tribe. Never take the easy shilling. Always leave a lucky penny on the table for the next man and never, ever lie to anyone.'

Taking a sup of his Powers, the old man continued, 'Always keep in the back of your mind that we, your mother and I, you and Elaine and the children and your sisters, if they ever come back home from Dublin, have to live with these people. We've been here for years and we're not going anywhere.'

His dad would never have got into such a mess. He wasn't greedy. He was gentle and open. He loved the simple things in life, the Burren, the cliffs, the GAA. He was so proud of the Merchant and, unlike many Irish fathers, he told him.

The Merchant loved him for his tolerance, his calm and his ability to joke at the most difficult situation, but most of all he loved him because he was his dad and he was always there for him, even when the Merchant had no time for him. He'd always say, 'Don't worry, Kevin, you must have loads on your plate. Just call around when you have a bit of time.'

He hardly ever did and now he wanted him back. He'd give him all day and all night. He thought his dad would always be there—as he always had been.

EVERYONE LOVES A FUNERAL

He took a deep breath to make himself as broad as he could, as hand after sweaty hand clasped him. The ritual was alien to him. He wasn't prepared for any of this.

At one point, his mother was swamped by five members of the same clan. She disappeared into the vortex of their grief. The pungency of damp overcoats overwhelmed them all. The place smelt like a bookies.

He continued to calculate his downfall as somebody's husband gave him a bear hug.

'Be strong, take your time and don't do anything rash,' whispered a mourner, one of the dozens he hardly recognised.

Fr O'Mahoney swung the incense once more. He was trying to clear the place so that he could get home for *Nationwide*. You don't think they are like the rest of us, but they are.

But still they came. The line ran past the collection boxes and snaked around the Statue of St Jude—the patron saint of lost causes.

The family hadn't spoken much in the past three days. Apart from crying, they had hugged a lot and focused on making sure the sandwiches were made, the drink was bought and the aunties put up. His mother had grown bigger since the news, making the funeral arrangements and preparing the death notices, which his father had become so fond of reading as he got sicker and sicker. The death notice is a fine art. It signals the type of person you were. Not too over the top now. Simple, dignified, solemn.

'Everybody loves a funeral.'

His mother was bang on. Everyone turned up and the mother gave him a nudge when, as predicted, the town's official Banshee appeared from over the pew.

Every town has one. There is just a type who loves a bit of grief.

The Merchant only caught the relic of Padre Pio out of the corner of his eye as his mother reluctantly slipped it into her handbag. By then the Banshee, who hardly knew his dad, was whispering in the hushed, lispey tones of the pious, like a hundred Mary O'Rourkes wittering in unison, uttering devout incantations to yer man with the bleeding hands.

His father's old friends approached. They were the men of the 1930s, who were born into an Ireland of perennial underperformance. Theirs was the generation for whom the mailboat called. They were McAlpine's Fusiliers and the Dagenham Yanks rolled into one.

They lived their lives in towns none of them had ever heard of before they landed in Holyhead, strange-sounding places like Nuneaton, Bromley, West Bromwich, Hounslow and Stockport. The old men, stuffed into their over-sized navy Crombies, were back to mourn a decent man who, while a class above them, had always done everyone a good turn and looked after his own.

The Merchant turned from the old men to the decapitated Christ at the Seventh Station he had first noticed at confession years ago. He loved confession back then. It was part of the Saturday ritual wedged between hurling practice and an afternoon working on his uncle's bog.

There's something very comforting about the idea of confession. He could do with a bit of forgiveness now. In fact, the whole country could do with forgiveness for their debts.

He remembered the anxiety of waiting for his turn and counting the seconds as the penitent in front of him mumbled about unspeakable acts to the priest who went through the motions. His hushed blessings were always drowned out by the giggling, that unique and uncontroll-able giggling that can only come from the combination of church and six 13-year-old boys.

Then there was the ritual of comparing notes. 'What did you get?' 'Jesus, six Hail Marys, a Hail Holy Queen and a pair of Our Fathers.' Fr Moore was always the hanging judge of the place, doling out heavy sentences for tiny misdemeanours such as Macaroon bar thieving, which everyone knew was 'allowed'—and even expected—at that age. Anyway, the whole process of getting away with it appealed to him as a child.

As more arrived to offer their condolences, he found himself trying to pinpoint exactly when they stopped going to confession, him and his mates.

An old flame squeezed him and breathily kissed him on the ear, with the lingering intimacy of a former girlfriend. Perhaps it was the smell of fags and foundation, within sight of the confessional in which he'd made up heinous crimes to savour the essence of redemption, which triggered his memory.

They stopped going to confession when they understood what slow sets were for. He tried to stay calm in the face of the same lads, who now lined up to shake his hand, offer a few words and demand a few scoops with him after. But they too would have to find out.

'Sorry for your troubles, Kevin.'

It was Richie, his best friend and the man to whom Kevin had promised cash back before Christmas. Kevin knew Richie was stuck, what with Dell closing.

'He was a great man, a true man, the auld fella.'

'Do you remember the last time we all went to Croke Park?'

'Will we see you for one across the road?'

'Just the one and then yez'll all come back to the house for a few.'

'Rightso, Kev. Hang in there, man. You know we're always here for you. The lads will always be here.'

Oh sweet Jesus!

Most of the lads were not well-off and had given him their life's savings and even borrowed on his advice. What would they do when they found out the money was gone, their houses were on the line and that he had got a kickback from that sleeveen at National Irish to set up the loans in the first place?

They went back years, and yet he had led them all up the garden path.

His sister's blotchy eyes lowered slowly. This was her signal to the mourners to move on, she'd heard enough. It must have been something she learned over the years at parent-teacher meetings. Instead of telling some pushy cow that her child wasn't good enough for honours French, she'd just lower her eyes as the congenitally ambitious mother wittered on about how Saoirse was going to take a year out and work as a chalet girl in Chamonix after the Leaving.

'Honours French would be a great help on the Alpine piste,' she gushed.

His sister found that dropping her eyes slowly to the floor cut the conversation. It had the effect of making the speaker self-conscious and embarrassed. The gesture must have come from something deep in our Darwinian heritage, in the same way as raising your eyebrows signals disbelief.

Wherever it came from, it had the desired effect. The mourners moved on quickly.

His mother insisted that they would grieve like strong farmers— stoically. They were different; they had their dinner in the evening after all. Jackie Healy Rae was right all along about the plain people and dinner, and whenever he was right, his mother was happy to be wrong.

No one ever had 'dessert' in their house, or sat on a 'settee'; they asked for the 'loo' not the 'toilet'. They never said 'pardon'. They were not like the rest of the yahoos—a cut above, almost Planters.

The priests—his mother had drafted in and paid for three of them—coughed and spluttered and, because none knew how to turn

off the fancy new lapel mics, everyone heard them. The parish knew—
without even registering it—that a concelebrated Mass beat the sole
practitioner hands down. The local church works like an upmarket law
firm, the more partners who enter a meeting at the same time, the more
the client should be impressed. An altar full of priests is like a meeting
full of equity partners. Like a clatter of lawyers, a clatter of priests is
designed to impress.

The Merchant of Ennis knew all about these lawyer types because the
bigger his operation got, the more lawyers he met. He needed more and
more of these guardians of the law to sign off on the legality of something that was verging on criminal. But he wasn't alone and neither were
they. In fact, the whole country was coming down with lawyers by the
end of the nonsense. Ireland had fallen victim to a pandemic of
solicitors and its posher and more virulent strain, barristers.

The throat-clearing concelebrants made dignified grieving difficult.
His mother kept using the word 'dignity'. Appearances are important.
Ireland has always been like this. Even now, when the economy is
grinding to a halt, a significant proportion of official concern centres
on what others think of us.

Had we, the whole country, ever really been able to stand on our
own two feet, without constantly looking over our shoulder?

THE LAST RITES
The pub across the road was jammed for the customary few jars after
the removal. When you take people out of the church, the natural
flowing lexicon of Irish grief disappears and we get all tongue-tied and
anxious. It's only temporary because by the third pint we are back in
our professional bereavement councillor groove, but initially we say
whatever comes into our head and some, in an effort to lighten the
load, ignore the death completely.

The bar smelt of wet dog, Shake 'n' vac and chips.

'Jaysus, there ye are, man. Sorry for your troubles, but I was just
thinking of his face the day ye gave them hoors an arse-kicking in '97.
D'ya remember, Kev?'

'Oh I do, Richie. Dad was proud as punch.'

'Dirty fucks nearly ran straight home, with their banners up their
holes! And ye bating forty shades of shite outta them.'

Richie was pissed. He had been like this since Dell closed.

'You're right there, Richie, it was the craic.'

'Ye should have seen the fucks. Hadn't seen that look on anyone's face till the Deise were hosed down be the Cats last year.'

'True, true for you, Richie.'

'Jaysus, Kevin, you're some man for wan man, and ye'll stand tall after this. What ye havin', Guinness?'

'Three pints, Josie, and a Ritz.'

'C'meer, I know I shouldn't be saying this today of all days, but how's business?'

Before he could open his mouth, the question was answered for him as Richie, like many nervous people, had to fill the silence.

'I know, I know. Don't tell me about it. I wasn't going to mention it but things are a bit tight, Kev, ye know, with the place closing and all.

'In point of fact,' blurted Richie again, using the strange syntax the Irish employ when they want to be taken seriously, 'it's really a world-wide thing, isn't it, Kevin? No one's fault, really?'

The Merchant of Ennis still hadn't spoken.

'Not to worry. We bate them back in '97 and you takin' no prisoners and we'll bate them agin.'

Nobody would ever let him forget it. The day he became '97 Kevin. The day he walked out onto the pitch at Croke Park. The day he carried the hopes of the village on his broad shoulders. The man who led them out and put them on the map.

His mother was so proud, in her new rigout, listening to Nancy Griffith in the minibus. They were all there. No one would ever forget it. Everyone knew '97 Kevin after that. Everyone wanted a piece of him that night, even gorgeous Elaine Flannery whom he went home with, her gazing at him with the glazed flirtiness of seven vodkas.

No one would forget St Patrick's weekend 1997. Everything he'd ever done since stemmed from that match. It propelled him. Every deal, every introduction, every development was sealed with a few jars and other lads reminiscing. He pretended he couldn't remember, self-deprecating, but he remembered every move.

Three minutes to go, a goal and two down. All over. Local fellas, eight pints to the good—who couldn't hold it any longer—leaving before the whistle for a piss. Heads down.

'You're only a fuckin' choker, Rice, never had any balls, all mouth.'

'Captain? Me hole.'

Free in. He rises, takes and moves left, towards the corner flag on his poxy left side—bollix. Past two. Keeper's coming out. Pick your spot. He hits it hard and fast and bang, top corner. The flags go up. Christy Burke's flares erupt. The San Siro comes to Croker. Christy from down the road had been waiting for that since the trip up North to buy gargle, bangers and slabs of Twixes off the Prodies in Enniskillen.

'Only two in it,' screams his dad from the line.

He looked so big then, his dad. He was only a sparrow when he died.

'C'mon the 'Garritt, for fuck's sake!'

Last puck. It's so loud. Ref checks his watch, sliothar bobbing around in centre field. No one wants it. They're hiding. A blur. *It's mine, take the fuckin' thing.*

'Don't swing out, Kevin, don't be dumb.'

The veins in Fr O'Mahoney's face are popping.

Now it's quiet, all quiet, desperately quiet. It's almost slow-motion. Same again, to the left first, past the 20 m line. Have to come inside, couldn't risk it. A point won't do. The goal narrows. He feels the breath of Chops Walsh hot on his shoulder, spittle on his neck, hand on his jersey, dragging him back. Choking.

Don't go down, ref won't give it. Come inside. Drop the shoulder. Pull the trigger.

Oh sweet Jesus!

They all wanted to talk to him. The presenter with the bad wig on local radio had him on all Sunday morning. Auld wans kept phoning in, and Elaine winked at him through the raised pint glasses, pointing outside to the car park. Things would never be the same again. Onwards and upwards. Ballygarritt GAA Abu.

Now it was all over.

He knew what was coming and so did they. The pleading look in their eyes, desperate for some news. They wanted to hear it from him. Even though the horror stories were all around, they hoped that they'd be fine with him. They didn't know the half of it yet. He could only look nervously into his pint. He was, after all, their man. Everyone trusted '97 Kevin with their life and their money. Now with his dad gone, he was on his own.

When he bought the big site and put up the big house, with the first electric gates in the county, no one begrudged him. This was a first. But that's what they expected from a man at the top of the community.

Sure weren't the local Cumann crawling all over him to run next time out?

Being with Kevin Rice was half the battle for them. He conferred status. Proximity to the Merchant of Ennis was crucial. Knowing what he thought and doing what he did was almost as good as being the real thing.

'D'ya think so? It'll turn around? Next year?'

'Fuck, that'd be mighty, and the houses out the end of the town too, ye know the wans that were just put up?'

Jesus, he had forgotten about them. How did it all get so mad? He was the bricks and mortar version of the Pied Piper. He led half the village into all sorts of property deals. Worse still, these were syndicates—so in a matter of days, the real cash would have to be stumped up.

The locals were happy enough to trust his spoofing about the market turning around and 'hold on for a little while and you'll be grand', but the fine print of the contract was very clear. One of those lawyers would hammer it home any day now.

At the time, he didn't point out the small print to anyone and even if he had done, they were so immersed in the craze, they wouldn't have noticed. These little Donald Trumps would have followed him to the end of the earth and back. Sure didn't he send Killamatra flying in '97!

'The banks, ye say? Are they all right now, Kevin? Jaysus, they were fierce tight there earlier in the year. Criminals is what they are. Breaking the back of the working man, and they living the high life up there in Dublin.'

That was a change of tune from a few years ago when no one even talked about the banks. They were just there to give out cash for any hare-brained idea and if one of them didn't back you, the next one would. But now someone had to take the rap.

The next day, as the coffin went into the ground, the depth of the grave shocked him. It was such a long way down.

Dad was down there all alone, and he was up here, also isolated, for the first time in his life not knowing which way to turn.

Chapter 6 ᴏᴠ

| **SHYLOCK**

ON RIALTO BRIDGE

'What news of Rialto?'

'It's the same story as in Marino, Portobello and Pimlico,' said the Merchant.

'You know what this means, friend?'

'Yes. You'll get your brass and I'll get outta this mess.'

'Precisely, my friend.'

They both stood on Rialto Bridge. Each one looking down separately, seeing the reflections in the canal, two heads bobbing in the watery filth between the goslings, the Dunnes shopping trolley and the cans of Dutch Gold.

The Merchant of Ennis lit up a smoke. Shylock asked for one. They both inhaled deeply. The two of them had a funny habit of exhaling from their nostrils.

Through the smoke, from the crest of Rialto Bridge, they could both make out—beyond the Luas track—the first block of their development. This was where they were going to make a fortune.

Shylock would make the loan and take his cut and the Merchant of Ennis would use the money to pay off some of his debts back home in Clare. This way he could salvage most of the empire, pay off the local investors and keep going. Shylock was a genius when it came to money. Not the sort you'd go for a pint with, but good with figures.

This was the breathing space the Merchant needed and, more importantly, with the cash that these sales generated, Shylock would refinance the Merchant's whole portfolio from Marino, Pimlico and Portobello out to the retail park in Newbridge and, of course, the empty estate out on the Ennistymon Road. They could buy time. Because the development had the government as its key investor, they were both certain that the State wouldn't pull out of the deal. This was a flagship public private partnership, after all.

The State was the last cheque writer and had always stood behind its developer friends. The Merchant and Shylock gambled on the glad-handling and the culture of the Galway Tent to save them.

'It'll be like the first investment in the toll bridge, man. We'll make a fortune,' Shylock had told the Merchant.

'Same idea, man. These PPP—public private partnerships—are Fianna Fáil's way of looking after their mates. We take a small piece of the action 'coz the banks prefer a consortium to one big investor these days. We just wait till they rehouse those scobie fucks somewhere else. Then we sell the flats as canal side chic—Dublin's Little Venice or some other shit like that—to some rich NCAD twat with a degree in graphic design and Daddy's money.'

Shylock did a calculation. He was lightning quick.

'It's gold plated, man, and more importantly for you, you'll be square with all your other shit, no strain, man,' he said, smoke coming out of his nostrils.

Now here they were, umbilically linked, Shylock and the Merchant of Ennis. Tied together by the Rialto deal.

The Rialto project was very simple. It involved all the necessary ingredients. All they had to do was let it cook and allow the magic chemistry of greed, fear, leverage and aspiration to do its thing.

Shylock had graduated from flipping mortgages in a grubby mortgage broker outfit above a Chinese restaurant in town, where he learned all the most sordid tricks of the trade. Now he was respectable, he'd moved from River Island to Hugo Boss and was putting together consortiums for the big boys.

Like the rest of us, he had come a long way and he had no intention of going back.

NO GOING BACK, NOT BACK THERE
He had started straight after school in 1997 in one of the many mortgage brokers that popped up all over town as the property thing took off. He was only a kid. He was born in the third week of June in 1980, nine months to the week after the Pope kissed the tarmac on Dublin Airport and told the young people of Ireland he loved them.

His ma was very young, only 17 at the time. He lived with his nan and his ma all his life. His da scarpered. Bad enough getting someone up the pole at the Pope's Mass, but hanging around afterwards was a bit much to ask. Anyway, there was no work in the 1980s, so what could he have done?

When his da came back after getting drunkenly nostalgic with Jack's Army during the 1994 World Cup in Orlando, she and Shylock had moved on and the da wasn't welcome around their place. And his American mullet was shocking. Ma laughed with Shylock and said you couldn't have something like that living in the house. She was dead right.

Ma missed a part in *The Commitments* by one audition but that was her luck, his ma, always just about getting things and then having those things ripped away from her.

It wasn't going to happen to him. When he got his breaks he took them and when he saw his opportunities, nothing would stop him. The bosses of the mortgage broker's saw this in a matter of weeks. They would give Shylock the worst leads, the most hopeless cases, and he would be back in a day or two with a sale, a fully signed up mortgage application, plus insurance. No one else operated like this. None of the other trainees who spent all their wages in Copper Face Jacks came close to him. He could close any deal. When they boozed on a Friday, he would ask them for the potential clients who hadn't jumped that week. He offered them commission off his commission if he could reel in the client. For these Ross O'Carroll-Kelly types, who inhabited the nether regions of the finance world, Shylock was a soft touch—a chippy weirdo who worked all the time and listened to 1980s ska on his MP3 player.

But deep down he scared them. The way he watched them. The way he moved quickly, spoke in short rapid-fire sentences and drew little diagrams linking deals together. It was as if he had figured everything out before they had realised what they were playing for. It was as if he was in the heads of the people who were on the other end of the phone.

Shylock understood rejection. He understood that people just wanted to be loved and when you were desperate and coming to a mortgage broker, trying to scrounge together the money to buy your starter home in Dunleer, he knew what you wanted. He also knew what people would do to get cash. He had the sixth sense that all deal makers need. Shylock, in Ireland of the boom, had what it took to go far.

THE MIDDLEMEN AND THE CHAIN

The mortgage brokers had a direct line to the banks and their endless supply of easy credit, and they also worked with the developers. In some cases, the bosses of the mortgage brokers were on the boards of well-known estate agents.

The difference between Shylock and the other mortgage brokers is that he could see how the whole thing fitted together. The manic, spidery diagrams he drew as he spoke to some first-time buyer on the phone were his way of following the cash around. He was at the bottom, but he knew once he had seen the summit, he would figure out a way of getting there.

Shylock was always asking: Who is making the most? He understood that the poor first-time buyers on the phone looking for the best deal from him were at the bottom of the pile, becoming more and more addicted to easy money.

Working from the top down, Shylock followed the cash. In 1999, a developer bought a site for €2 million with money borrowed from Anglo Irish Bank. The site was 10 acres of virgin land out in Deckland. There was no planning permission but as it was a 10-acre site, the developer could apply for 10 units per acre. Back then, we were still talking about three and four bed semis in the new estates of Deckland. There were no detached houses or apartments. Ultimately, Shylock would be providing finance via the mortgage broker for these homes, but while that was his bread and butter, his prize was much bigger.

He understood that the developer got planning permission for 100 houses and the houses would sell for €200,000 each. That meant his top line would be €20 million from selling all the houses. Shylock started to salivate.

The 100 sites in the overall estate cost the developer €20,000 each. He sold them for €200,000. On his lunchbreak, when the others were sitting in Stephen's Green flirting with each other, Shylock went onto builders' websites to get an idea of how much it cost to build each house. He checked the figures with his uncle who was a chippy on the sites. They came to a figure of €60 a square foot to build. So the 1,000 square foot houses were costing €60,000 to build plus the €20,000 it cost to buy the land. Fees for the estate agents, the architects and the lawyers cost about 12 per cent, so that was another €20,000-odd. But still the developer was making about €100,000 on each house. Then

Shylock thought about VAT. That was 13 per cent, so the developer was making close to €80,000 pure profit on the house.

Shylock did some quick figures in his head. The developer was making €8 million on an investment that cost him €2 million in cash. Wow.

But it didn't cost him €2 million in cash because he borrowed the cash from Anglo Irish and, more to the point, he was getting paid almost straightaway. Shylock had noticed that all the calls that came in to him from first-time buyers were due for completion in 12 months' time. That meant that the deposit had been paid already. So the developer was getting the deposit, which was 10 per cent of the cost of €200,000 per house, upfront. That meant he had the entire site cost covered before he built the estate. All he had to do was build four show units, and the other people born around the time the Pope arrived here—the Pope's Children—would queue up and fork out the deposit and the developer was in the clear.

Shylock also recognised that while the developer was financed by Anglo Irish Bank, most of the mortgages he was arranging were financed by Bank of Ireland. But then when he was buying shares in Anglo Irish, which had to rise as it was the financer of these developers, he also noticed something else. The biggest shareholder in Anglo Irish Bank was Bank of Ireland, so the banks were together in this little scam.

The more Bank of Ireland financed these types of Deckland mortgages, the more money it made, but the more money Anglo Irish Bank made too. And the more money Anglo Irish Bank made, the higher its share price went and the more money Bank of Ireland made on its shareholding.

Shylock was amazed by the simplicity of the whole thing. As long as he kept feeding the suckers in at the bottom, the more the big lads made at the top.

And that is where Shylock wanted to be.

He wanted to be lending to the big fish at the top of the chain, rather than the little fish down here. But he was smart enough to know that if you can get money off poor people at the bottom, you can get multiples more off rich people at the top.

So he had to learn the tricks of the trade.

PYRAMID SELLING

Down at the bottom, the mortgage broker works on the basis of commission. The punters who phoned up looking for advice were not getting advice at all, but were tangling themselves up in a web of deceit.

For Shylock, the game was simple. The mortgage broker put an ad in the *Star* or ran one of those pay per click ads on the website of Daft.ie or Myhome.ie. The first-time buyer innocently called up, ostensibly looking for advice about which mortgage was the best to take.

Then Shylock went into overdrive. The broker was paid by the bank, which ultimately provided the mortgage on a commission of 1 per cent on every deal. When Shylock started out, the normal price of a new house in Deckland was €200,000. This went up to €300,000 by the time he'd moved on. So at the end, the broker company was getting €3,000 per house and the individual salesman who nailed the deal was getting a quarter of that figure. Shylock was taking home €750 personally on every mortgage he managed to sell.

So Shylock's motive was not to advise the people who rang but to sell to them. He queried why the people who were supposed to regulate this industry, whoever they were, allowed this stuff to happen. How could the biggest financial decision of a young couple be entrusted to a snake oil salesman who was in it for the commission? But what did he care? That was a problem for our politicians to figure out.

Every week there was a leader board listing which salesmen were doing the best. The weekly target for each broker was to close six sales. That would be €18,000 profit for the company, minus the four and half grand Shylock was taking for himself.

Some of the salesmen loved meeting the clients, taking them for lunch before taking their cash. Shylock never bothered. Why would he? He'd never see them again, so fuck them and their shitty little hopes and dreams, their decking, their Ford Fiestas, their car seats and infuriating little princesses, their crèches and their two-week holidays in Majorca. Sign up and disappear.

He advised on self-certified income statements. This happened when the banks got sticky about someone who clearly didn't have the income they claimed. He found a way they could sign a statement claiming that their income was sufficient. Everyone knew they were lying, but to get the business done Shylock told them to sign that their income was €80,000. He then came up with a little scheme to move whatever money they had into different accounts at different times in a week. The same €5,000 could be seen five times in the same week in separate accounts, so it looked like the guy had €25,000 in various accounts, each searching for the highest interest rate.

Shylock loved these people with self-cert mortgages because they were financed by the subprime outfits such as 'Moneyzone' that emerged in Ireland in 2002. They always charged the self-cert guy twice the interest rate for his mortgage because the big banks had rejected him. In many cases, the big banks were shareholders in these subprime outfits, but no one was to ever know!

This meant that Shylock got a bigger commission and, more crucially, these financial delinquents at the very bottom had to buy mortgage insurance, which he also got a cut of.

He could never figure out what financial model said that you charge the riskiest mortgage—the self-cert one—the highest interest rate and expect to be paid back. This seemed to almost guarantee default. But what did he care? No one asked him to offer aftersales service. We were all big boys now and anyway, he was taking his cut off the top.

As always on a Friday when the rest were heading to Ron Blacks, Shylock took his commission and headed for home on the 123 bus that meandered through the city, starting in Marino and terminating in Rialto.

He pulled out his notebook and started to make the connections. He scratched out a pyramid. At the bottom were broke Decklanders paying 8 per cent interest on a mortgage for a semi-D in Enfield. They paid the company 1 per cent of the total price, which is why the bosses of the company were driving fuck off motors and hanging out in the Shelbourne. He took his cut too.

He then drew an arrow to Bank of Ireland, which was offering only 1 per cent interest on deposits but charging its clients on average 5 per cent. So it was making free money: 4 per cent profit straight off the top. Then he drew a line to the developer. He was building the houses, making a fortune and buying more land to do exactly the same. But where did his money come from? That's when the arrow pointed to Anglo Irish Bank. It was financing the developer, but because the developer was selling off plans and Shylock was facilitating it, there was no risk. He, Shylock, at the bottom of the pile, was underwriting and minimising the risk at the top by signing up all the little people. He then drew a line from Anglo Irish Bank to Bank of Ireland. They pretended to be in competition, but Bank of Ireland Asset Management was the biggest shareholder in Anglo Irish, so if Anglo Irish did well, the top brass at Bank of Ireland looked very clever. And all because they were part of a pyramid scheme selling overpriced houses to poor commuters in the new suburbs.

It was all so simple. Why did they not see it, the fools on the bus? Why didn't the people on the streets, the lads drinking in the barge pub in the summer sunlight, see that they were the eejits at the bottom?

Shylock looked again at his piece of paper. Where the developer and the swanky brass of the banks were at the top, he drew a little spindly man like the one in the kid's game hangman, which he hated because of his dyslexia. That was him. That's where he was going—to the top.

As the bus headed up the canal, he folded the piece of paper back into his notebook and stuffed it into the pocket of his jacket.

From the second seat from the front at the top where he always sat, he watched the city change as the bus moved from street to street, 'Rat Race' by The Specials—his ma's favourite song—blasting out of his headphones.

That Rat Race shit wasn't for him. No fuckin' way, man.

Chapter 7

MISS PENCIL SKIRT GOES TO KILBARRACK

CRASH

Her phone rings. Where is it?

The traffic is brutal as always on Mondays. The squeaky sound of the wipers is getting on her nerves as she tries, faithful Tweezerman in hand, to pluck her eyebrows. This manoeuvre is difficult as she is in first gear, foot permanently on the clutch to avoid the irate account director in his BMW 5 series who is trying to cut her up.

He is raging and looks straight ahead, greying temples, not catching her eye. He knows she's there. In fact, he knows she is in the right and he is in the wrong. That just makes him more irritable. He barks orders at some poor graduate trainee back at the office. He is shouting into that strange piece of Lego stuck to his ear. This makes him look like a manager in a call centre rather than the Master of the Universe he would like to be. Someone should take him aside and have a word.

She pulls a face in the mirror, arching her brows. Are they too dark? She'd never noticed their colour until the last time she got her caramel-blonde highlights done but now she's obsessed. *Are my eyebrows too black?*

She shouldn't have done it at home. What was she thinking, dyeing her hair at home? End of January. A case of no money and too many direct debits. 'Casting' by L'Oréal—'coz you're *not* worth it—should come with a chemical warning. Maybe she overdid it. Most of the time it worked, she sometimes even looked like Nina Persson rock chick chic. But today she catches herself in the mirror and Myra Hindley stares back at her.

The wipers are getting louder. It is the soundtrack of Irish commuters, the grating sound of a worn wiper in a car that is 4,000 miles past its last service date and would need a Janet Jackson-style makeover to pass its NCT.

The front seat is crammed: hairbrushes, makeup, clips, Nicorette and Converse trainers. She shouldn't treat her vintage vw Beetle like this—after all, it is costing her a fortune per month.

Where is that bloody phone? The BlackBerry vibrates. She's leaning right across the car now, groping around with her tiny hands for her bag on the passenger floor. This is quite a stretch, but she's straining all 5 ft 4½ in. of her. She can feel her skirt hitch up around her ass. There it is, in the side pocket of her Orla Kiely bag, ringing away. One last dip and she'll have it.

Like a diver taking a breath before a descent, she looks up, sees that the traffic's stuck on the far side of the yellow box and dives, deep over the passenger seat, past the packet of Kleenex, the nail varnish, plump-up lippy and broken earrings. She has it!

Suddenly there's a bang and then a horrible scraping, crunching metallic sound. The contents of the passenger seat—scratched CDs, old packs of Marlboro Lights, *Vanity Fair* and *Hot Press* magazines and a shirt she was returning which was too big (yesss, the Elizabeth Hurley raisin diet is working)—slide down on her head.

Oh no, she's stuck.

She can't get up. Her stomach muscles are aching from that Pilates class she did last Friday. She has no strength.

Yer man is out of his Beemer in a flash, incandescent. Before she can straighten up, he's towering over the passenger window, glaring right up her skirt. She's lost her left shoe in her unsuccessful battle with the clutch. She cocks her head at a 45-degree angle, wedged as she is between the passenger seat, a Marks and Spencer's avocado and prawn sandwich wrapper and the glove compartment which opened on impact to reveal a Domino's Pizza flyer and two unpaid parking fines.

She smiles, raises her eyebrows as if to say 'shit happens'. He is not even looking at her. He is stretched across the bonnet, checking her out-of-date tax disk.

There's no shame in a size 17 neck, she thinks. He should really wear a bigger size shirt as the little folds of pinched fat pucker just under his Terry Wogan collar. Bad choice: white collar, blue shirt makes him look like an American accountant facing a massive fraud charge—you know the type of story tv3 news has on last before the celebrity gossip roundup.

She inelegantly leverages herself up, practically impaling herself on the gear stick. She finds the missing shoe, gets out of the car and straightens her pencil skirt, pulling it down as close to her knees as it will go, but it's still stuck up too far.

'Hey, like, I'm so sorry.'

'Have you seen my car?'

'Sorry, I didn't see you.'

'That's not fucking surprising; you were stuck under the seat. What were you doing?'

'It doesn't matter. It's a long story. What are we going to do now?'

Better play dumb. She can't afford this but when he is wearing a red tie with the Roadrunner on it, how can she possibly take him seriously? And Jesus, it has been a long few days. She hasn't been home since Friday. There was the annual off-site weekend conference event, followed by a meeting this morning in Limerick and she's only getting back to Dublin this wet Monday afternoon.

Christ, it's all coming back now. What was she thinking of last night? All that and now this!

'You'll be hearing from my solicitor.'

Stupid prick.

OFF-SIDE AT THE OFF-SITE

How could she have done it? I mean, the Aussie from accounts! In front of everyone!

But office 'away days' bring out the worse in all of us.

In January 2008, business was still booming. Miss Pencil Skirt was working in PR.

Because they had nothing better to do with all their cash, she was asked to organise an off-site event in a new spa hotel where the 'team' could go and bond with the bosses.

If you haven't been on one of these, don't worry. You won't be at one now because, like queues in Brown Thomas, they are so 2008. Up to last year, they were all the rage. Now they look like yet another one of those excesses that we got caught up in like many of our fads in the boom, such as having a holiday home in the country, a place to get away from it all when, in fact, most of us had just come from the country and couldn't wait to get out of the place.

Workers, who spend their entire day dreaming of being somewhere else, are forced to get together under the guidance of an over-enthusi-astic human resources manager who speaks in 'booklet English'—a strange corporate Esperanto learned by people who did Biz Org in their Leaving Cert.

Even the description 'human resources' should warn us. At least when these places were called personnel departments, you could have the satisfaction of knowing that you were considered a real living, feeling person. You might not be as important as the manager in the accounts department but at least you were a step up from the filing cabinet. When you went to Personnel with personal issues like a death in the family, a holiday query or a request to go on a spoof course, the idea that your entire worth was being assessed, costed, calculated and determined by a simple input/output equation was not signalled directly.

Sometime in the mid-1990s, the corporate world decided to dispense with the pretence of Personnel—the pretence that your whole person was in some way of intrinsic value. Instead you became a resource, like the filing cabinet or the electricity that keeps the building lit—a human resource but a resource nonetheless. *Hi, my name's Grainne. I'm a resource.*

These days, even as the economy is collapsing around us, human resource departments are still coming up with initiatives culled from gobbledygook MBA textbooks which are always down-sized, company-wide, task-specific, people-centred, goal-orientated, growth-targeted, client-focused, time-saving, knowledge-enhancing, audience-appropriate, team-building, earnings-driven, profit-sensitive, carbon-neutral, dim-witted bullshit.

The conference theme is 'Knowledge Management—How to leverage know-how in a hostile environment'. God knows what it means but that doesn't matter because it's Showtime. The weekend will be Glastonbury for people who work in quoted companies, with Dad rock, dangerous liaisons and soggy canapés.

These are bread and butter gigs addressed by marketing gurus, self-help charlatans and even economists who've rebranded themselves as futurologists. Yet all these actors are mere fluffers for the main act, which is always the right-on, I'm one of you, ordinary-guy CEO. Even now, when everything is going pear-shaped, part of the corporate story always has to be progress; you too can make it. Reach for the stars. Realise your potential.

At half past eight, the pushy PA, who's been with the CEO since 1998, takes over proceedings. She's got that scary look about her, like a

German anti-nuclear activist from the 1980s with angular glasses, spiky plum hair and a clipboard.

She's Irish but has been in the us for three months so she says things like 'ball-park', 'touch base' and 'in the zone'. She also has a habit of saying, 'ya know what?' in response to every question she's asked. For example:

'Would you like a cup of tea?'

'Ya know what? I won't.'

Ten minutes before the 300 workers—described grandiosely as 'associates'—arrive to pay homage to the corporate gods, the stage is full of skinny lads in Converse high-tops, drainpipes and black T-shirts (the worldwide uniform of seasoned roadies who are always dry in that 'just-Earl-Grey-for-me' reformed alcoholic way). There are cables and bits of duct tape everywhere. At 8.50am, there is the soundcheck.

The chief executive—who has also spent time in the States, bounds in all chummy and practises his nonchalant, spur-of the moment, off-the cuff, learned-off-by-heart speech. He is media-trained to within an inch of his life, right down to the phoney pauses, drum rolls and inserted gags.

These conferences always open with a blast of U2's 'Beautiful Day', cue dry ice and a light show worthy of a mid-1980s prog-rock stadium gig. The CEO takes to the stage to thunderous applause, coffee-to-go in his hand. He says something entirely predictable like 'Yikes, now this is scary.' The crowd laughs uproariously, the sort of forced howl Ceausescu used to get.

He starts the verbal high-fives immediately, congratulating everyone for targets met and standards set. He refers to the head office as Redwood—an anodyne suburb of St Louis—saying how Redwood 'respects' Dublin (thanks, we need that) and reaffirming that the people are the company, that without the people they'd be nothing. By satellite link up he introduces us to a black receptionist from Illinois with Alicia Keyes braids. 'Dioneesha Wilkins is the face of the company,' he smarms. 'She's been employee of the month six times and it's hundreds of ordinary people like Dioneesha who make this company great'— which is obviously why Dioneesha has to get the bus to work.

He does a Bill Cullen and gives the crowd his life story—wrong side of the tracks, hard-working mother, kitchen-table wisdom and penny apples—it's all standard rags to Ritz-Carlton stuff delivered in that 'Jesus Christ Superstar', would-you-believe, evangelical CEO tempo. The chinos are slightly loose, pushed down by the paunch. He has an open-necked pink aertex with an ad for the world's top-selling incontinence drug on the sleeve. He looks like an overweight caddy. He wears jewellery. You just know he has a copy of *Foreigner 4*. There's a hint of a mullet.

All the talk is of winners, going the extra mile, digging deep, being there for each other, listening, the 'go-to-man', being counted, respecting the opposition, the importance of Number 1, merit, co-operation, potential, uniqueness, diversity, systems, integration, loving the company, loving your work, loving yourself. When you put it all together, it's about nothing and everything. Churchillian, it is not.

The second part of the speech—introduced with a video of underprivileged people to the background track of the pumping 'Right Here, Right Now' by Fatboy Slim—is about the latest fad: corporate social responsibility. Normally, there will be a message from some Irish tax exile who is a large shareholder about the need for the corporation to look after the community, to give back, to share and to be a part of the community, which explains why he resides in St Barts and comes home to Ireland to deliver speeches on corporate social responsibility and open pro-celebrity golf classics.

At this stage, everyone but the top brass of the company is texting each other, finding out what room everyone is in or who's not playing paintball this afternoon.

Most of the girls are thinking of the massage they've booked for the afternoon before the big night and whether there's time to pop into town and change those new shoes that are killing them. Silent texts flash up in the darkness all over the hall, which has been designed with a galaxy effect ceiling. The only lights are the spots picking up the beads of sweat on the forehead of the corporate Sun God on stage.

Time's dinner?
Massage this aft?
R u listnin 2 dis shit?

COLLAPSE
The corporate conference market was the fastest growing segment of the Irish hospitality market. In 2007, it grew by over 50 per cent. It has collapsed completely.

And the impact of this slump is being felt throughout the economy. Most worryingly, the impact has been savage on some of the enormous hotels that have been built around the country in the past two or three years. Few things evidence the boom better than the explosion of spa hotels catering for people who want to spend their weekends in a glorified kettle with a bar and an expensive restaurant with a celebrity chef's signature on it.

In Ireland, the property boom was coincident with the collapse of Church vocations. Thus demand and supply intersected at the sweet spot where deconsecrated seminaries miraculously reinvented themselves as new golf and spa hotels.

The first Irish revolution saw the Catholic Church—enriched by donations from the poorest population in Europe in the 1940s and 1950s—buying these places from down-at-heel Protestant landlords. Possibly this felt like payback time for some. The Church ended up owning the gaffs of the Ascendency whose ancestors had introduced the Penal Laws precisely to prevent Catholics owning this type of thing.

In the second great transfer, the enfeebled Church sold the mansions on to syndicates of the lapsed but rich grandchildren of the cowed peasants whose donations paid for them in the first place. These syndicates, rarely involving anyone with any experience of the hospitality sector and financed by local banks, went mad building all classes of golf course and spa across the country. They tried to out-spa each other with all sorts of phoney cultivations like 'moss rooms' and 'tropical rain or monsoon shower effects'. In the grounds, Corpus Christi processions gave way to VIP-sponsored celebrity golf tournaments in late May.

We are now in the phase of the third great transfer of the Irish gentry's houses. These places are bust and the developers have handed the keys back to the banks, who in turn have handed them back to the State. By way of the farce called NAMA, our government has decided to bail out the banks so the State is about to give us the bill. So with perfect symmetry, these useless golf courses are back in our hands, the grandchildren of the people who bankrolled the Church to buy them and the great-great-grandchildren of the people who worked the land to generate the cash for the Ascendency to live on them in the first place.

FOLLOW THE MONEY
In the same way as the houses have now reverted to us, whether we want them or not, a circular flow of cash is evident throughout the economy.

If we follow this circular flow, we can see what can happen quickly to an economy as integrated and small as ours.

Let's take the collapse of the corporate hospitality market as an interesting microcosm of the greater economy. We can see how one small change in confidence can have dramatic effects on places and jobs that seem to have no real connection to each other.

Miss Pencil Skirt's PR company's main client was one of the big mobile phone operators which was doing very well in the boom. We are a chatty bunch and were sending more texts and spending longer on the phone than any other nation in Europe. Yes, there was a worry that we might be reaching saturation point, but in 2008 there was no real cause for concern.

But like all mobile operators, the company was carrying lots of debt, which it borrowed to roll out the infrastructure and buy the mobile licence. Equally, the PR and marketing budget was huge because as there is no real difference between the phone companies, the only way to distinguish themselves was by constantly arguing that there *is* a difference via advertising messages on billboards, on the radio and TV, in the papers and online. If the truth be known, the mobile company was less about telecom technology and more about advertising. It had to constantly be inside the head of a fickle user, doing deals, giving bargains and, most of all, keeping the account. This is particularly the case for corporate accounts. Big companies spend a fortune on mobile phone bills and if you can keep these accounts, you are in business.

In late spring 2008, the operator begins to experience a falloff in some big companies, particularly estate agents and builders. Revenue starts to plateau but, as Irish wages are rising, costs are rising significantly. Also, the huge debts the company has are being rolled over all the time to reduce the interest rate cost. In September of last year, credit suddenly dried up. This lack of credit in the economy hits the company in four ways. First, its debt-servicing costs rise. Second, the corporate phone accounts are pared back by their clients who are also struggling. Third, we all start looking for bargains to reduce our mobile bills. Fourth, the company's share price tumbles, reducing its size and therefore reducing the other way it used to raise money, which was by issuing more shares.

So the accountants storm into the boardroom and advise the chief executive that she has to cut down on all spending to get the books back on track.

Miss Pencil Skirt, whose salary rose last year for the fifth year in a row, took out a mortgage only two years ago. Why wouldn't she? Everyone else was doing it.

THE SYNDICATE, SPRING 2008

Meanwhile, in Donnybrook, an estate agent is talking to a doctor in a cafe. The paperwork is ready for signing. The syndicate will have to put up only a tiny amount of cash. The bank has cleared the 80 per cent financing. The hotel is generating cash and, most crucially, the corporate market is booming. The spa is full most of the time and the course will benefit enormously from the appearance of Padraig Harrington next year. The Diarmuid Gavin landscaping has already got it into the *Irish Times* weekend section, adding enormously to its cachet in Dublin 4. It was mentioned last night at the dinner party.

The deal is done.

The avaricious doctor was frustrated that people with considerably less education than himself seemed to have become millionaires just by borrowing, buying hotels and flipping them on. He wants in on that game and in March 2008 NCB stockbrokers published a report saying that any slowdown would be brief. The softness of the market, according to the estate agent, was an opportunity to buy. And why wouldn't he trust the director of one of Ireland's leading property outfits? After all, he'd known him for years. They were in the same year in school if not quite the same stream.

He now owns a hotel.

THE SYNDICATE, SUMMER 2008 TO FEBRUARY 2009

By June 2008, the phone company is feeling the pinch and it starts to cut back. The accounts decree that there will no more sports sponsorships and no more away days for the team for now. It tries to keep redundancies to a minimum at this stage, assuming that the downturn will be modest and the young population will start chatting again soon. All its calculations on profitability rely heavily on this demographic dividend that the Pope's Children are supposed to give Ireland.

The first the hotel's receptionist hears of the cancellation for January 2009 is the email, curt and direct. This year's do is cancelled. The hotel moves to drop its price, but the email refers to something called 'blanket company policy'.

The hotel, in an effort to balance the books, pulls advertising from the local paper and puts some of the local staff on reduced time. But the reduced hours make it impossible for the barman to pay the mortgage he has just taken out on a house in the new estate, Ossory Court, outside town. It's smarter financially for him to go on the dole and get the State to pay his mortgage interest via mortgage relief. Then he will sell his new place—it's only eight months old—and see what happens. He can always pick up a nixer here and there. It's bound to be temporary.

The roadies see work drying up. They're normally flat out at this time of the year but the gigs aren't happening. Without the gigs, the hotel is empty. There's no one in the spa and the golf course is a wilderness. But both have to be maintained. The hotel had marketed itself as a 'destination' hotel for the corporate sector. Now there is no corporate business.

The doctor gets a call from the estate agent to explain a clause they had overlooked in the prospectus. It referred to the difference between the notional value of the hotel and the overall debt. It says something about the bank having recourse to cash if the value of the hotel fell below a certain level. But they'd never discussed that. It was always assumed that the only problem was how to best dispose of the capital gain from a tax point of view. This is why he put the hotel in his name not a company name, because he would only pay 20 per cent capital gains rather than the 30 per cent corporation profit tax. He's on the hook and the hotel is haemorrhaging money.

Miss Pencil Skirt is also feeling the pinch. Her company became too dependant on fees from the mobile company which is now drastically cutting back on its PR budget. In turn, her company is not giving any business to the advertising company which now has to lay off staff. These redundant workers, who used to buy newspapers every day, now simply go online. The newspapers get hit twice, both in advertising revenue and circulation falls, which means that even if there is advertising next month, the price of that has to fall too. The paper's marketing department, which used to make a fortune in commission, is also slashed. The first thing to go in the dwindling marketing department is the expense account at its favourite restaurant in town. The restaurant, which had just won a Michelin star, had been all over the papers and its celebrity chef had featured on a TV programme, can't get money from the banks to tide it over this drop in business. Without working capital, it can't pay its suppliers. The first to get hit is the butcher, who is owed €20,000. And on it goes, around and around in a downward spiral.

Miss Pencil Skirt can't quite understand why her boss is not speaking to her. They used to be such good friends, whispering conspiratorially. But the wind has changed. Everyone is nervous.

In the end, even she was shocked by the head of human resource's use of language.

'We have to talk to you about your role with regard to the current economic climate.'

Pathetic.

The long faces and the manager's weasel words about it being a 'business decision' made her feel that these people could never hurt her. What was she losing sleep over?

They droned on.

'It's nothing personal and although the market is soft out there, someone like you should not have a problem.'

She was remarkably calm throughout and it was they who squirmed, embarrassed by their behaviour. She had the upper hand and she knew it. She was resigned but free and not half as hassled as she thought she'd be.

She gave back her company badge and swipe card. And walked, if not confidently, at least unbowed out into the sun.

KILBARRACK, MARCH 2009

The man in hatch 7 was getting increasingly agitated.

'I wouldn't have signed that if I had known . . .'

'Well, you'd have known if you'd read all the forms. You're going to be here for a while.'

The place could kick off at any time.

He had his head in his hands. He was at his wit's end. He was vaguely familiar, but she couldn't place him. She'd definitely seen him before. Here amongst the hatches, all was a blur.

It reminded her of her first day in secondary school when she didn't know anyone. She had clutched her schoolbag—the one with her name on it—tightly. My God, so many people, so many strange-looking people who seemed to know what they were doing and where they were going. She was completely lost. The girl formerly known as the head of PR was way out of her depth.

She hadn't realised it was a 'ticket pulling system'. So she had to start all over again. When the next number came up it was 39. Her ticket said 143. But that's the system: either you know it or you don't. One thing was clear: she'd better get to know it quickly.

Back at hatch 7 the argument continued.

'But it's not worth anything. Haven't you heard of negative equity?'

'Sorry, sir, that's not my problem. A second house is a second house. Investment or not. Whether it's worth a million or nothing.'

'What are you saying?'

'Keep your voice down. I'm saying that it affects your welfare position.'

'Jesus fucking Christ! I can't believe this is happening.'

'Please, stand aside and wait for an inspector.'

She's afraid to catch his eye. She didn't expect to see someone she recognised, especially here. She had joined the ranks of the one in sixes. That's the one in six or 15 per cent of the workforce who are likely to find themselves unemployed in Ireland when this depression beds down.

Oddly she hadn't made the link between the two offices—once she'd left the old one, it was only a matter of time before she turned up at her new one. The day she was told that it was all over at the upmarket chrome and steel office on the docks, the last thing on her mind was the dingy dole office in Kilbarrack with its grey plastic seats, its interminable queues, hatches and forms.

She had become used to views out over the Liffey and beyond to Howth. You could see the mountains of Mourne on a good day. This was her world. It was their world, the graduates of the late 1990s. These were the Pope's Children, the children of the boom. They weren't equipped to deal with the welfare office in Kilbarrack.

So she devoured 'What to do if you think you are about to lose your job' and 'What to do the day you lose your job' in the *Independent* and similar articles in the *Irish Times*. She absorbed everything about job cuts in the news. Poor souls. She could never understand why public sector journalists in RTÉ, who can't be laid off, thought it acceptable to doorstep people at the gates of mothballed factories when they'd just been let go. She was surprised someone hadn't told the interviewers with the silly little self-important mics to just piss off. What purpose did these interviews serve? You were hardly going to get a redundant bloke with kids at home saying, 'Sure it's great. I feel fantastic, never better. Thanks for asking.'

At the beginning, the former head of PR looked on the bright side. At least she didn't have kids and crèche fees. She had a mortgage, but she'd manage for a while. She was one of the lucky ones, really. But still she regarded 'the unemployed' as being different to her. She wasn't one of these people, was she? It just didn't sound right. She had an honours degree, for God's sake. She half expected someone to come up and tell her it was all a weird UCD experiment to assess people in stressful situations.

At first, she had joined LinkedIn, set up a Twitter account and updated her Facebook page. You've got to keep connected, the articles said, but with whom? For what? Networking, that's what it was all about, the man said on the website. She realised how many others were in her position from the number of LinkedIn and Facebook requests for her to be friends with other people. People like her, from her year in college, who hadn't bargained for this and didn't know what to do.

But it all changed quite quickly. It had never crossed her mind that she might have to wait in a dole office for her 'Jobseeker's Benefit'. People like her just didn't go on the dole. It was her friend who suggested it to her. She didn't know what to do or where to go. So like thousands of others, she went online.

A week after her last day at work she found herself in the Kilbarrack Social Welfare Office. She self-consciously joined the queue for 'New Enquiries'. A handwritten sign on a sheet of paper was helpfully taped on the wall, with an arrow pointing towards two hatches at the side.

Over the weeks, the office had to employ a man to direct hundreds of bemused new arrivals. What was a trickle had turned into a flood. She turned up at 10.45am. There were 11 people in the queue ahead of her but a line quickly formed behind her. She was relieved she didn't live in the city centre where the queues of new applicants stretched down the street and regularly featured in news reports and photos. The last thing she wanted was to be spotted.

She sat reading the *Times* business section, looking for a job and wondered how, with a degree and two postgraduate diplomas, she had come to be here. After seven years in London working for two of the world's five largest PR companies, she had come home. She excelled in this glittering new role. Everything was moving in the right direction and she'd breezed through her mortgage application with help from that highly efficient but rather distant mortgage broker.

But now, inexplicably, she was sitting beside a chain-smoking single mother in a tracksuit who, unlike her, was taking everything in her stride.

They glanced at each other—the novice and the pro—and smiled. The younger woman, sensing her unease, told her not to worry, just to make sure all the forms were filled in correctly and to be sure to get her rent allowance. The PR Queen, who was in designer jeans and cashmere—wanting to appear casual but not destitute—was offered a squashed Johnny Blue.

'We'll be here for ages, love. Smoke?'

'Why not? Thanks.'

Here she was applying to the Irish government for handouts, and now going outside to share a smoke with a girl she would have crossed footpaths to avoid three weeks ago. It was surreal, she thought as she accepted the smoke, but she'd better get used to this. She dragged deeply.

Jesus, she loved smokes. As the nicotine found its way into her veins, things began to calm down. Edel, her new best friend, was a mine of information. It was like learning a new language, this form for this, that form for that.

This was a bizarre experience, truly. She was becoming one of them. She felt bemusement rather than depression at her predicament as she went back in and looked around, not wanting to catch anyone's eye, but intent to see the lie of the land. The new arrivals were easy to spot. They sat and stared blankly like people do on the Tube. Only the hardened ones in the trackkies chatted away, hoop de hoop earrings flying everywhere as they nattered about Jordan and Peter Andre.

The familiar man at hatch 7 was still complaining, 'But no one told me about that . . .'

This made her nervous. *Please don't shout*, she thought. *It's so undignified.* Even here, middle class girls still clung to such things as dignity, still worried about what is and isn't acceptable behaviour and still tried to preserve the fragile standards of their upbringing as everything was falling apart.

A row of people waited to be seen. As each person was served, they moved a seat to the left. It was like musical chairs but without the music and their present would be acceptance of their claim. At the top of the queue was a hard woman with a Benson and Hedges face and lank dyed black hair pulled back in a ponytail—the Kilbarrack facelift. She fidgeted. In fact, everyone was fidgeting.

Miss Pencil Skirt had arrived with no idea what would happen. Would they take her off to an office for an interview? Having read the online information, she was armed with a folder containing her P45, her P60, her last three months' payslips, the Social Welfare card she was sent on turning 16, the letter she was given at work outlining her termination by reason of redundancy, the letter she signed agreeing her redundancy payment, two job applications in case she had to prove she was looking for work, her passport and driving licence (in case they wanted 'ocular proof' that she was who she said she was) and her application for the Jobseeker's Benefit, which she had printed off from www.welfare.ie. There was no way they could say no to her. She was the best-prepared dole applicant that had ever walked through the doors. She couldn't help it. That's just the way she was.

When it was finally her turn, unlike the others who snarled, she smiled and said 'Good Morning' to the surprisingly helpful matronly lady at the hatch. The Matron looked relieved to be dealing with someone from her own class. She took her form and looked at her sympathetically.

'Oh. You're one of the New Ones.'

'Yes, I suppose I am.'

'We get all sorts in here'—pointing to a knot of overweight girls in pyjamas—'That lot would buy and sell you.'

Edel was in the middle, cackling.

'Then we get people like you who shouldn't be here.'

She talked in a 'we're all in it together' way, as if it were the Blitz they were dealing with and not grubby local financial meltdown.

She didn't need to see anything in the carefully prepared folder except for the cold termination letter and, after checking that she had paid enough 'stamps'—whatever they were—the Matron finally said, 'Wait to hear from us. Applications are taking about five weeks to process.' The PR girl was relieved. According to the papers, in places like Trim they were taking 15 weeks.

She nodded to Edel as she headed out.

'Sorted, love?'

'Yes, I suppose so. I suppose you could say that. Thanks for the smoke.'

'No strain, love. Later.'

She stopped by the noticeboards at the door. After all, she had a day to fill. There were posters for MABS for those in debt, Samaritans ads for those who needed a friend, CDVEC courses for those who had the energy, extra payments for the long-term (5 years) unemployed, Leaving Cert Applied courses for those at the bottom, One Family for Edel and her mates, Threshold for those about to be thrown out of their 'dream home' and a mental health agency for those who couldn't cope.

This is Ireland. This is our country, she thought. *What has become of us?*

She became aware of a presence. He was flicking through the Threshold leaflet. He was a bit too close for comfort. Someone who didn't value personal space too much. It was the angry guy from hatch 7.

Oh!

Yes, it was *him.*

It was him all right. He'd lost a few pounds and his hair was a bit greyer. But it was definitely him—the same guy she had crashed into over a year ago.

'I'm still waiting for that solicitor's letter,' she quipped, flicking her hair.

He squinted and then smiled. He remembered her and now they were bonded like so many thousands of us in a way that neither of them would have thought possible the afternoon she drove into him.

He mellowed. It was over. That era was past.

'You'll be waiting a while.'

'Why?'

'He's on remand.'

Chapter 8

BREAKFAST ROLL MAN'S U-TURN

UP THE BONDI JUNCTION
How in God's name did he do that?

The nurse looked quizzically at him and his limp arm. Nothing in Bondi had prepared her for the sight of a young man, his skin red raw from the sun, suffering from almost third degree burns. There he was, sweltering in a sweaty Waterford GAA strip with unflatteringly tight acrylic nicks, ankle socks and white boot-runners. He must've looked a sight on the beach beside the body beautiful surfers.

There are two types of people on Bondi Beach. The beautiful people and the Irish.

The first species is the sculpted, toned, buff Aussie surfer. All sun-bleached hair, bright white teeth and toned limbs, like milk-fed cattle. Just the right proportions, strong features, physical perfection . . . and that's just the straight blokes!

Gay men built like Bette Midler's backing dancers in outrageously skimpy budgie smugglers ignore the Elle MacPherson clones doing tai chi as they wait patiently for the right waves. They catch their own reflection in the perfect symmetry of the board: long, smooth and sleek. Many have taken advantage of the 'unisex Brazilian' for $60 in the Body Express beautician on the strip just above the beach. The back, sack and crack wax business is booming.

Bondi is a homage to the body. The shops on the strip advertise body piercing, tattoos and all classes of massage designed to enhance your physical appearance. Just the place for the Irish to feel at home, then. No pressure.

The exercise bars on the beach are a vehicle for the turbocharged vanity that dominates Bondi. The bars are a bragging opportunity for

the most beautiful of the hard-torsoed ones. Lifting yourself up effortlessly places you firmly at the top of the hierarchy. It speaks of graceful,
unforced muscle control and, of course, denial. By levering yourself
upwards in one uninterrupted feline movement, you have achieved
virtue. You're no ordinary gym bunny. You have reached an elevated state
of physical grace. You know you are being watched, envied, admired.
Healthy mind, healthy body. You are Adonis and you're probably tantric.

Adonis fears ugly things. Which is why the sight of the second
species must've been, for him, like an Indian seeing Columbus for the
first time, peering out from the jungle, some distant cousin of human-
ity. For Adonis, seeing the second species on Bondi could only have
reinforced his belief in evolution. *Sometime*, he thought, *millions of
years ago, we were related*. He shudders in the sun, causing little con-
tours of muscle to harden on his oiled back.

The second species is us, the Irish, in our GAA jerseys, huddled
together so as not to frighten the natives at the far side of Bondi, not
knowing how to surf, swim or strut: the O'Neill's football, step one
haircut and socks give it away. The faded teenage tattoos on freckly
backs are another tell-tale sign, particularly as what was once a shark
just above the shoulderblade now resembles a beached whale, deformed
on skin stretched by too many Hula Hoops, pints and Pot Noodles.

The nurse examined him. The arm was broken all right, but it had
been broken for hours. Why hadn't he come sooner? Nothing could live
in his pickled body. He is marinated in beer, stewing away in his own
juices, festering from the inside out.

She slips on her swine flu mask to obscure the fetid stench of that
heavenly combination of Castlemaine XXXX and 40 Major. Did they not
teach these people that booze dehydrates? She'd seen bad cases before,
particularly after the local Aussie Rules derby on Australia Day when
the bogans from the western suburbs flock into King's Cross to
celebrate something called 'Australianness'. But she'd never seen a case
like this. This lad must have been drinking for hours in the midday sun.
How could you do that to yourself?

For this lad who, like most of his generation, was brought up
knacker-drinking flagons in wet fields or damp bus shelters, the idea of
gargling in the sun with his mates—and frightening the beautiful
queers of Bondi into the bargain—must have seemed like paradise.
Indeed it was, until they'd hopped on the 333 bus back to Bondi

Junction. A few spliffs, more jar and then the Wii for the craic. It was turning out to be a brilliant Sunday, yet another one in his new life in Oz as far away from Waterford, dirty building sites and unemployment as possible. Within two days of arriving, he'd got a job with an Irish builder who was starting again in Australia.

He should have gone straight to Emergency after it had happened. But first, he was anaesthetised by grog so it didn't hurt at the time and, second, he had no residency. The Aussies were threatening to throw people out and by the time he'd realised how serious the arm was, he was sobering up to the reality of deportation. Third, how could he explain it?

'How exactly did this happen, Sir?'

'Well, you're not going to believe me, Nurse, but here goes. We were playing tennis on the Wii. I was going for a big backhand to win the set, straight down the tramlines. But he had driven me over to the corner of the court and I was hoping to hit it on the run, lots of topspin. I drew back the arm, ready to smash the ball as it came over the net. But I didn't see the corner of the microwave that we had brought in from the kitchen 'coz, well, we had the munchies, you know what I mean? All I remember is the crack as the Wii console flew into the air and my arm snapped in two.'

The nurse couldn't hide the smirk. Her shoulders were now shaking, heaving up and down as she tried not to laugh. Jesus, she loved these young Irish lads! These drunk wannabe Roger Federers.

She'd noticed a huge increase in them over the past few months, presenting for all sorts of dodgy injuries. They were hilarious, so human and yet so vulnerable, sitting there in their tight GAA shorts, sobering up, looking down forlornly at their injuries, thinking, *How will I pay the rent? There's not much demand for a one-armed plasterer.*

GENERATION EXODUS

Breakfast Roll Man was in clover. Not only had he sold up at home, but now with all these young fellas coming over, he had a ready-made, under-the-table workforce. All he had to do was drive up to one of the Irish bars in Bondi Junction, put up an ad and he'd have a full team of plasterers, electricians, plumbers, brickies and labourers—all refugees from the crash at home. He hadn't intended going back into the business so early but with so much Irish talent around, looking for work, Breakfast Roll Man figured he'd be mad not to get back in the game. His latest recruit, Waterford's answer to Roger Federer was just one of these thousands of young people on the move. They are Ireland's new exiles: our Generation Exodus.

In every town and village in the country, we are seeing the scurrying footprints of Generation Exodus. One of the most fascinating barometers of the Irish economy is published not by the ESRI, the Central Bank or any of the many stockbrokers paid to monitor the state of things, but by the GAA. If you want to understand what is happening on the ground in every town and village, go to www.gaa.ie. As well as fixtures, news, updates and analysis, the GAA's website is a mine of sociological information. One monthly gem tells us who is transferring from which club and where they are going.

For the last few years, the club transfer list was pretty standard, reflecting young players moving around the country to where they were working or studying. So lads would transfer from clubs in Dublin to Cork or Waterford, depending on jobs. Obviously, much of the movement was to Dublin clubs as the capital sucked in resources to fuel the boom.

However, in recent months, something new has been happening. We are seeing a huge increase in young men moving from Irish clubs all around the country to clubs abroad. This barometer—let's call it the GAA Club Transfer Index or GCTI for short—doesn't lie. More significantly, the huge surge in emigration it reflects will not be picked up by official statistics for months, if not years.

According to the GCTI, emigration is on the increase from all over Ireland and it is particularly prevalent among the under-30s. What makes the change in the index all the more startling is the dramatic turnaround in fortunes between the beginning of last year and now. In January 2008, not one club player transferred to a club outside Ireland. By late autumn 2008, over one-third of all transfers involved lads leaving the country and signing up for clubs in London, New York and Australia. This has continued throughout 2009.

So Paddy is moving again. Historically, it has always been so. When things are going well here, we come home, and when things turn down, we go. Such migration patterns are not normal. For example, in the 1980s Ireland and Spain suffered from the same level of unemployment—19 per cent.[1] This lack of opportunity prompted 400,000 young Irish people to leave the country.[2] By contrast, the Spaniards hardly budged.

Over the years, the GAA has been a brilliant indicator of economic and demographic trends. In the 1980s, emigration in rural Ireland was so severe that many villages couldn't find 15 young men to field a team on a regular basis. Equally, the boom years were a bonanza for the GAA. New clubs opened to cater for the huge outward move to the new suburbs of Meath, Kildare and the peripheries of all our main towns.

Wherever a series of new estates was built, GAA clubs followed, as did outside decking, Woodies DIY and Domino's Pizza. For a while, these new suburbs in 'Deckland' thrived. Glamorous 'GAA Mums', ferrying kids around all weekends, county flags flying from their people carriers, became a political block fêted by all parties. Communities formed quickly and the centre of these new neighbourhoods was the ever-present GAA club.

Whereas in the boom the GAA picked up the effervescence of modern Ireland, today it is pointing again to the depopulation of the country as those who can leave do so. And leaving is precisely what we are doing.

The swing back to emigration has been phenomenal. At one stage these young people were told they would inherit the earth. Only a year ago, in 2008, Bank of Ireland was trumpeting the fact that Ireland was the second richest country on earth; now we are scraping the bottom of the barrel again.

If you want to see this mass movement of people, Dublin Airport is the place to go. Up until last year, the most conspicuous species in the airport was the stonewashed East European arriving full of hope and not a little fear, imagining their new life. They wanted to be part of the Irish Dream.

But with mobile phones, texts and Skype, immigration now is not the exile it once was. You go, you see and, if not quite conquer, you try to make it. People are well informed; they know the score, unlike the old days.

BREAKFAST ROLL MAN TOASTS PAT KENNY

Sitting back, looking out at the surfers in Bondi, Breakfast Roll Man raises a glass to the man who made it all possible, the man whose actions prompted Breakfast Roll Man to sell everything.

'This one's for yer man off the telly.'

They all pissed themselves as the waitress brought the next round.

'Have one for yourself, love. We're not paying for it. Pat Kenny is!'

She burst out laughing, not knowing the joke but, as she'd just arrived over in Sydney from Galway, she at least knew who these raucous Dubs were talking about. It was bound to be funny.

In 2007, Breakfast Roll Man had been getting a bit concerned about prices and the lads on the site started telling him that the quality of building work was plummeting. He'd never been that greedy. He'd had five great years, years he hadn't really expected. In 2002, he hadn't the arse in his trousers. By the time he sold up at home, he was rich even by Australian standards.

The family was young and secure. He had cash in the bank and he was about to get involved in a big apartment complex in Rialto. But things didn't seem right. The banks were too keen and no one was asking the normal questions.

Then he saw it on the front of the *Star* that morning in July 2007. And that is what tipped him over.

Breakfast Roll Man worked on principles. There was right and wrong. There was common sense and there were things that you just didn't do. That's the way his ma and da had brought him up.

The first thought that struck him about the story was that this was like the film he'd seen years back, *The Field*. It was wrong for yer man the Bull McCabe to go terrorising the poor widow woman for her field. That just wasn't right.

It wasn't right for Pat Kenny, who everyone said was an intelligent man, to try to take part of his neighbour's garden. According to the paper, to win the case Kenny would have had to get up on the stand and openly say that he had always intended to grab his neighbour's land.

Sweet Jaysus, thought Breakfast Roll Man, *what's the country coming to? They'd hang fellas off the nearest tree for that years ago. So yer man was about to admit that when he was sending his neighbour Christmas cards and the like, he was secretly planning to take his land.* Breakfast Roll Man decided it was time to sell up everything because when people started robbing neighbours' gardens, it was all going to end in tears.

The more he read about the Pat Kenny case, the more he was convinced that the market had peaked and that only lunatics and headcases would be bidding now.

Where Breakfast Roll Man came from, your neighbours were your mates. They were your people and they looked out for each other. You never grassed on each other, even if a lad was red hot. You lent each other money, as opposed to robbing each other. Sure there were rows and arguments but they were about important things like snooker, football and dogs. You married your neighbours, drank with your neighbours and went to each other's parents' funerals. That's what you did.

If someone was in trouble, you stood up for him even if he wasn't entirely innocent. The point was you knew him, you knew his kids and even if you didn't particularly like the lad, he was better than someone you didn't know at all. That was the way it was. It was something called community.

In Breakfast Roll Man's world, only junkies robbed their own neighbours. And they were scum. Not as bad as the pushers but stupid scum all the same. Didn't they see what gear did to people?

Anyway, proper people didn't rob their neighbours.

THE U-TURN

The Kenny case fascinated him. The idea that a grown man would put locks on the gate of another man's land and not give him the combination shocked him. But it also made him laugh. He imagined the lad off the telly, the lad with one of the biggest jobs in the country, waiting behind the window to see the reaction on the face of his neighbour when he couldn't open the lock. *Spying out the window like a mad aul' wan and then he interviewing politicians about morality. Mad fuckin' country,* thought Breakfast Roll Man.

And what about other details like the lad off the telly having a go at the neighbour's Moldovan gardener, some young lad called Vanyo? Breakfast Roll Man imagined Vanyo on the blower, talking to his mates back home in Moldova when they asked him what the Irish were like.

The reports in the *Star* were hilarious. You couldn't make it up. The lad off the *Late Late*, Pat Kenny, pushing his neighbour off the land that the neighbour owned in the first bleedin' place. And the neighbour an aul' fella of 75-odd, whom he'd known for 20 years.

Then yer man Kenny goes to court and contests a case for 'squatter rights'. *Imagine that,* thought Breakfast Roll Man, *'squatter's rights— only 'head the balls' and fellas from weird sects what has taken over a house go for squatter's rights, for Jaysus' sake. Can you imagine all the craziness and the jealousy and the small-time greed involved? Imagine the conversations, the schemes and the pettiness.*

Breakfast Roll Man concluded if two rich men were scrapping and one of them the most famous lad off the telly like that, this stuff was going on everywhere. If this greed was taking over the country, it was time to get out—for your sanity as well as your bank balance.

The Pat Kenny Case was in the papers on 31 July 2007, just before the builders' fortnight's holidays. Breakfast Roll Man was on his way to Alicante with the Missus, her ma and her ma's new fella. Things were going full tilt. But Breakfast Roll Man—who always went with his gut feeling—knew it was wrong. He could see that the thing was mental, young lads arriving on the sites demanding a grand a week; builders, who were lads he knew from the sites years back, buying tower blocks in London for tens of millions of euro; and the lad off the telly—who was on a fortune, big money—buying a poxy little combination padlock to keep his neighbour off his own land. That was it!

Breakfast Roll Man's da had always said get out when you're on top, not that he'd ever been on top. But that never stopped his da, Git Dunne, from giving out advice at the bar in the Submarine.

It was a sign. It was Breakfast Roll Man's epiphany, his apparition in Lourdes. Things wouldn't be the same again. The country had gone completely mad and he, Breakfast Roll Man, was wise to it. At first he was going to get out of the big development he'd just started but then he reconsidered and said, 'That's it, out of everything. Sell it all.'

Just before he got on the plane, he rang his bank and cancelled the Rialto deal and told them to find a new developer. A few of the apartments had been sold off plans and the build was going ahead. There'd be loads of builders would jump at it.

The bank was cool. It didn't care—business was booming. They asked him if he was sure. It was a sweet deal, said the lad on the other end of the phone. He'd been with the bank for years and they'd done well together. The banker wanted to understand why he was selling everything, the sites, the developments, his few houses around the town and the few he had abroad.

'Are you sure? There's at least three bar in that deal for you.'

'I know what you're saying but I just want out. Leave it for the next fella. There'll be plenty of deals.'

'OK, your decision. By the way, what changed your mind so quickly? Just out of curiosity?' said the banker.

Breakfast Roll Man paused as he was on the top step about to board the plane. He looked at the faces around him, going to their mortgaged second apartments in Alicante. He looked at the airport and the queues and the chaos of Ireland and then he looked down at his copy of the *Star*. Pat Kenny's face looked back at him.

'You don't want to know! You wouldn't fuckin' believe me if I told you anyway.'

PART II

Chapter 9 ～

ADDICTED TO MONEY

I f you were in any doubt that this recession is an equal-opportunity destroyer, then spare a thought for the Irish cocaine dealers in negative equity. No one is safe from the recession, no matter which side of the law they're on.

In the past few years, the mad twitching and gum chewing of the cocaine user have become commonplace in Ireland. In 2006, an RTÉ documentary found traces of cocaine in 90 per cent of the pub toilets in suburban Dublin. While cocaine might have been the narcotic of choice, demand for all drugs soared. According to the Gardaí, the drugs market in Ireland was worth as much as €1 billion by 2008, one-third of the national health budget.[1]

The documentary showed that there are lots of drugs about and it also revealed the democratic nature of the economy. When things are good, everyone and anyone can make money. That is as true for the guy selling wraps of cocaine as it is for honest tradesmen. We may not like to think a successful economy can breed successful drug dealers, but a rising tide lifts all boats, even the ones laden with Bolivian marching powder.

By the same token, when things go bad, we all go down together. The dealer gets caught out like everyone else. Like the first-time buyer stretched by rising interest rates, or the developer with the troubled portfolio, the dealer finds himself at the wrong end of too many deals. The only real difference is that in the drug economy, bankruptcy often has decidedly terminal effects.

THE MIRROR
All economists love their models. It's an opportunity to show an economic theory in action, using a reference or example that people know well. The problem with theory is that it is distant from our

day-to-day experience. So for our purposes, I am going to use the model of a drugs cartel and explain how it works. We are then going to look at the banking and financial sector and see how it works. The idea is that the comparison will help us better understand the chinks in the banking system that contributed to our current situation. It's not as big a stretch as you might imagine. After all, banks deal in that most addictive of substances, money.

We will look at the similarities between the two 'dealers': those who trade drugs and those who trade money. We will follow our chosen drug, cocaine, from the mountains of Central America to the dinner parties of Ballsbridge. We will also trace the journey of cheap credit from its source in countries like Germany to a sofa dealership. You may not find all the similarities pleasant, but they may fascinate you. You may even find it so hard to distinguish the two, that you will not be sure whether the banking game was the blueprint for the drug cartel's business model, or vice versa.

One thing is certain, both substances—drugs and easy money— create an initial euphoria, followed by dependence. As entire countries can become addicted to money and easy credit, this is a highly danger-ous situation. In both cases, the dealers—the drug gangs and the banks—make a fortune, while the bill is picked up by the taxpayer.

In short, nice work if you can get away with it.

THE DEALER
When things were going well, the dealer thought the sky was the limit. With frightening speed, he graduated from selling hash to Es and, ultimately, cocaine. Coke is where the real money is.

In the drugs trade, they say 'you can't dance on Es'. What they mean by this is that Ecstasy is not an easily diluted drug. As it is pill-based, it's not possible to buy a block of MDMA, mix it with other white substances and thus convert 1 gram to 5 grams. The producer can do this, but the dealer, who sells to the user, doesn't have the technology. Cocaine, on the other hand, is a powder. Powder can conceal a multitude of sins.

All the dealer has to do, if he wants to maximise his profit, is to dilute the pure drug with other substances. One popular solution is Nu Life, a homeopathic product intended to help hay fever sufferers. The sort of thing he might pick up at a chemical-free holistic medicine shop. That and a little caffeine and our dealer is in business.

The sums are simple. The reasonably-sized dealer can buy a kilogram of 80 per cent proof cocaine (the dilution starts early) from Central or Latin America. He will, as they say in the trade, 'dance' (dilute) on this a minimum of five times, turning it into at least 5 kilograms. To do this, he will use bulking agents like Novocaine or Lidocaine, which cost him €700 a kilogram—substances dentists use to numb the gums.

Thus, from the original 80 per cent proof drug, the average Irish drug user is lucky to get 12 per cent proof cocaine. This can drop as low as 8 per cent during the Christmas period when demand outstrips supply. That's when the dancing really happens, with dealers doing Michael Flatley impressions to match Graham Norton's caravan *Riverdance* in 'Father Ted'. The dealer is making money hand over fist.

Much like Shylock the mortgage broker, during the boom the cocaine dealer was having it both ways. He could expand his supply to meet the soaring demand without having to worry about increasing costs—the higher the demand, the more he danced and the more the quality of cocaine on the street collapsed.

The dealer started to notice this increase in demand during the summer of 2005. At that point, most people ordered a gram of cocaine at a time, so he spent hours making up dozens of 1 gram wraps. These retailed for €70.

Soon he saw a change develop in buying behaviour. The 'one-er' replaced the gram by 2006. A 'one-er' is a €100 wrap containing a gram and a half. As consumption rose, so too did the size of the deals that the punters wanted to do. They wanted more and more of the stuff. He was beginning to find his horizon expanding, fast. He started ordering larger amounts from his source further up the chain.

By 2007, demand for the 'one-er' was supplanted by the 'Garden Gate'. The Garden Gate is an 'eighth of an ounce', or three and a half grams. His clients were obviously going bonkers at weekends. But the demand was there and the dealer could either meet it and profit, or lose his customers.

Then, overnight, as with property, the drugs market collapsed. The dealer's phone stopped ringing. As credit dried up, so too did the demand for cocaine. It is, after all, a rich man's drug. It's a reward for success, of which (thanks to negative equity and rising unemployment) there was precious little in Ireland's suburbs all of a sudden.

Now, let's follow the trail and see how the cocaine got here.

HONDURAS

A wonderful thing about generations of Irish emigration is that we have ended up nearly everywhere. When Jovani—my guide in the jungle by the ancient Mayan city of Copan—heard I was Irish, his face lit up, and he asked me if I had heard of John Gallagher. When I said no, he was visibly disappointed. 'But John Gallagher discovered us,' he said.

In 1834, John Gallagher, an Irish adventurer and soldier, was fighting as a mercenary for the Honduran independence movement. In the early part of the nineteenth century, Latin America was full of Irish adventurers. It was a good place to make money, if fate and inclination took you there. Many fought in the Latin American wars for independence and most stayed on afterwards. Gallagher apart, though, not many of them hung on in Honduras.

The most striking thing about the Mayan statues in Copan, high up on the border between Honduras and Guatemala, is their Asiatic features. The stone figures look almost Chinese, not unlike the relics from ancient Ming Dynasty sculptures.

All around, the descendents of these people smile openly from beneath their wide-brimmed Stetsons. As our Nissan pickup climbs higher, the villages get poorer, the air thinner and the people more Asiatic-looking. The Spaniards didn't even bother mixing with them and so the last of the Mayans look much as they did when the first invaders crossed the Atlantic.

After a while the road disappears, becoming little more than a worn brush-covered trail. So too does much of the pine forest, cut down by illegal loggers. The rest of the journey is made on horseback. The sturdy beasts and the dexterous guide pick their way over rocks and past gorges and up and up again towards the villages at the top where the air is thinnest, the sun strongest and the growing conditions perfect.

This is the heart of the cocoa industry. This is the start of the journey that will culminate in Ballsbridge society hostesses snorting white powder through rolled-up fifties right after the main course to avoid anything dangerous like dessert.

Dozens of Indians in brilliant white shirts and cowboy boots are chopping down the plants with razor-sharp machetes. There are four harvests a year. Unlike crops farther down the valley, cocoa doesn't need that much water, just sun. Old men chew the leaves to give them extra energy, while the local kids play what looks like a 58-a-side soccer match barefoot in the dust. This dustbowl is the cradle of the cocaine-dealing world.

Here the cocaine is pure, 100 per cent—nothing added. All around, attached to the corrugated shacks, are little stills where locals ferment leaves for their own consumption. But, much like the logs from the pine forests, the vast majority of the cocaine is for export.

So the trail to Europe begins back on the horses that brought me up here, and goes down the hill, into the Nissan pickup trucks and on to the cocaine factories of Central America, then out into the wider world.

There are any number of ways to bring coke across the Atlantic. But we must choose one entry point, so let's pick up the thread again in southern Spain, after the big guys have taken their cut and passed it on.

HALFWAY HOME

The flight from Dublin is on time. If it weren't for the dozens of golf clubs clogging up the conveyer belt as herds of greying Irish men in identical slightly-too-tight tan slacks and extra-large Leinster jerseys jostle for position, you'd be out past Customs and in the hire car in minutes.

One bar owner on the Costa del Sol said he realised that Ireland was screwed when middle-aged Irishmen like these golfers—who four years ago would play a round of golf, sink eight pints, have a singsong and then go to bed—began to turn up in his bar, jumpety and running in and out of the loos, sniffling incessantly and then asking him where they could find hookers! But these guys are the users, not the dealers, so let's leave them to Marbella and the rest of the Costa.

Despite the unscheduled delay, there's hardly any traffic on the road north, towards the Alpujarras.

The road twists and turns past orange groves, small farmsteads and large walled villas with electric gates and British-registered, blacked out Range Rovers. Once you get up a little bit higher, you can see the view over the hills, beyond the golf courses and out to the Mediterranean. Few places are more beautiful than this and yet fewer are more danger-ous. We are now in the fulcrum of the European drugs trade.

Every line of charlie that an Irish person snorts off the cistern of a pub jacks has come from this area. The Irish gang that dealt them the gear in Dublin, Cork or Limerick sources its stash here.

THE PYRAMID STRUCTURE

In terms of structure, the banking business and the drugs business are surprisingly similar. Once demand and distribution are sorted, the rewards can be huge.

While I am explaining the drugs pyramid, don't forget the banking game. As with cocaine, credit reaches street level and your back pocket via a number of channels.

Keeping the Irish supplied with cocaine is not an easy task. It needs financiers, agents, collectors, transporters, money launderers, big dealers, little dealers, tax advisors and, above all, a reliable source of the product itself. This has given rise to a vast underworld economy and network that is vital for administering the business.

Remember, this is not some minority pursuit. A €1 billion drugs trade in Ireland implies that every man, woman and child in the country is spending between €200 and €250 a year on narcotics. Given that most people are not regular users/abusers, this figure implies that hundreds of thousands of people are spending significant sums on drugs every weekend. In terms of turnover, the drugs business in Ireland is one of our biggest importing sectors, rivalling any legitimate trade you can name.

The first thing the drugs barons in Dublin do is form a syndicate to put up the cash. In the past, big Irish drug dealers used to work solo, but then they realised that everyone would benefit if they put up the cash in syndicate. As in every business, there's a discount for volume. The bigger the order, the better the deal for each member of the syndicate. They pool their resources in order to get a 'cocktail' (usually a mixture of hash, coke and heroin) delivered. The Irish barons, by working together, can order as much as 5 tons at a time, setting them back something in the region of €15 million.

For the purposes of balance, as we are following cocaine from Honduras to Spain to Ireland and all the way back to a low-level deal on O'Connell Bridge, we will also follow a block of money on its similar journey.

Like the drug dealers, the money dealers of Ireland source their product from outside the country. First, they dole it out to their corporate friends at a preferential rate. Ultimately, however, the money finds its way down to the streets, ending up in places like PC World or Land of Leather in the guise of a zero interest rate credit deal, diluted by hidden costs and charges, not dissimilar to the cocaine fortified with Novocaine.

In banking terms, the drugs barons pooling their resources is the underworld's equivalent of a syndicated loan. This is where a number of banks pool their resources to borrow a much greater sum than any of them need individually. In this way, like the drug dealers, they get a better deal. So, when they lend this money out to punters for mortgages or as holiday home finance packages, they maximise their margin on the difference between what they paid for the money and the rate at which they lend it to you and me.

But like the drugs game, the money supply has to start somewhere.

If the cocaine trade begins high up in the vertiginous heights of the Honduran mountains, the Irish money trail begins on the Brandenburg plain in Germany.

BERLIN

Sitting here in Starbucks, at the bottom of Unter den Linden, it is hard to believe that it's been 20 years since thousands of stonewashed, be-mulleted Easterners marched though the Brandenburg Gate, past the Wall and on to freedom.

This is the capital city of the country with the most extraordinary savers in the world. Germans saved €250 billion more than they spent last year.[2] This is the Irish financial industry's Honduras. Like the cocoa farmers chewing leaves while most of their crop is exported, the Germans harvest the money, then move most of it on.

Our banks 'buy' these savings from the German banks for a period of three months. They pay less than 2 per cent for this money, which they then lend to us at a routine 5 or 6 per cent. They also sell it in large deals to more unscrupulous dealers whose customers the banks would normally never touch. As we go down the chain, at every stage a money dealer takes his cut so that the money that left Germany with a price tag of 2 per cent ends up being repaid by the poor addict who misses a payment on his hire-purchase LCD flat screen in Drogheda at the very profitable rate of 28 per cent!

THE CHANNELS

In the drugs world, if the syndicate is well known and has a good reputation, it can get 'bail'. Bail is leverage, where the initial suppliers of the drug, the Colombians, Guatemalans or Hondurans, agree to accept half the payment now and half later. You've got to be big and have a triple A record in the drugs game to get terms like this.

In the financial world too, the same type of arrangement exists between banks and finance houses. So let's imagine that AIB wanted to buy money from a large German bank in order to finance expansion into the 100 per cent mortgage market. It buys the money 'on margin', meaning that AIB just puts up a small percentage of the cash, promising to pay the German bank in full once it starts making money on it.

A bank can only get that sort of deal if the supplier believes it is good for the cash. Again, it'll need to be triple A rated.

So in both worlds, 'bail' is given to the big guys. They are getting their gear on trust.

Back in the drugs world, once the syndicate is sorted, the drug barons contact an agent. The agent is himself close to the next rung on the ladder, the broker, who organises a price for the syndicate. Normally this is referred to as an 'on the floor price'—literally, the price of the drugs on the floor of the Spanish warehouse, with a broker's fees included.

At this point, the 'cutting' process accelerates. Now everyone starts to make their profits from the deals. The cocaine was 80 per cent when it left Latin America and value continues to be lost as 'fees' are extracted at each transit point.

In the banking world, the same process begins. As soon as the pure money leaves Germany, a network begins to take their cut.

In finance, this agent/broker axis is the job of investment banks and, lower down the food chain, stockbrokers. An investment bank working for AIB will respond to their request to raise money by facilitating a deal with another large investment bank in the market. Both will take their cut and AIB will get its money, which will then be dealt to money-lenders further down the chain.

The investment banker operates the same way as a drugs broker. He takes an order from a client and contacts another broker, gets a price, whether it is buying or selling, and both brokers make a few quid on the twist.

QUALITY CONTROLLED

Both investment bankers and drugs brokers need to know the quality of the product they are paying for. The drugs broker has a chemist. The chemist rates the purity of the consignment, gives it a triple A stamp and takes his fee. The investment banker's equivalent of the drugs broker's chemist is the rating agencies. By rating companies, banks and countries, the rating agencies should give investors peace of mind— promising them that what they buy is of good quality, unlikely to default and so won't cause them any sleepless nights.

If the rating system fails or is compromised in any way, the foundation of every transaction collapses. Consider the drugs world. What would happen if the chemists were actually paid by the supplier to rate bad stuff as good stuff? What might the syndicate in Dublin do to a stamper who lied about the quality of the gear because he was in the pay of the supplier?

This was not a concern in the banking world. Perhaps nobody ever watched a Mafia movie. In the US subprime disaster, the rating agencies were paid by the banks to rate the junk they were selling as triple A. In reality, some of the assets in this AAA toxic cocktail were worthless. Subprime debt, loans to people who had neither means nor intention of repaying money, were packaged with reliable securities, then given gilt-edged ratings by agencies in the pay of the banks.

In the Irish case, a huge amount of the credit was used to buy overpriced houses when there was absolutely no connection between the price of the house and its value. We too needed someone to validate the price paid, to say: 'This is correct. This two-bed terrace in Monkstown is indeed worth €1 million. Your money is safe here.' This is where the estate agents came in. They were responsible for valuing houses. Bizarrely, these valuations were given credence even though, like the rating agencies, an estate agent's fee was directly related to the price of the house. So, house price inflation was in the interests of the estate agents: higher prices meant higher fees. The banks and the estate agents were hand in glove, working to hoodwink the punters.

This situation is the result of what is known in economics as moral hazard. When a regulator, or an estate agent for that matter, has a financial interest in a transaction that they are meant to be refereeing, their objectivity is fatally compromised. From there it is only a hop, skip and jump to the Irish situation.

You can see how, in both cases, the price of the drugs and the price of the credit is escalating before it hits the streets. Inevitably, as the price rises, the quality drops.

DISTRIBUTION IS EVERYTHING

Once tested and paid for, legitimate hauliers transport the drugs back to Ireland. In many cases the drivers have no idea what is hidden in their cargos as the drug lord uses fake companies, importing all sorts of stuff from Spain—clothes, shoes, fruit, spare parts for our new Spanish-built trains. Runners are paid to constantly watch Customs and Gardaí at our ports.

Because of EMU, the Irish banks don't have these problems. Both their product and business are legal. The only problem the trade has is risk, something that started to rear its ugly head in 2007. As the Irish market became riskier, foreign willingness to lend to us declined. By October 2007, Irish banks were finding it harder and more expensive to borrow money for a period of three months (which had become the lifeblood of their business model at that point). Nobody was prepared to lend to the Irish banks for so long a period any more.

Funding could now only be accessed through the overnight markets. The banks borrowed today to pay back tomorrow, always hoping to be able to borrow the money again the next day. This was completely unsustainable. In fact, it is a credit to the dexterity of the bankers that they managed to do so for as long as they did.

But eventually the shit did hit the fan, on that fateful night in September 2008. We can be sure that the banks weren't joking when they told Brian Lenihan they wouldn't last the week without the government guarantee.

GETTING WORSE AS WE GO DOWN

Based on what we know about the dealer's business model, it's probable that the cocaine snorted at the dinner party in Ballsbridge (or, for that matter, a GAA club in Kerry) is at best 12 per cent cocaine. If you want to gauge the purity without rolling up a crisp fifty and ramming it up your nose, just observe how much food is eaten. The guy pushing the asparagus round his plate has the best wrap (or the one with the most Lidocaine).

If the drug barons use their own network of dealers, their stuff will end up being dealt in bars, nightclubs, on the streets or even over the phone. There are also hundreds of small-time dealers who buy a bit in bulk and then cut it up and, as a freelance operation, make their living. More typically, many young fellas are on a wage from the drug lord:

organised like a corporate sales force, each with his own patch, his own client base and his own modest commission.

Everything at the bottom of the chain is contaminated. Most of these guys are users as well as dealers.

Banks work the same way. Let's return to our AIB example. The bank sources a huge amount of credit on the market, in order to boost its domestic loan book business. Let's use the 100 per cent mortgage craze of 2006 and 2007. Like the drug dealer spotting the rise in cocaine consumption in nightclubs, the bank sees a gap in the market.

In Ireland in the Noughties, this niche was the stressed out first-time buyers who needed a 100 per cent mortgage. The banks used our friend, Shylock, the mortgage broker, who (as we saw in Chapter 6) took his cut while masquerading as a chummy advisor to the buyers. So the first-timer buyers paid for Shylock's cut via higher interest rates that were masked by turning the mortgage into a 35-year debt trap rather than the usual 20-year sentence.

Although the poor couple had parted with 8 times their combined income for a shoebox in Gorey, they still had to furnish the thing. So the banks agreed to give a credit facility to the likes of Harvey Norman, and they kill two birds with one stone, making money each way. Harvey Norman became the dealer of last resort.

MIND YOUR LANGUAGE

Another similarity between the drugs and the credit rackets is their use of language designed explicitly to exclude and to signal to other dealers that they are on the inside. All industries have their unique jargon, as anyone who's ever tried to buy a computer knows. This insider patois is an essential coding mechanism to confuse the addict and the outsider.

For example, in the drugs game we might have 'a score for a four timed kicked box on the lay'. Alternatively, a banker might favour impenetrable argot like: '40 basis points over Euribor for a buy side bar'.

Both are clear to the dealers and opaque to you and me. That's the intention. We are supposed to be excluded. The first means that in Dublin a kilogram of cocaine that has been bulked up four times, so is probably now about 12 per cent proof cocaine, will cost you €20,000 but the bigger dealer will give you credit to purchase it.

The second, the banking jargon, means €1,000,000 in cash from a bigger bank will cost you four-tenths of a percent over the prevailing wholesale interest rate that the ECB is charging.

Confused? You are supposed to be!

While you cope with that mystery, I hope you'll excuse me while I get 'a laid bar of Pollen and turn it into soap'. If you're still thinking when I return, perhaps you can join me in 'shorting the market because the CDS spreads on the sovvie have exploded'. Clear as mud, you'll agree.

THE INDULGENT COPS

Given that there's so much money to be made, it's easy to see how there is always the incentive for a greedy banker to risk blowing the balance sheet.

This is why we have a Financial Regulator. It's why we hope for enlightened politicians who realise a nation of credit junkies is not a good idea. In the same way, we have a drug squad, as a nation of narcotics junkies is not a good idea either. Unfortunately, in Ireland we did not possess even the few good men at the top who might have called a halt to the madness.

Let's go back to our drug barons. In recent years, you may have noticed the upswing in armed robberies in Ireland. Why would drug lords, who were making a fortune selling gear to the 'mad for it nation', need to rob banks? I blame the cops.

If the Guards intercept a drug shipment, it sets off a chain reaction. The dealers can't pay their bills. The suppliers, the gangs in Colombia who have their men in Spain, don't like being defaulted on.

Retribution tends to be both swift and vicious. The terrified Dublin gangs know that they'll never do business (and likely never breathe) again. So when the Drug Squad seizes their assets, they rob banks in order to pay their debts.

Thus, despite the sophistication of the network, the secrecy of the gangs and the ubiquity of the users, the Guards manage to disrupt the trade by going after the dealers and watching them like hawks.

Can you imagine the vista if the cops had been so deeply corrupted that they were on the side of the dealers, turning a blind eye at Customs and discouraging anyone from asking questions about the huge amount of drugs flooding onto our streets?

Many good gangster movies are about this appalling landscape. Usually the hero of the film is the straight cop who takes on his own system as well as the gangsters. Think of genre classics like *American*

Gangster, LA Confidential or *The Untouchables*. The good cop, bad cop line makes for great drama and the moral of the story is that something can always be done.

Now consider the Financial Regulator in Ireland. The banks are dealers in cheap credit who act in their own self-interest. The Financial Regulator, the Department of Finance, the Central Bank and ultimately the government are supposed to be acting in the interests of the people. Their job is to ask questions, apply the law and keep cheap credit to a manageable level on the streets. In Ireland over the past five years, what did they do? Worse than nothing. They fêted the bankers, the dealers of cheap credit, and treated them as paragons of the new elite and the venerated creators of a New Ireland.

So despite the government trumpeting about a special task force charged with regulating the show, there was only lip service. The first Regulator, Liam O'Reilly, was subsequently given a board directorship of Irish Life and Permanent. One might make the analogy of the wolf in the henhouse, had not all the hens long been cooked.

In the drugs world it is not uncommon for the big barons to help each other out, but you'd expect CAB to have a thing or two to say about large deposits materialising overnight. In the world of Irish finance, particularly at the top end, nothing happens. Worse still, when the crime is unearthed, the culprits retire (not resign) on full pensions while the shareholders get wiped out! You couldn't make this stuff up.

But this is not fiction. It all happened. The challenge now is to follow the money. We must piece together who gave money to whom and who lent that cash on to whom. So let's do that. We will follow money from the typical zero interest-rate sofa seller pedalling credit to people at the lower end of the market all the way up the chain to the very top of the pyramid, where the 'Credit Barons' who started the whole thing are teeing off at the sixteenth hole at the K Club.

IT'S ALL IN THE PRICE

As we can see, in the drugs game, the closer you are to the top of the chain, the better the quality and the cheaper the drug. By the time the drugs reach Ballsbridge, O'Connell Street or Portarlington, the prices have exploded and the quality has collapsed. This is why the business is so lucrative and why so many dealers get involved. You are literally paying through the nose that you're damaging.

Now think about the financial business. The bottom of the pyramid, where the people with the worst credit ratings look for cash, is precisely where the quality is at its lowest.

It is typical for those who borrow down here on apparently 'easy' plans to end up paying well over 20 per cent interest rates, with very strict rules about payment schedules. If they miss a payment, the penalty is huge.

Like the addicts at the bottom of the drugs chain, the addicts at the bottom of the money chain pay exponentially more for less.

Contrast this sort of deal with the top of the tree and consider the price and terms that members of the 'Golden Circle' were asked to pay to bail out Sean Quinn and Anglo Irish Bank.

In summer 2008, Sean Fitzpatrick had a big problem. But so too did the Department of Finance, the Irish Stock Exchange, the Central Bank and the Irish Financial Regulator. Sean Quinn, the billionaire, had taken a huge position in Anglo Irish Bank, some 29 per cent of the total bank. He was about to sell his position because he had lost a fortune on it. Having started buying at close to €18 per share, the price was now €11. He wanted out.

But this meant that nearly 30 per cent of the shares of Anglo would come on the market. This would cause panic in the markets and the share price would tank. A parachute for a billionaire had to be found.

The authorities were all made aware of this. For the parachute to work, no shareholders could know. Therefore, those who police the Irish financial system were highly cognizant that some stroke was about to be pulled.

After informing the authorities, calls were made to Seanie's Golden Circle mates, all wealthy men who owed him one. Here we see clearly the difference between the prices, terms and quality of money at the top of the tree and the conditions at the bottom.

Each of these wealthy men was offered the opportunity to borrow €30 million from Anglo Irish Bank, showing no collateral or intention to repay. Most crucially the loans were on what is called a non-recourse basis. This meant that if the price of Anglo shares went up, they won. However, if the price of Anglo shares collapsed, there was no obligation to pay anything.

At the top, money is cheap, plentiful and the terms favour the borrower. At the bottom, money is expensive. The terms squeeze the borrower and are stacked in favour of the lender. So every time an addict signs up to a zero interest rate sofa deal at the bottom, profit goes back up the chain and is siphoned off at every stage.

The people at the very top can get the money to bail out Sean Quinn on a no-obligation basis precisely because the people at the bottom are paying so much.

What we have is a financial pyramid, a Ponzi scheme that became so powerful that it was deemed, when the crisis came, 'too big to fail'. Like a Latin American banana republic, one industry had been allowed to become so big, to extend its tentacles so deeply, that it had taken over many levels of government and brought our country to its knees. Not even the drug dealers were so cavalier with their business.

Chapter 10 ~

THE BEST WAY TO ROB A
BANK IS TO RUN ONE

M any years ago, when I was at university, I ended up trying to get into some class of a ball one wet Thursday night. Maybe it was the Fresher's Ball. Sorry, it is all a bit hazy now—the intervening years have been hard on us all.

Whatever it was, it was on in the Mont Clare Hotel, just outside the back gates of Trinity College. Now the term 'ball' was stretching it.

In truth, the 'ball' was a glorified disco—a backcombed, midweek, tenner-a-head version of a Debs with lots of taffeta, lots of cleavage and lots of promise.

In the late 1980s, the hotel was a bit down at heel. No one had any cash to do the place up. It was Dublin pre-Ryanair, pre-Temple Bar, so the short-hop weekend break that we all know now hadn't yet materialised. I suppose hotels in town survived on Irish-Americans, a few travelling salesmen and the odd person up from the country for a match or a bit of shopping.

We hired our dinner jackets and bow ties at a small place beside the Central Bank (which is still there) and five of us stopped off in the Stag's Head for a few before the event. One jar led to another and, before we knew it, we were well on and the ball had started. So off around College Green we headed, into the Lincoln Inn for a quick sharpener and then on, steaming, to the Mont Clare.

The bouncer, a huge lad, took one look at us.

'Sorry, lads, not tonight.'

'But, but . . .'

'Yez heard me, yez wasted gobshites.'

'But here's the tickets.'

'Not in that state, bud.'

'C'mon, man!'

'Yez are annoying me now.'

He glanced beyond me to two giggly Arts students.

'Ladies, come in out of the cold. Cloakroom's on the right.'

He looked down at me.

'You, Redser, you're barred. Now off—get away from the bleedin' door.'

There we were—in monkey suits—with nowhere to go. Yet we were undefeated. We were fuelled by the unquenchable optimism of the drunk. There had to be another way.

One of the lads had an idea. He'd worked in the Mont Clare the previous summer and knew if you sneaked around the back and up the old lane, there was a way in through the kitchens where the exit door was always open for the rubbish to be taken out.

It had to be worth a go.

So in we squeezed, through a corrugated iron fence, looking for the kitchen door, past the wheelie bin full of bottles and the pile of fag butts where the kitchen porters had grabbed a few drags between shifts. We were on the right track, but a bit the worse for wear. Through the door on the left and down the stairs. We were in.

'Shush!'

'OK.'

Another door, around the corner and up another staircase. It was a big hotel after all, and the gig could have been anywhere. The key was to get as far into the interior of the building as possible and as far away from that bouncer who'd murder us if he saw us. In fact, he'd murder me first.

'Let's push through this door.'

Strange. We must have ended up in the accounts room of the hotel, because it was full of computers and in trays and out trays. There was also a table tennis table, which seemed out of place but could easily have been there for staff working double shifts. Then there were more computers and whiteboards.

I'd worked in hotels before, but none was like this. Even though everything was out of place, we seemed to take it in our stride. When you're a bit wrecked and gutting for another pint, it all seems logical.

'Let's try the lift. We're probably in the basement and the gig is upstairs.'

Into the lift I got, dinner jacket, bow tie, black brogues—smoking. The lift jolted upwards before the others could get in. The lads were still downstairs. I could sense, this was it: the doors would open and I'd slip into the ball unnoticed.

THE HEIST

The doors opened just in front of my face agonizingly slowly.

I looked at them, startled, and they looked at me, equally bemused. I saw the batons first, then the flak jackets, then up to the caps and right back down the pristine seam of the navy-blue trousers to the black Doc Martin shoes.

'Jesus! Evening, Guard.'

One of them smirked, looking me up and down with my dinner jacket, bow tie and a cigarette.

'Evening, Mr Bond,' he laughed.

'What are you doing here?' I blurted out, confused as to why cops would be in the Mont Clare Hotel at half-twelve on a Thursday night.

'Shut up,' barked the grumpy one as he grabbed me.

'C'mon, lads. I was only trying to get into the gig.'

'Do you know where you are?'

'Yes, of course I do. I'm not that hammered.'

'Well, you'd better explain that to the Super down at Pearse Street because you are under arrest for trying to rob the Anglo Irish Bank.'

The Irish Bank of Commerce had just changed its name to Anglo Irish Bank and was situated in a rather inauspicious corner of Clare Street, opposite the Davenport Hotel, just up from Pearse Street Dart Station. It shared a side entrance with the Mont Clare Hotel.

The five raiders in tuxedos had stumbled into the not particularly secure bank, rather than the hotel, via one of its exit doors, and had been captured on CCTV parading around the building looking for a last pint.

Luckily for us, the Guards saw the funny side of it and, after a few hours in Pearse Street, they released the five dehydrated and freezing would-be robbers in monkey suits.

That was my first experience with Anglo Irish Bank. But not to put too fine a point on it, we were clearly considerably less successful at robbing the bank than the people who ran the place. It seems security was never high up on Anglo's list.

THE GAME

Fast forward 20 years and I am in a monkey suit once more, surrounded by bankers. It is late but at least this time I'd come through the front door legitimately.

On Thursday, 20 November 2008, the O'Reilly Hall—a donation by Tony O'Reilly to his Alma Mater—was rocking.[1] It had been a successful night. The booze was flowing and the black tie made everyone look fitter, younger and maybe more distinguished that they had any right to be.

The old boys of UCD had made a few good speeches about combating the recession. They appealed to our sense of patriotism. The entertainment came from a wonderful tenor from Kentucky who sang 'My Old Kentucky Home'—which is always the opening song at the Kentucky Derby. Given the number of senior Irish bankers in the room—all graduates of UCD—and what had been exposed about their gambling habits in the previous weeks, maybe a betting anthem was aptly chosen.

The great and good of Irish business and politics were there. Michael McDowell worked the room constantly, as did the heads of many of our quoted companies. Given UCD's position as the national university, this glittering array is hardly surprising. There were a few interlopers like myself but non-UCD alumni were few and far between.

Seanie Fitzpatrick was sitting two tables away from me beside his fellow Anglo director and Brian Cowen's confidante, Fintan Drury. Spirits were high. Ossie Kilkenny, U2's former accountant, was pressing the flesh and cracking jokes, but the normally ebullient and always friendly Fitzpatrick seemed a bit out of sorts.

In the light of what was to be revealed about him and his covered up personal loans four weeks later, it is hardly surprising that he had other things on his mind. Yet at the time, the legendary Seanie charm was occasionally on show as he moved from table to table, winking and squeezing shoulders.

If there was strain, there were only brief flickers of it. He spoke to his wife at length, whispering in her ear the way we all do with the person we're closest to.

He looked slighter than I remembered him from previous meetings. At a certain stage he appeared to stare far away into the distance as if trying to come to terms with the enormity of what had happened to him. Holding his glasses in his hand up to his temple, he fixed on a spot in the distance. What was going through his mind? Had it all unravelled?

The last time I was there in the O'Reilly Hall, I was presenting at a business awards ceremony—a sort of Rose of Tralee for men with BMWs and K Club memberships. That was only 18 months prior to this evening. Back then, there were no moments of solitude for Seanie. He was everyone's friend. There was a queue of admirers coming to kiss the ring of the man who had changed Irish banking. Anglo Irish was a byword for the swashbuckling Irish and in the world of Irish finance, Seanie was the Godfather.

In the chummy circles of Irish business, nothing succeeds like success. Eighteen months earlier, the sycophants had lined up. Journalists who have subsequently damned him were there paying homage, as were competing bankers hoping to be noticed. Captains of industry and builders, of course the builders, many of whom were made by Seanie, paid homage too. One wonders how many of them ring him now for the odd round of golf.

As Fitzpatrick stared out into the dark, the orphan of failure was making her unwelcome presence felt. He knew what was about to come. He understood what happens in our country when the pendulum swings. No matter how much sweat went into the ascent, the drop is always precipitous.

But that was 'the game' he had spoken about so often. In a 2007 interview he had commented that that's all it was, 'a game and it's about winning'. He suggested that he got into the game of banking because he had been refused a modest mortgage in the 1970s.

That night, his momentary solitude revealed the inner torment. There are some things you just can't bluster through. Yet Seanie was still the chairman of a bank and that bank had backed many who would never have got a start anywhere else. Surely they'd remember that when they came for his head? Surely someone would speak up for Seanie? After all, he spoke up for them.

If you talk to people in Dublin who've done business with him, you won't find many who will speak ill of him. In the notoriously bitchy circles of Dublin business, this is what makes Sean Fitzpatrick intriguing. How can a man like this, who—so the story goes—practically bankrupted the country, have so few enemies?

What drove him? Because in the end, it is difficult not to conclude that it was something more than commerce that fuelled the house of Anglo. Was there was a greater motive that went way beyond money? It was a game, but why did he risk everything to win?

THE PLAYER

Prior to this, my only proper dealings and comments on Anglo Irish Bank had been two years ago in 2007 when I wrote the following in my last book, *The Generation Game*: 'Anglo is little more than an out of control hedge fund leveraging itself and its clients into property. When the market finally gives up, these outfits tend to go belly up.' I was advised by my publisher's lawyers to take the name Anglo out, as we would be sued for telling this truth. So the sentence read 'Certain well-known Dublin banks are now little more than out of control hedge funds leveraging themselves and clients into property.' (Maybe this is yet another example of the bad law protecting the few to the detriment of the many. But for that I don't blame Fitzpatrick; the finger of blame is more accurately pointed at the courts, the bar and the barristers.)

I met Sean Fitzpatrick a few times before. In fact, I have to thank him for a dinner in the now defunct Commons Restaurant in Dublin. This was payment in 2002 for a talk I gave on the impending disaster in Ireland if we kept inflating our bubble. I must've looked pretty stupid when things went on ever upwards in 2003, 2004, 2005 and 2006.

I had also met him at a TV interview we were to do—on, of all things, banking ethics—when Seanie was warning the government about too much interference in the banking system and regulation after the DIRT scandal. This was back in 2003.

I had shared a platform with him in 2005 when he spoke of the absolute need for Irish banks to remain in Irish hands. This was, in the light of what has subsequently happened, a revealing speech. Seanie spoke passionately about the need for us to prevent foreign takeovers of Irish banks. He drew the distinction between foreign shareholders and capital which he needed, and foreign management which he didn't want. He said at all costs foreign management must be blocked. He explained his thinking explicitly in the context of a crash in the Irish property market. He couched his terms suggesting that if there were problems, it would be far more preferable to have local senior management teams who could pick up the phone to the Minister, ring around the big guns and try to put a rescue package in place for Ireland than for the bank's foreign headquarters to do so.

In short, he was saying that when it all crumbled, it would be better that our own banks were around to lean on the State to do the right thing by them, not necessarily do the right thing by the people. How prescient was this? If we contrast the behaviour of the Dutch-controlled ACC in bringing big developers to heel with the Irish banks who are adopting a softly, softly approach, we can see the evident difference in attitude.

There was also the small matter that foreign managers might see the shady dealings that were going on between the banks in Ireland. Such clarity would call time on their little scams of moving money around in the case of Anglo, Irish Nationwide and Irish Life and Permanent, or just endemic and repeated overcharging as in AIB, or simply reckless lending at the end of the boom, as evidenced by Ulster Bank and Bank of Ireland.

Did he see it all collapsing? He certainly was more worried about the consequences of what they were up to than many, yet why was he compelled to push the boundaries? That day, he spoke about his children and what might happen to them and their generation if the banks imploded. How could the man who more than anyone else endangered the system by backing the most reckless of developers have not realised that he was part of the problem?

THE REVELATION
Sean Fitzpatrick was always extremely engaging and easy to get along with, much more accessible to journalists and without the layers of media handlers that is normal for bank chiefs. Having worked in the banking game for years in London, I'd say he was one of the most down-to-earth senior bankers I've come across. He was on top of his game.

That night at UCD in November 2008 was different. Sean was agitated and by the time we chatted he had probably had a few too many. We bumped into each other. There was a bit of a stand-off initially. He made a big deal of the fact that I had said hello to him first. He was adamant that he hadn't sought me out. Well, why would he, as my views on the banks and the economy were well known?

That said, he was keen to put me straight on a few things I'd written about the banks. This wasn't too surprising as I'd been writing more than my fair share about them, particularly in the weeks running up to and after the guarantee.

Seanie sat me down, bottle of beer in hand. We had a few more in the course of the hour. People were already leaving. The huge hall was emptying out. I know this because his wife was worried about his diabetes and came over to the table a few times. It was getting late, she said and, mothering him, whispered to me that he had to be up in the morning. But he wasn't budging. He was in sparkling form, on fire.

Fitzpatrick the salesman was in full force. He has an intense but not threatening way of holding your gaze. It is charming and almost paternalistic. You are falling under the Seanie Fitz spell. You are being love-bombed and you feel that you are the only person in the room. He looks at you from over his bifocals with his twinkly brown eyes and you believe him.

He explained why Anglo didn't need any cash injection and how he and his team would go on the road and raise private capital. They didn't need the government, and the international markets understood the Anglo model and the Anglo culture.

I didn't tell him about my breaking and entering episode, or about my conversations with Brian Lenihan before the guarantee when I'd concluded to the Minister that sometimes you have to save the bad banks to save the system.

I was too busy listening. Seanie was on a roll. Most interestingly, he spoke about how he had built the bank from practically nothing and how Anglo had changed the way the country did business. For him, the success of Anglo and the success of the country went hand in hand.

Then he paused and said something more revealing than anything about tactics, relationship banking or the Anglo model.

At the time, the word was that Bank of Ireland or AIB would take over the limping Anglo. This was anathema to him. Bank of Ireland was always seen as the Establishment, almost the Ascendancy, bank. Many described it as a Church of Ireland bank while AIB was seen as the ultimate bureaucratic bank. He railed against these big banks, claiming that Anglo did things differently. There were the layers of bureaucracy that the other outfits demanded. If you wanted a deal done, you went to him. These other guys weren't bankers; they were time-servers who'd wrap you up in red tape and never take a decision.

Then he came closer, right up to me, squeezed my arm and practically hissed between clenched teeth, 'No fucking Protestant is going to take my bank. No fucking Protestant is coming near us. Those establishment fuckers and Bank of Ireland have been running our country before we came along and those fuckers are not going to bring me down. None of them are ever going to look down on us again. We are the outsiders and this is our moment and those fuckers don't own us any more.'

This was a moment of truth, because this is what Sean Fitzpatrick had been fighting all his life and I'd never seen it. He was the Godfather. He was the boss of a new power—the man they all wanted to be. He was the reckless genius who had built Anglo from nothing and yet, he hated them, the other banks.

As far as he was concerned, they were the Dons, no matter what their religion, they were the rulers of a financial network, easily as closed off and hierarchical as the drugs cartels that bring cocaine from Central America to central Ranelagh. Seanie couldn't join their club so he had resolved to beat them. He, as the Godfather, had played a different game, one with higher risks and greater returns and by the end, they would come knocking at his door.

No, it wasn't about money—as Fitzpatrick had said many times over—it was about something much more, something much, much deeper.

Chapter 11 ~

| THE GODFATHER

DAVOS, 2006

Rupert Murdoch being frogmarched off the premises, out to the freezing snow, is one of the funniest things you will ever see. It is made all the more hilarious by the fact that the media mogul, possibly the most influential man on earth, is being manhandled by a spotty teenager, a conscript in the Swiss Army.

Obviously when you tell the average Swiss conscript to allow people into the hotel only if they have identity tags, the soldier takes this as gospel. No one, no matter how important, is allowed to pass.

Rupert Murdoch made the embarrassing mistake of trying to test the resolve of the Swiss Army in public. Didn't he know that these guys were chosen to guard the Pope for a good reason? That reason is unflinching discipline.

What made the encounter unusual is that the soldier had no idea who Rupert Murdoch was and Rupert Murdoch had no idea how to react when refused. The mutual incomprehension on both faces was priceless.

Murdoch was trying to get into the Google party after hours at Davos. Apart from the gabfest, Davos is about networking and parties. The giants of Wall Street vie with each other to see who can host the best bash. Who knows, Murdoch could have been there to make a gargantuan offer to the diminutive founder of Google, Sergey Brin, who floated around his own party endearingly like a self-conscious gatecrasher.

Maybe that was Murdoch's aim, but we'll never know because our Swiss guard was having none of it. But that is one of the things about Davos, the high and mighty of the corporate world are all there, doing deals and giving each other the chummy high fives of people who know they are at the top of the heap.

Earlier that day, in a cramped hotel foyer, Peter Sutherland, chairman of Goldman Sachs and BP, chatted to Hank Paulson, then the

US Treasury Secretary, and Robert Zoellick, the head of the World Bank. Sitting nearby, casually dressed in jeans and runners, was Tom Friedman, the highly influential *New York Times* columnist, who was chatting to the editor of *The Economist*, while at the table next to them was Ehud Barak, then the Prime Minister of Israel, drinking what looked like a Harvey Wallbanger with his wife.

The Godfather had come a long way from the man who'd been refused a mortgage in the 1970s. Not only was he the boss of the new power brokers in Ireland, but here in Davos, amongst the big boys, his genius was being recognised. In January 2006, as he trudged through the snow and looked up at the imposing Rinerhorn and out over the heated open air swimming pool, he knew he had made it.

At the World Economic Forum in Davos in 2006, Mercer Oliver Wyman, the most respected banking outfit in the world, named Anglo Irish Bank 'the best-performing financial institution in the world'. This is the Oscars of the corporate world and the Godfather was walking away with a gong.

He had grown his bank's profits from practically nothing 15 years earlier to nearly €700 million. His bank was now making more profit in a day than it did in a year back then. 'World's best-performing financial institution' also meant the world's best-performing CEO. The Godfather had reached the summit.

He had got to the top of the business, a business he didn't have any right to get to the top of. His family was not the Cosa Nostra; they were small players. However, in the previous 20 years, the Godfather had operated the most ruthless machine, which not only eclipsed that of the other Dons but set the tone for the entire business. The model was growth. Simple as that.

He had quadrupled Anglo's balance sheet in the previous five years, up to €45 billion. Another five years of that and he would run the biggest bank in the country.

He had changed the game and the world knew it. He was the man and the others, even the established families and blue-blooded businesses, knew that all deals would have to go to the Godfather first.

His lieutenants were the smartest, best trained and most aggressive. He bought their loyalty with cash, much more cash than the others were prepared to pay. More than anything else, the Godfather understood the psychology of the game.

It was about winning and, in a small town when all the money was counted, what really made a difference was whether you were on top or not.

This ruthless attitude unnerved the older banks. They had been used to carving up the market in Ireland between them. For years, the bosses of the established banks were the Dons of the Irish financial world. Central to the old status quo was that people knew their place. The Dons had a conveyor belt of lieutenants and deputies from families and schools they trusted.

In the old days, Ireland was cosy. Everyone was vetted. People knew who was who. In many cases at the top, they had married their sons and daughters off to each other and, up until a few years back, the *Irish Times* wedding announcements served as a forecast of who was going to be who in the years ahead. It was the Irish mergers and acquisitions page.

The Dons always knew that marriage was a good way of forging alliances and propagating the system. That was until the Godfather arrived, and with him a whole new way of doing business and a whole new cabal of businesses. The Godfather had expanded into a range that they had never touched and, by bringing in new businesses, he had created new players.

These new players unsettled the old establishment. For the old-timers, the new entrants were trigger-happy, erratic gamblers. They drew too much attention to the game. But most of all, the old establishment knew what the new lads were: a threat. The old Dons were scared.

In the old days, the key to the game was to be always low-key, softly spoken and highly discrete. No one had any interest in unwanted attention. The Cosa Nostra played its cards close to its chest. And that was the secret of its success for generations. A quiet word here, a firm reprimand there. The women were never flashy. Parties were understated even while the profits flourished. The Irish banks and the clans who ran them were solid and institutional.

When they were caught red-handed, as they were for diverting massive amounts of DIRT tax into secret accounts so that the ordinary people could avoid tax, the old Dons put their hands up, shuffled a few deckchairs and carried on as they had before. Contrition works when you are at the top.

If one of their lieutenants decided to go over to the dark side and blow the whistle on their activities, the reaction was also well planned.

Initially silence was the policy and then gradually the man, no matter how upright he was, would be the victim of a smear campaign to prevent him working in the town again.

He may go to the press, but that would pass and, ultimately, the Dons found that in general, journalists in the town were so easily purchased there wasn't too much to worry about. They had their franchise and it could be protected without too much effort. A few calls, a dinner here and a drink there and all would be well again. There was very little in a small town that corporate hospitality couldn't buy.

As for the government, the old Dons knew how to handle it. They were smart enough to co-opt the State into their world, so much so that no piece of legislation had been passed in 20 years that might be detrimental to the interests of the banks. In fact, the State had taken so well to deregulation that the Dons sometimes mused that Ireland was not so much a State with a banking system, but rather a banking system with a State attached to it. And, on the face of it, they had a point. In 2004, the 'big six' banks had assets of about €300 billion, twice Ireland's GDP. By early 2008 this figure had risen to nearly €600 billion, over three times Ireland's GDP.

The Dons also knew how important it was to have the State's incriminating fingerprints evident at any crime scene that might present itself. So for example when the DIRT affair came to light, the Dons made sure that the Central Bank, the so-called policeman on the block, was up to its eyes in the scandal.

The cops could hardly come over all high and mighty if they knew and were involved in the crime all along. And by giving a former central banker a board position, the Dons could ensure that everyone in the club was singing from the same hymn sheet.

The government too needed the Dons. Who else could finance the budget deficits of the old days if not the Cosa Nostra with its web of contacts and salespeople all around the place? If the State needed money quickly, as we did in the 1980s and early 1990s, whom did it go to but the big moneylenders? Irish banks were financing more than half the national debt throughout the 1980s.

So the old system was moving along nicely as it always had done, until the Godfather and his new methods came on the scene.

Initially, the old Dons saw him as a mild irritant. They were happy enough to let him grow his patch. How could a Mickey Mouse outfit like Anglo Irish Bank, with a rundown office beside the Mont Clare Hotel, threaten the glittering headquarters of Bank of Ireland, AIB or Irish Life and Permanent?

He was brash and a bit nouveau but because he was on their radar screen, they were happy to leave him free to do his own little deals.

After all, they smirked over a few gin and tonics, what was he doing only leasing photocopiers? In their hubris, what the Dons of the Royal St George Yacht Club failed to see was that the guy who was leasing photo-copiers today was the aggressive businessman of tomorrow. The Godfather was cultivating a new tribe with every deal, and with every 'yes' on a loan application he was building loyalty, creating a new class.

THE CARTEL

The Dons heard that out on the street, the Godfather's hungry lieutenants were bidding aggressively for business. But as far as they were concerned, that would only keep their own middle-ranking men on their toes. Anyway, the old Dons concluded that they didn't want the business the Godfather was interested in, despite the fact that it was profitable.

They were in the mass distribution business. They were dealing credit, buying it cheap, taking a cut and passing it on to the credit addicts below. Credit was the drug that every economy needed and these Dons were the Cosa Nostra that controlled this drug trade.

They had the distribution network of banks in every small town and village which was essential for getting the drug onto the streets. The easy credit, which they made their money from, had to get to the credit junkies somehow and they had dealers in each and every small town. More significantly, due to their extremely smart stewarding of the business and knowledge of the locals' small-town prejudices, they had managed to turn these small-time credit dealers into pillars of the local establishment.

What did they care about some upstart like the Godfather on the make? Eventually he would have to buckle under their power, bend at the knee and show respect. Once he showed respect and no one had to lose face, they could all continue in the old-fashioned way. Who knew, maybe there were areas of common interest between the old established families and the Godfather? After all, business was booming. Why fight when the cake is getting bigger? Also the Dons worked on the basis of as little public squabbling as possible. That only attracted attention and heat. Hotheads were to be avoided.

Gentlemen behaved like gentlemen, even if they were glorified dealers, pushing easy credit on a nation of potential debt junkies.

The Godfather surrounded himself with a new type of lieutenant and went after a new type of business. Once he had graduated from car and office supply leasing, he went after anything that was tax driven. He financed car parks, hotels and shopping centres, anything that was made more palatable by a tax break.

This distinguished him from the other Dons. But what really set him apart was that he took a piece of the action. They'd never touch the merchandise. The Godfather figured that the best way to make money was not only to lend money to people but, once he lent to them, to get them—his clients—to work for him.

So he encouraged the lieutenants in Anglo's ranks to start taking personal positions on the deals they were financing. It was this that ultimately attracted Shylock, who was then still flogging mortgages and taking a cut. But he was dreaming of the big time, watching and waiting.

By cutting his lieutenants in on deals, the Godfather kept them focused and keen. Most crucially, he wanted them to do things with him they'd never do with the Dons. This made them loyal. Once they had crossed that Rubicon, there was no turning back. They were blood brothers, ready to break whatever old rules there were, ready to go the ruthless extra mile for money.

Around the town, in bars after work, the smarter competing lieutenants got wind of this new opportunity to make a personal fortune. Not surprisingly, some of the established Dons' best men jumped ship to the Godfather.

The old Dons continued with their age-old rules about what could be financed and what couldn't. They took their time. They were not in the business of making mistakes. They certainly hadn't got to where they were by being rash.

THE ART OF THE DEAL
The Godfather had other plans. He saw the weakness in the old structure. If he financed the tax-driven deals, he could cut himself in on the deals easily.

To see how this worked, let's take the example of a shopping centre in a provincial town that none of the old Dons could be bothered chasing. Furthermore, as financial snobs, they certainly could not countenance breaking bread with the type of people they deemed to be yahoos who were doing deals down there in the sticks.

The Godfather, on the other hand, sought out these new players and cultivated them, knowing that they were hungrier and more aggressive. He also knew that, as a result, they would pay him handsomely for his cash.

So the land where a shopping centre would be built could be bought for, say, €50 million. Once the place had planning permission, the value of the entire project would increase to €75 million because the local politicians would ensure that they blocked any future development of retail parks in the vicinity. The local politicians could be convinced by the local muscle. That's the way things worked. You scratch my back.

The Godfather had to cultivate these relationships but he soon realised that a few rugby matches or the All-Ireland Final would make those little guys ecstatic and keep them onside. As the man who is now chief operating officer of Anglo said, when he was an ambitious lieutenant dealing with posh clients in London which the Godfather targeted in later years, 'If you take someone to a British Open, the Grand Prix and then to Wimbledon, there will be a point when they owe you one.'

The tactic he used later to great effect in Mayfair and Knightsbridge was honed and perfected in Ennis and Galway at GAA matches, point-to-point meetings and local golf classics.

It was a small price for the rewards that were to come and it kept the new players in his pocket, which is where he wanted them.

The revalued site was pure profit and, as it had the new capital allowances for tax, it meant that anyone who was an owner in such a deal could have a huge tax write-off. So the Godfather was making his players, his lieutenants and himself rich while at the same time minimising everyone's tax bill.

He was only playing the game, but he was playing at a higher intensity and paying better than anyone else.

In a deal like this, which was the typical blueprint for the Godfather's activities, he would probably have arranged for Anglo to finance €40 million of the loan. He would put a syndicate of his friends together and, along with the local builders, they would make up the €10 million cash down. This would make up the €50 million.

He normally got his 10 per cent of the cash down from his friendly private banker—a small-time moneylender with big ambitions who went by the name of Fingers.

So already they were in clover. Whatever capital gains he got were taxed at a personal rate of 20 per cent because his mate Charlie McCreevy had reduced capital gains tax. This move, which generated huge turnover in the market, also jaundiced the nature of Irish transactions. Developers realised that it would be much more profitable for them to take on these huge loans in their own name and so they did.

This easy money attracted all sorts of new players to the Godfather's empire. He was taking bets on new players and in turn when they got rich, he got rich. When Moya Doherty of *Riverdance* fame needed €29 million to buy the most expensive house in Martha's Vineyard, she turned to him; when former colleague Paul Pardy needed help raising €150 million for a hotel project in Florida, he rang the Godfather.

He signalled his intent to change the rules when he bought a smaller moneylender with the funny Austrian-sounding name of Ansbacher in 1996. This moneylender had been in trouble with the government for facilitating the tax and financial skulduggery of a former golden circle.

The established Dons, although they knew all about this and in many cases were involved, didn't have the balls to buy such a contaminated moneylender. The Godfather was different.

THE WEDDING MARQUEE

Two years after Davos, on the day of his son's wedding, things were falling apart. But it was all about appearances. After all, he had been fêted at Davos, the deals had got bigger and bigger and today he was in the Ritz-Carlton, still in the middle of everything.

The Dons would assemble and pay their respects. It was to be a celebration. The Godfather and his wife had known their future daughter-in-law for years and she was from a good family, good people.

But still he agonized over his speech. As he looked out over Powerscourt Gardens to his beloved Greystones and the sea beyond, he worried about the tone. He thought back over the previous helter-skelter five years.

The wedding would have all the new players as well as their advisors, the lawyers, accountants and auditors. The speech had to hit the right note.

His wife of 30 years told him not to worry. He was a family man—solid, hardworking and successful. His vices were few and his capacity for hard work and good deeds legendary.

Now that he had proved himself, it was important to be magnanimous. He needed to speak of responsibility, of the community, of the need for love in the family and, more importantly, between families. His people would be there. So too would the other Dons, but they were now looking to him for leadership, not the other way around. He was the Boss, the *Capo di Tutti Capi*.

Looking beyond the roses to the immigrant Iraqi radiographers mixing the mimosa, the Godfather surveyed the scene. They'd come a long way since his son's birth and he wasn't going to give up easily even once they had relented and made him their spokesperson. When they could no longer ignore him, the Godfather was made the President of the Irish Banking Federation in 2000. The old Dons needed to keep their heads down after the DIRT tax scandal and Anglo had not been involved in it. The Godfather, still operating a much smaller outfit than the Dons, could serve a purpose for them.

And he didn't disappoint in his inaugural speech, announcing the introduction of the new Code of Ethics for a banking system that was under the spotlight following recent scandals. Just when the moneylenders were taking flak, he pronounced:

> The key to it all is the same key that has always underpinned a strong banking sector confidence. Or, to use a word not much in vogue nowadays, trust. And our industry has to face an unpleasant fact where the word trust is concerned. It has been undermined in recent times, to a point where the image and perception of banks has been badly damaged.

He would have been lying if he said that he got no joy from seeing the old establishment squirm under the spotlight. His own bank's cleanliness allowed him to twist the knife in a little.

He was the new type of moneylender and the world knew that in his hands, the Irish banking system was safe, and more than safe—it was thriving.

The industry of which we are proud must do everything in its power to ensure that we do not warrant in future the degree of criticism that has been meted out to us in recent times.

As he looked back, he began to chart in his head when things started going his way.

While the Dons got bogged down in petty scandals about over-charging small guys for fees, he was moving ahead. The deals were getting bigger and, at the time, he was putting more of his personal money into them. And when that wasn't enough, he put the bank's shareholders' money, in the Godfather's name, into these ventures. The bank was now breaking all the rules by being on both sides of a trans-action. It was the moneylender to the deals and its top brass were the partners in these deals. It wasn't a bank; it was a personal investment vehicle.

Yet the Godfather continued to speak like an altar boy. He announced that:

The principles of integrity, confidentiality, professionalism and compliance are the most basic of modern banking and we have gone to some pains to ensure that they are at the heart of this Code of Ethics.

As he ushered the other Dons into his son's wedding, he was orches-trating the next moves. He spoke publicly now about the need to keep the moneylenders in local hands, to keep at bay some of the bigger syndicates that were operating outside the country and wanted a piece of the action. He had no problem with their money, just with their generals.

The Irish Cosa Nostra was quite big enough. He had seen what happened when a tight circle had been opened up to others in the past. It was all right letting new guys in at the bottom—that sort of com-petition was good—but it was crowded enough at the top. He was still sure the Golden Circle loan could be pulled off and they'd all get out of this.

Today was a wedding, a celebration. It was time to be generous—time to look to the next generation.

THE EURO PYRAMID SCHEME

By the time the attitude of the established banks changed it was too late.

The Godfather and his crew were making fortunes and grabbing new business. They had bet on new players and the new players were thriving. When he picked these new players, many of them were on the floor. He bet on the man, not just the project. He looked them in the eye, sized them up—made sure he was protected in case the deal went wrong—and shook hands. Anything was possible.

The Godfather understood the nature of the game more than anyone else, better than the older Dons who hadn't realised quite how much the rules had changed when Ireland had entered the euro.

The Godfather's players would continue to be profitable as long as there were more and more new players coming in at the bottom of the pyramid. All they had to do to get the big guys out at the top of the scheme was keep the money flowing in at the bottom. It was simple really.

The Irish Cosa Nostra could do this because they had found a new source of external funding. Up to 2000, the Dons' ability to expand was always limited by money. They never had enough money to make the system bigger. They were constrained. They only had as much money as there was in the country.

They had to ration what deals they did, with whom and for how long. Also, getting money into the country was difficult. There were all sorts of controls and problems at the border. They had to smuggle money in and out. That's how the old Dons got caught with what became known as the DIRT scandal. They simply couldn't get the cash out of the country quickly enough. Somewhere along the line, someone made a mistake and the scam was exposed.

But all that changed with the advent of the euro. From the perspective of the country's moneylenders, the dealers in easy credit, the euro meant that an infinite pool of money became available. The Cosa Nostra really didn't care what currency they dealt in. After all, they had operated all the currency exchanges up to then. They were both moneylenders and moneychangers. But even if the money-changing business was badly affected by the euro, some of the Dons saw an opportunity. Despite this, they were still slow off the mark.

But no one appreciated the euro more than the Godfather.

He was on top of it from the start. If he could borrow as much as he wanted from international banks and moneylenders, particularly in

Germany, he could keep the conveyor belt of new players going. It was akin to a drug baron getting a new pure source of cocaine or heroin. For the banks, joining the euro was the same as the drug baron dis-covering the Golden Triangle or accessing the complete stash of Pablo Escobar. Germany was the stash. Since 2000, German savings had been climbing steadily, and their money needed somewhere to go.

It changed the game and it meant that the distribution network the old Dons had built up was no longer necessary.

From his mortgage brokerage, Shylock watched the Godfather. It was nearly time to jump ship; the Godfather was leaving the Dons far behind.

The Godfather turned his attention from small-time borrowers. Why would he bother maintaining a costly sales force of dealers, middlemen and go-betweens? This was the old way of doing business. Why lend €10,000 to someone you don't know and can't charge huge fees to, when you can lend €10,000,000 to someone you know and who will pay you a fortune for arranging the loan?

The Godfather was making much more money with much less hassle. His business model was sharper, quicker and more profitable. He was still a moneylender, but a highly focused moneylender. His number of employees was a fraction of the big two banks. He had far fewer lieutenants and far fewer customers. His reliance on the big deal meant he had very few relationships to maintain. His top 50 customers accounted for the majority of his business. So they were easy to keep track of.

Much more significantly, he had changed the way the world did business. By the time he was accepting his accolades at Davos, he was the man everyone wanted to talk to.

He had worked the system and broken the stranglehold of the Establishment on the banking game. Financial power in Ireland had moved from the yacht club to the golf club. Anyone could play golf and everyone did. Now, thanks to the Godfather, anyone could get credit and everyone did.

As he looked at himself in the mirror to fix his bow tie before the speech, he knew he had changed the system. He had almost won the game. The former photocopier leaser was the toast of Davos and now, if he could pull off this Golden Circle deal, he would still be on top.

The wedding band lowered the music. The Godfather's moment had arrived. He scanned the tables. He saw his friends, the new players, and his enemies, the old Dons. He saw his power structure in front of him, the lawyers, the accountants and the developers. He surveyed the new elite and their children—like his son—about to inherit the world, living in Europe's fastest growing economy.

He glanced down at his wife. She had been with him through everything. She squeezed his hand gently. She had made sure he had taken his insulin earlier. She whispered to him what he already knew as he spread out the few notes he'd made. He was a brilliant speaker, a brilliant communicator and a man on top of the world. He cleared his throat.

'Unaccustomed as I am to public speaking . . .'

The place went into uproar.

But the clock was ticking.

| THE TURF WAR

HOW TO BANKRUPT A COUNTRY

In June 2006, Shylock walked into the Godfather's office to report for his first day of work.

The first call he made was to the Merchant of Ennis, who was looking for a big break. The country was full of Merchant of Ennis types. They'd emerged over the previous 10 years, as they had morphed from builders and auctioneers to developers. They were having a go and rolling the dice. They had discovered that they could sell anything they built at a profit because the Dons who were funding them were also making sure that the buyers at the bottom of the pyramid had access to plenty of credit to meet their exorbitant asking prices.

The new Merchants were the Godfather's people and they loved him, and in a way he loved them too. One thing was clear: they could not thrive without each other.

The Merchant needed money because he couldn't keep up with the opportunities. The old Dons didn't move fast enough for him, they didn't seem to understand that time was money. The Godfather did, and had his lieutenants, people like Shylock, ready to do business with them. Shylock's terms were usually more extortionate than the other lenders', but Shylock was quick. The Merchant had his answer in a few hours rather than a few weeks. When you were a new Merchant, competing for deals with other new, aggressive Merchants, speed was everything.

The Godfather's attitude to Shylock and lieutenants like him was totally different to the old Dons'. He let them do the deals and take some of the profits for themselves. This way, he figured, they would get up in the morning keener, more focused and driven by their own back pocket, as well as by the desire to do well for the clan and the company.

Shylock moved from the mortgage broker to one of the old Don's banks briefly in 1999. He tried to make it in the old way, the way 'respectable' people made it. But he couldn't stand it. It wasn't for him, all that arse-licking.

So in 2001, he moved back to the brokerage game. No, it wasn't as glamorous as working at the headquarters of AIB but he was making more money and, for him, that was all that counted. He was also honing his craft.

When he moved to the Godfather in the summer of 2006, he couldn't believe his eyes. He had never been in such an environment before. The deals were so big. When he was with the old Dons, records were checked, loan to value ratios were stringent and Shylock, no matter what he thought of the deal, had to get it past the credit committee who would ultimately sanction the money. This was the security regime the old Dons had put in place. Remember, they had too much to lose by making elementary mistakes. They had nice lives, nice families. They had earned the respect of their community so what value was it for them to be humiliated because one small-time go-getter got in too deep?

The Don's credit committee, with its cold scientific approach to numbers, ratios and forecasts, was the core of the organisation.

These guys were the bouncers at the door of the old Don's firm. Like bouncers everywhere, their favourite thing was to turn away new or unknown Merchants with the line 'Sorry, regulars only.' They were the keepers of the gate. If you got through them, you were away. Shylock hated them. They came between him and his commission.

With the Godfather, there was none of that stuff. His game was to get big as quickly as possible and get the cash out into the market—as much of it as possible. The Godfather only cared about margin, as did Shylock. The more money he loaned to the Merchants, the more margin he made. It was all about volume. Shylock was made up.

This company changed the nature of what it was to be a money-lender. It became part of the deal itself. The moneylender became the Merchant and the Merchant was tied up with the moneylender. With both of them parties to the deal, both had a stake in things going ever upwards. Deals were accelerated, not delayed, facilitated not queried. To see how well this symbiotic relationship worked for the Godfather, we need look no further than the price people were willing to pay for a piece of his company—the share price, which rose from 50p in the old restricted money to €18.50 in the new money.

Interestingly, Shylock, despite seeing what was going on, preferred to just lend the money, stay on one side and take his commission from the loan. The lads on the floor, some of the Godfather's most trusted cadres, thought he was mad. They assumed he had no balls. But they all acknowledged he was good at his job. He never missed a trick.

THE TURF WAR

The old Dons realised the game had fundamentally changed when the business they used to rely on started to go to the Godfather. He played the game harder and faster than they were used to. He didn't play by their rules—he had invented his own. The old Dons were beginning to look stupid. He was showing them up so much that even their normally compliant shareholders were starting to make themselves heard. They were losing support. Every quarter, the Godfather was making more money and taking a bigger market share, while the Dons, who had started the business, who had let this upstart in, were being left behind.

The new Merchants were flocking to him and they were in the ascendancy. They were the people the government wanted to be seen with. They were the success stories and they were gaining influence where it mattered. Everyone knew the Godfather was the man and the old firms were not at the races. He was inside the tent pissing out, and they risked being outside the tent, pissing in.

He was too big now to be taken out. They should have done it years ago, but they had too much hubris back then, and now they had left it too late to beat him, so the only option left to them was to join him. They were sick of being sneered at.

In 2004, the old Dons changed tack.

Out went the reliance on organic growth and their corporate motto changed from 'slowly, slowly catchy monkey' to 'fuck it, the early bird catches the worm'.

You could feel the change everywhere. When Miss Pencil Skirt went to her bank to look for a loan to buy a vintage vw Beetle, she expected some resistance. After all, she had no credit history as she had just got a job and had only arrived back from London the month before.

There was not only no problem, but a young man with a mop top at the bank asked her whether she'd thought of buying her own place. She was a perfect candidate, he told her. They had a new interest-only mortgage on offer which could be stretched out to 30 years.

She took the leaflet. She thought, *Why not?*

The Dons opened the credit taps. It is hard to understate the change this had on credit availability in Ireland and to overstate the risk the old Dons were exposing themselves to in their headlong rush into battle with the Godfather.

They abandoned all the old rules and started to hoover up money from all over the EU so they could also lend at the breakneck pace set by Anglo.

The Godfather didn't mind. The banks' lending was pushing up house prices and that suited him. He was in bed with the developers and if they could charge €500,000 for a two-bed shoebox, then he and his developer friends were making easy money. By trying to compete with the Godfather, the other banks were only making him stronger.

In 2004, the net foreign borrowing of the Irish banks, which can be seen as the amount of extra credit they introduced to the Irish market, stood at 10 per cent of GDP. This figure had remained fairly steady for the previous decade. By 2006, this number was 40 per cent of GDP.[1] In 2008, when the whole sorry mess finally exploded in all the Dons' faces, the figure had reached a ridiculously high 60 per cent of GDP.

The Merchant of Ennis could get anything financed. He had started the big development outside the town on the Ennistymon Road and was now getting clients into the gold rush in Varna in Bulgaria as well as the student flats in Leeds. The banks lent for anything, any scheme he came up with. All it took was a few pints, the usual forms and the money appeared.

Between 2004 and 2008, the balance sheets of the Irish banks doubled from €300 billion to €600 billion: €300 billion of growth in four years.[2] And very few shouted 'stop'; the couple that did were dismissed as doom and gloom merchants who didn't understand the new paradigm.

All hell had broken loose. No deal was too big, no Merchant too dodgy or hare-brained not to be financed. The Irish streets became the scene of the biggest financial splurge the Western world has ever witnessed.

The Dons got together and turned on the printing presses, cranking them up to full throttle. They threw everything in their power at the economy. They stopped at nothing to show the world who the real boss was. The Establishment would beat this new upstart at his own game. To do this they needed to make the level of profits the Godfather seemed to be throwing off effortlessly.

The entire nation was their target. If they couldn't find enough opportunity in Ireland, they would create a new type of Merchant of Ennis. This new Merchant would buy up houses abroad with money that was borrowed from outside the country. The people, even the Merchants, were only pawns in this game. They were all potential addicts and if the Dons could just get enough of us on the drug of cheap credit, they might just claw back the market share gained by the Godfather at their expense. In so doing, they could regain the respect and status that they felt was their birthright.

As the banks dived in, the amount of funding they received from overseas increased by 750 per cent. By the top of the boom, Irish banks owed €125 billion to foreign savers—over three times the Irish national debt.[3] This is how national bankruptcy happens.

THE KNOCKING SHOP
Where were the Regulator and the Central Bank during this madness? Where were our politicians? Did they not understand that the country was being destroyed by the banks? We were a battleground about to be flattened by this war.

Were they not supposed to be warning the banks and then ultimately stopping this mad turf war that could only lead to tit-for-tat lending? Who was in charge?

There were guidelines on lending that were being broken every day, so why did no one do anything about it?

As the turf war got more out of control and the reputation of the country as a financial centre was being ruined, not only by our own banks but also by the financial weirdos we allowed to operate here, where were the financial police?

They were supposed to be keeping an eye on things, but not only did they turn their backs, they invited in all sorts of new chancers. In an effort to set ourselves up as a low-regulation, 'no questions asked' global financial centre, our regulators managed to turn our country into a financial brothel, attracting all sorts of economic deviants who wouldn't be allowed to carry out at home the sort of acts they were up to in Ireland.

Ireland became the Patpong Road of international finance. And our regulators were prepared to perform unnatural acts to bring the business here.

We became an international centre for the most abnormal financial behaviour and, in the process, the Regulator, the Central Bank and the Department of Finance have destroyed this country's reputation as a safe place to park your money.

If you have no idea what was going on here, under our noses and with the connivance of the authorities, consider the case of Depfa Bank. This gives you a flavour of what we were doing.

FROM MIDWEST TO WILD WEST

'This is the death of the German banking system.'[4]

These were the words of Deutsche Bank chief executive Josef Ackermann, on seeing the problems faced by German lender Hypo Real Estate following the meltdown of its recently acquired Dublin-based subsidiary, Depfa Bank.

So let's take a look at Depfa Bank and see if we can discover the source of Herr Ackermann's dismay. Consider what the Irish authorities allowed this bank to do.

You've probably heard something about it, this Depfa outfit. The name might be vaguely familiar from the business pages. Like many crime scenes, the location seems innocuous enough. Walk past the Luas road works in the IFSC, across the road from Gen Re, the global reinsurance company that is being investigated for fraud, around the corner from the former O'Brien's sandwich shop, straight across from the train station named after James Connolly, our socialist hero, and there lies Depfa Bank—a basket case of a bank that moved its headquarters to Dublin to involve itself in twisted and deranged financial acts that, alone in Europe, Ireland not only tolerated but encouraged.

This small firm became a boiler room operation for one of the most delinquent episodes in European financial history. The losses in the Irish-regulated Depfa rocked the German government in October 2008.

Three years ago, 5,000 miles away from Ireland in snowy Wisconsin, USA, the school board of Whitefish Bay met to discuss how it might plug the gap that was emerging in the pension funds of its teachers. The board was also worried about paying for the upkeep of its schools in the district, which needed new pitches and playing fields.

The board chatted to a local investment banker who had himself been a pupil at Whitefish. He suggested that the school board might think of borrowing and then using this borrowed money to put together an investment of complex bonds that would return them enough to cover all their pension costs.

But where would they get the money? Who would lend to a small educational municipality in the midwest of the States?

It turned out that an Irish bank would be only too happy to lend to them. That bank was Depfa Bank, with an address at 1 Commons Street, Dublin 1, tucked away opposite the Vaults Pub. Depfa promptly lent the school board $200 million to buy an 'investment' that was issued in Toronto by the Royal Bank of Canada. So Wisconsin borrowed from Dublin to buy something issued in Toronto.

The asset they bought was a complex basket of IOUs issued by reputable companies mainly based in the US. In financial markets these investments are called 'collateralised debt obligations' or CDOs. This market in collateralised debt obligations was a giant IOU market, which allowed companies to borrow with impunity. But the trick was that in this basket of companies were some very good companies and some very bad companies.

The CDOs work just like cocaine: the dealer in Dublin buys a box of cocaine, then kicks it five times to make 5 kilos out of a 1 kilo box. He sells this as pure cocaine even though it is maybe only 12 per cent proof. But it looks, smells and feels the same as the real thing. And eventually, if they are only used to this stuff, the users can't tell the difference between the good stuff and the 'kicked' gear.

Similarly, a CDO is a blended basket of bonds; some are good, the real thing, and some are trash. The weakness of bad companies is disguised by the strength of the good ones. So when they are put together, the risks look less than they are. In addition, they pay more interest than ultra-safe government bonds.

So for the purchaser of these financial products, they have the huge advantage of paying out more than a government bond, but as they were borrowing all the money in the first place, the difference between the rate at which they borrowed and the return on this makey-uppey bond was 'alleged' pure profit. But the big risk was that some of the bad companies would default.

No one explained this to the school board. They were told they were buying something safe and that the risk of default was negligible. The rating agencies, which it has transpired are nothing more than a bunch of charlatans, gave these baskets AAA rating. Of course, as we've seen, they were paid by the banks that were putting together the baskets in the first place. So it was in the rating agencies' interest to keep the business flowing and give these things an AAA rating.

Back in Dublin, Depfa Bank was at the centre of this scam. It not only lent the money to buy this stuff, it took a fee as well, claiming that if there was a default it would guarantee the basket. So it also wrote the insurance that underpinned the investment, taking a commission for its efforts. This was all going on under the nose of the Irish Central Bank. In fact, it was all going on while Irish financial officials were being taken to lunch by the cowboys at Depfa.

In effect, Depfa said that it would be the lender of last resort. Of course as the markets were going up, Depfa thought that defaults would never happen and its bluff would never be called. The Irish Regulator looked on, saying nothing.

Depfa had moved to Dublin in 2002 to take advantage of our lack of regulation and low taxes. Like the pervert who goes to Pattaya for golfing holidays, Depfa went to Dublin to evade the German authorities while still carrying on like a commercial deviant. It had been a sleepy German lender for years. Its new boss knew that if it set up in Dublin, it could get involved in really hardcore stuff. By 2006, Depfa in Dublin, as the lender of last resort, was standing behind $2.7 trillion of these loans.[5] So think about this from an Irish standpoint: an obscure bank operating in the IFSC had guaranteed international loans worth 14 times Ireland's GDP.[6] To do this, Depfa was borrowing from everyone to cover these obligations. Its Irish executives took home bonuses of $30 million in 2006.[7]

During this time, Depfa did what all banks do: sponsored events and made donations to curry favour. It was a major benefactor to Concern. I think this stuff is called Corporate Social Responsibility. The one I like most, which probably says more about the investigative nature of our journalists than the delusions of Depfa's management, was Depfa's sponsorship in November 2007—when this out of control bank was beginning to feel the pinch—of the Association of European Journalists Annual Conference. You can just see the fearless defenders of freedom quaffing down champers provided by the dodgy outfit Depfa. Did anyone ask where all the money was coming from?

By 2007, Depfa had managed to sell itself to another German bank, Hypo Real Estate. The €5 billion deal, which was the biggest in Irish banking history—Depfa was an Irish bank—hardly registered as a news item. One wonders was the buyer fully aware of the business Depfa was involved in. Just to show you how little the cosy club has been upset by what has happened over the past few months, the law firm that acted in the Depfa deal, Arthur Cox, has recently been appointed legal advisor to NAMA. Yet its managing partner was also given the job of chairing the Financial Services Advisory Board in 2007 before the Irish banks imploded. What sort of advice exactly was being dished out?

Back in Wisconsin in 2006, everyone was happy. The school had the money to pay the pensions; the Canadians got their cut for putting the deal together; the salesmen got their commission; the Irish got their tax from a booming business; and the Irish Regulator went on European tours telling the world how we did it, when in fact he hadn't a rashers what was going on under the shadow of the renovated Connolly Station.

Then, bang! In August 2007, investors started getting twitchy about subprime defaults in Las Vegas, Alabama and Colorado. Everyone panicked and wanted cash. People began to realise that the American banks had been giving loans to people who could never afford to pay. The bad bonds issued by bad companies started to default. They never had any money in the first place and no amount of covering up could mask this fact.

The school board started getting calls saying its money was not safe. Not only was it not safe, but one default was having a domino effect on the rest. The phones started ringing in 1 Commons Street and for that matter at the Regulator's office in Dame Street. Depfa continued to sponsor events and august outfits like the Royal Irish Academy.

But the school board was not the only one getting unwelcome calls. The week Lehman's went under, Depfa, now the responsibility of Hypo Real Estate, its new owners, collapsed. Worse still, Hypo Real Estate was a mortgage lender and thus systemically important in Germany. The phone rang in the Chancellery in Berlin. Angela Merkel was furious. She understood the extent of the damage and issued a statement that

Germany 'will not let distress in one financial institution endanger the entire system'. She arranged a $64 billion transfer to Hypo to cover its losses and she demanded to know what the hell was going on in Dublin. How could a German bank be allowed to do this? What was the Irish Regulator doing?

The same night, Brian Lenihan was fielding calls. The Minister was alone, unbriefed and at odds with his senior civil servants. His huge dilemma was that if he issued a guarantee, would he have to guarantee Depfa as well? Depfa would bring us down. He had to wriggle out of this and called the Attorney General to get an opinion.

Yet during the same week, the Regulator—who was supposed to be on top of these issues—kept insisting that there was nothing to worry about in Ireland. As Lenihan was on the phone trying to get to the bottom of things, our Financial Regulator was on 'Prime Time' telling the nation how strong Irish banking regulation was.

The greed culture of Depfa, like the culture that spawned the turf war between Anglo and the rest of the banks, has almost bankrupted this country.

Is it any wonder that the *New York Times* called Dublin's IFSC the 'Wild West of finance'? And we are now supposed to cough up to pay for these cowboys?

Chapter 13 ～

| MANUFACTURING CONSENT

JAPANESE HOMOPHOBIA

When looking at what can happen to house prices in Ireland and the slump, you have to consider that so many countries have experienced this carry-on before. A terrifying case in point is Japan, and Japan's experience is made all the more scary because it was and still is the second largest economy in the world with a track record of extraordinary innovation. Up until the day everything went pear-shaped in the Land of the Rising Sun, people believed that Japan had found the elixir to everlasting economic vibrancy.

In 1989, the *New York Times* warned of an economic Pearl Harbor and added that 'forty years after the end of World War II, the Japanese are on the march again in one of history's most brilliant commercial offensives, as they go about dismantling American industry'.

Japan was experiencing the most inflated property bubble of the twentieth century. The land on which the Imperial Palace in central Tokyo sat was valued at more than the entire real estate of Canada—the world's second largest country. With paper profits from property back home, Japanese investors were busy buying up trophy assets in the US—from the Rockefeller Tower in New York to Columbia Pictures in Hollywood. The best-selling book of the year was Michael Crichton's *Rising Sun*, which he said he wrote 'to make America wake up'.

Corporate America was in the grip of a Japanese hysteria and both mainstream commentators and the political elites believed that the Japanese march to world commercial domination was unstoppable.

Today, 20 years later, the Bank of Japan has announced it is still fighting a deflation battle. This deflation followed a ten-year recession in the 1990s. Instead of taking over the world, powered by its roaring property market, Japan suddenly, and for most people shockingly, went into an economic crisis that lasted almost 20 years. How did everyone get it so wrong?

People say that pride usually comes before a fall and, in the case of the Japanese economy, this was certainly true. The Japanese property bubble lasted almost a decade and was driven by cheap credit, massive financial deregulation and a fair amount of pop-psychology as the herd reacted to the property boom. This led to almost panic buying, financed by a banking system that lent out money for just about anything.

What is interesting for Ireland is not that this happened, because it happened here as well, but what happened to house prices in Japan after the boom.

Prices roared upwards and then collapsed, ending up below where they started at the beginning at the boom. Property prices fell 70 per cent peak to trough in Japan and never recovered. Having been burned, the Japanese became homophobic—this describes not an attitude to gay men, but to investing in homes. They rejected the idea of ever buying other people's homes as an investment.

This is likely to happen here; development land is likely to settle back to 1996 prices and houses prices will continue to collapse. When we hear some property lads talking about green shoots—the lesson from Japan should be heeded.

'PRIME TIME'

On a 'Prime Time' programme in late 2003, I was debating with an economist—a spokesperson for one of the banks that was actively destroying the country by blowing the national balance sheet on property. I suggested that the entire façade was a 'scam', perpetrated by 'the banks and the developers with the connivance of the government, and far from being a sign of strength, ridiculously high house prices are a sign of economic weakness that will impoverish the country for generations'.

At the time, this type of analysis was ridiculed by many professional people who are now busy trying to rewrite economic history and their place in it. We all know what happened. There's no point getting into all that 'who said what, when' stuff now.

Over the years, it seemed to me—as I was doing my best impression of a Monty Pythonesque John the Baptist, screeching like a loon in the wilderness—that some of the top brass at the banks (and certainly the Godfather himself) realised that the whole thing would someday blow, but they were determined to milk it to the last.

AGITPROP

Crucial to the success of the strategy of mad lending was a well-orchestrated and incessant propaganda campaign. To keep the nation in a state of high alert, the banks employed propagandists with economics degrees. The propagandists did enormous damage to the reputation of the trade. Like dodgy plumbers, they gave all plumbers a bad name.

These propagandists used our respect or at least fear of science to dress up their nonsense. Like the proverbial 'men in the white coats', the propagandists donned the armoury of economics and adopted the quack pseudo-scientific language of the first-year textbook, such as 'demographic dividend' and 'strong fundamentals', to terrify the nation onto the property ladder. Having done this, the propagandists successfully disguised what the Dons and the Godfather were up to. When prices rose to ludicrous levels, they introduced the 'affordability index'. At every turn, they abused and reworked basic economics to justify the profits of the Dons. (If we had a tribunal for crimes against economics, the dock would be crowded with ghosts from the past and the charge would be simple: spouting drivel, dressed up as economics, to keep the Establishment safe.)

Like good propagandists everywhere, they knew what they were doing and understood that the media had to be their voice. The medium is the message, as they say.

Looking back charitably on this grubby episode in our history, maybe we can forgive them on the basis that they 'were only following orders'. The propagandists who took money for their flawed analysis can hide behind the excuse of 'I was just making a living'. He who pays the piper calls the tune.

On the other hand, the propagandists who didn't take a shilling from the banks, brokers, estate agents or property developers—and actually still believed all this guff—might be advised to reconsider their choice of profession.

Of course, once we bought into the property market, we had an interest in property price rises. What better incentive for someone to become a cheerleader for the boom is there than a financial interest in the boom continuing?

During summer, 2008, when, unbeknownst to all but a small circle, Sean Fitzpatrick was frantically making phone calls to his mates to lend him €300 million in order to bullshit Anglo Irish Bank's shareholders, I caught a rerun of the 1976 classic movie *The Outlaw Josey Wales*, starring Clint Eastwood as the eponymous hero.

During a particularly brilliant exchange, the bounty hunter Fletcher, hot on the heels of the outlaw Wales, comes out with an inspired put-down to the cowardly senator who is trying to pull the wool over his eyes in a cheap saloon. Realising that the senator is trying to spoof him, the tobacco-chewing Fletcher disdainfully hisses, 'Don't piss down my back and tell me it's raining.'

When I heard our own propagandists trying to convince us that all was well and that the fundamentals of the economy were strong, right up to the end, the expression constantly came to mind.

But then if you think of the pressure and the mood of the times, it is probably not that hard to understand why so few people could tell, smell or taste the difference between urine and water.

And it wasn't just the advertising that dulled our scepticism and heightened our senses; there was more going on, something deeper, about patriotism, something about the state of the country that we were naturally proud of, not being the victim any more, being a success. For generations, our narrative was the great little victim nation of Western Europe. For a brief period, we put this behind us and the burgeoning economy became an understandable source of national pride. Maybe this obscured our view; it certainly helped the regime. Before we examine this deeper stuff, let's look more closely at the basic propaganda. Like all propaganda, after the event, when it is exposed, there is a 'how the hell did we believe that rubbish?' moment. But when it was at full tilt, it was difficult not to be swept away.

THE BRIBE

We were bombarded by advertising exalting us to do the patriotic thing and buy a house. Advertising works and it pays the bills. Just ask the editor of any of our major newspapers who were shameless in their promotion of their own bottom line through their various property supplements, which were nothing more than debt pornography.

The media, rather than querying the boom, became an enthusiastic cheerleader. The media was selling the dream. The media, who says it exists to question, was manufacturing consent through its unwavering support of the property bubble. Why would it kill the golden goose?

Selling the dream means advertising and in the Ireland of the boom, did we advertise? In the immortal words of Mr Gogarty from the Tribunal, 'Did we, fuck'!

According to IAPI—the outfit that looks after all things advertising in Ireland—we spent a mindboggling €742,919,762 on property advertising from 2001, when the property market started to rocket, to 2007, when the market peaked. This is over seven hundred million euros, on advertising alone.

To put that figure in context, the cervical cancer screening bill for every woman in this country was due to cost €9.7 million.[1] The advertising bill for property alone would have financed every cervical cancer screening in the whole country for 77 years. This advertising spend on its own could have paid for the National Cancer Control Programme for the whole country, every man, woman and child for 50 years. It would cover every one of the special needs classes that were closed in the last Budget until the year 2115. Think about it: we spent nearly three-quarters of a billion euros not on property but on advertising for property. Imagine what we could do with this cash now. We spent three-quarters of a billion euros just to convince ourselves that buying property with other people's money was a smart thing to do.

But why did we need all this persuading if property was a sure thing, a sound investment that could be explained by supply and demand as the propagandists insisted?

Because we had to feel good about it as well as everything else. Like all fads and fashions, we wanted to keep up with the Joneses. The publicity is necessary to obscure the fact that this grubby little business of providing cheap credit and selling houses to people who don't really need them is essential to keep the banking Mafia in business.

The entire pyramid scheme is based on suckers constantly coming in at the bottom so that the lads at the top can get out with astronomical profits.

The message needs to be reinforced at every level, whether it is to a first-time buyer who is terrified by the incessant propaganda of not getting in the market or the status-obsessed professional close to the top who wants to show off and tell everyone just how far up the ladder he and his family have climbed. He too is terrified of what his colleagues and clients will think if he can't host a half-decent dinner party in his own home. In the immortal words of J. P. Morgan, 'Nothing so undermines your judgement as the sight of your neighbour getting rich.'

THE SCHULL STATE OF MIND

As you go up the scale, it is important to get inside the mind of the buyer, to ensure that they feel good about parting with a fortune for a pokey four-bedroomed Victorian pile in Portobello or indeed that dream, architect-designed work of art in Schull, west Cork—a town so posh that it has its own film festival without even having a cinema.

In fact, Schull is the pinnacle of the aspirant dream. Schull is beloved of retired BBC Controllers, David Puttnam arthouse souls, yachtie types with those weather-beaten upper class faces and Hiberno-Brits like Jeremy Irons who break out in a rash at the sight of an Irish bungalow. But Schull is where they want to be. It isn't a place; it's a state of mind. And much of the upmarket advertising was intended to reach out to the inner Schull in every upwardly mobile wannabe, making it not only acceptable but desirable to plunge into debt for a piece of this Nirvana of the mind.

The *Playboy* of property porn, which sucked up a huge slice of the advertising pie in Ireland, was the *Irish Times* property supplement. It so intoxicated its owners that they paid €50 million for the website *www.myhome.ie* at the very top of the market. The *Irish Times* is still the Queen of the genre. Even now, in the slump, she is still trotting out all classes of whimsy.

Advertising for Decklanders appeals to their sense of the practical and love of gadgets. In Ireland few things screech your class like where you stand on gadgets. Seven iPod docking systems at the breakfast bar in the kitchen will swing it for the likes of Breakfast Roll Man. He's the type of bloke who takes a mental note of the number of plugs in a room, calculating how many Gaggia coffee makers, LCD screens and Wii could be on the go at once. Deckland homes threaten to bring down the national grid on a nightly basis. In the new suburbs, advertising is simple. Size matters. The rooms are bigger and there is an extra bedroom, a home theatre. You could land a SWAT team in the kitchen.

These are all reasonably obvious selling points for those Decklanders on the incessant move upwards.

But for the discerning world of people who go straight to the property supplement of the *Irish Times* on a Thursday, buying a house needs to be something of virtue. In fact, the fewer gadgets the better. Everyone knows that antiques trump modernity anytime.

You are not just buying an inflated collection of bricks and mortar but something much more substantial. In recent months, as the market has tanked, the Queen of property porn has taken a new tack. She'll try anything, will the Queen and her new angle is quite a stroke. What chutzpah!

As she has desperately tried to keep the market from crashing completely in the past year or so, the Queen has spun the line that the person who is selling the house actually matters.

If you buy a house from a well-known writer or film director then presumably the inference is that you will become one yourself. The extra 300k on the price is justified on the basis that great art was conceived there.

So you can buy a house from a supposed Scottish rebel who, despite all the rather tedious stuff about the Left and social justice, is quite happy to take up residency in Ireland, presumably in order to avoid tax in his beloved Scotland. That tax might just have helped to bring a little bit of social justice to Easter Road. So in July 2008, Irvine Welsh was on the front of the *Irish Times* property section showing the cameras round his four-bedroomed spread with lovely polished wood floors in Rathmines.

Choose life. Choose a job. Choose a career. Choose a family. Choose a fucking big television. Choose washing machines, cars, compact disc players . . . choose the *Irish Times* property section.

Within the space of five months, writer Edna O'Brien was at the same game, showing her place in Donegal. So too was Deirdre Purcell. The writer Polly Devlin was telling anyone who cared how wonderful the area of Languedoc where she is selling her house is. One might be forgiven for asking, *If it's so wonderful, why would you be so keen to get out?*

Thriller writer John Connolly was in the same paper last year, trying to flog his gaff in Rathmines, as was director Jim Sheridan who, in April 2007, told all and sundry how fabulous his house in Dalkey was.

The house that he knocked down to build his cantilevered bit of Malibu Beach on Coliemore Road was perfectly good, and had stood proudly against the elements opposite Dalkey Island since my dad was a boy. But during the boom, good just wasn't good enough. Houses had to be breathtaking, unique and awe-inspiring.

And maybe, just maybe, their lingering talent will rub off on the next owner. Maybe you have a *Trainspotting* in you which will be released by the knowledge that Irvine Welsh once lived in your house, or maybe there is the script of a *My Left Foot* lying dormant in some part of your brain which will be miraculously sparked by the essence of Jim Sheridan which might linger long after he's gone.

You have to admit, there is a certain genius in this opportunism.

The incessant advertising was, of course, like all advertising, designed to manipulate and it worked. The €700 million was well spent, because the banking Mafia who were at the top were making this type of bread in profits every year—each. Spending money like that in a small country like ours can buy you a lot of admirers; you can get a lot of people 'on message' for three-quarters of a billion euros.

One of the more insidious parts of the agitprop was the idea that the boom was patriotic. To criticise the way the banking Mafia had taken over economic policy—so much so that what was good for them suddenly became good for us—was seen as anti-Irish. It was unpatriotic to be sceptical about the logic of rising prices and the excessive borrowing that entailed. When the Dons and the Godfather, together with the politicians, wrapped themselves in the green flag, it was very difficult to stand against the hype.

But despite the Mafia's huge use of advertising and their use of propagandists to piss down people's backs and tell them it was raining, thousands of us privately did worry. I was just someone who had the opportunity of doing this in public. But in bars and kitchens all around the country, many realised that something was not quite right. We could see our neighbours and friends were up to their eyes in debt and worried about what might happen.

Rather than being ecstatic zealots championing the economy and not worrying about the evident signs of craziness, many thousands were simply swept along, albeit hesitantly, half-expecting a crash, but not knowing when it would come or what it would feel like when it did.

THE MICHELLE SMITH TEST

Over the years, I always wondered why so few people, particularly those who'd been around a while and had seen these cycles before, publicly questioned the boom's foundations. These were people who could see the direct link between property supplements, the bottom line, the interests of the estate agents, the banks and the conniving lawyers who wrote the small print, which caught out so many.

Were we wilfully neglectful, stupidly optimistic or just infatuated by the novelty of success?

The boom was real. It was beneficial for the country. People got richer. In fact, according to the EU, Ireland even became more equal during the boom. Initially, credit allowed us to achieve things that, without the new money, we would never have dreamed of.

We produced more graduates, educated more people and spent more on health and social welfare than we had ever done before. We hosted hundreds of thousands of fellow European migrants who would never have had the chance of earning a crust without the Irish boom. Ireland, though probably not intentionally, gave these people a chance of a better life. At a time when Ireland is accused by France and Germany of being anti-European, we let people from Eastern Europe travel and work here freely. In contrast, France and Germany wouldn't let them in. In practical terms, we did more to foster European integration than the rhetorical champions of Europe who said one thing but acted differently.

During the boom, lots of people got lots of things that they had wanted for a long time. Liberal Ireland got equality legislation. The Left got welfare increases. The Right got tax cuts. The old conservatives still had the Constitution to defend them, while the new liberals had freedom. Up North, the spoils were also divided: the Provos got the Minister for Education, while the Unionists got guarantees. Down here, farmers sold sites and workers got pay rises. Young people got better jobs and old people got better pensions. Everyone got something. Ireland improved dramatically and this improvement was real.

All the cars, the houses, the new companies, the workers, the hospitals, the roads and trains and the Luas, they were all real. There was nothing fake about the traffic, the commute, the profits, the bonus structures, the restaurants, the Asian fusion takeaways, the lifestyles, the Michelin stars, Riverview, Electric Picnic and stamp duty. It all happened and it would not have happened without the boom and the borrowed money.

But why were we so slow to twig that the whole thing was a bubble?

Let's introduce the 'Michelle Smith test', which suggests that when something seems too good to be true, it turns out to be exactly that; yet at the time, the majority is not prepared to confront the truth.

Back in the summer of 1996, after years of languishing in the doldrums, having won zero plaudits, the Irish economy started to motor. So too did Michelle Smith. After years of mediocre performances, she started winning—and not just winning—she started destroying the opposition. Like the booming economy, Michelle Smith's performances were real.

Our economic experience was as real as Michelle Smith winning three gold medals at the Atlanta Olympics. She did get into the pool and she did swim faster than anyone on earth. She was enormously brave. She did devote her life to swimming and got up at 5am for years while the rest of us were comatose. She did go through the physical pain barrier and the emotional rollercoaster of being a champion.

There was nothing unreal about the feeling she must have had when she touched the wall before everyone to win gold. Nor was there anything fake about the collective pride we felt in her. In typical Irish fashion, I watched the performance in a pub and we drank to her. She was the real thing, Rathcoole's answer to Michael Phelps.

But her improvements were so dramatic that there was always a niggling doubt. How did she improve so quickly? (How did Ireland grow so strong so quickly?) How did she hide it? (How did we delude ourselves?) Did she not see that people would question it? But maybe she gambled that people would want to share in her success so much that we would all buy into the idea that someone could improve so much naturally. She probably thought that she could disguise it from the doping agents. Maybe she thought that everyone else was doing it, so why shouldn't she try it too.

Now think of the economy during the Celtic Tiger years. Deep down, we probably knew that we were on the edge, but we thought we could get away with it. We believed in the 'soft landing', the easy slowdown, the calm descent from such altitude. We believed not because we found it credible but because we found it agreeable. We never thought that we would be rumbled. Like Michelle, we never dreamed that we would fail the most exacting test of all, the one that comes in a credit crunch when the world twigs that you have been faking it all along.

IN THE LAND OF THE BLIND

We knew that there were problems but we were enjoying the ride so much that we suspended our faculties.

When I first heard people question Michelle Smith, my initial reaction was that she couldn't be fake because I imagined the systems were so sophisticated that she'd be found out straightaway.

Similarly, when the solidity of the boom was queried, many intelligent people suggested that the global financial system was so sophisticated that if there was a unique question mark over Ireland we would cease to be financed.

When some people questioned Smith's wins, particularly the swimmer Gary O'Toole, they were vilified. When O'Toole questioned the performances, even the normally placid Bill O'Herlihy had such a conniption that the smoothest of all presenters cut O'Toole off with the immortal line: 'We now have to go over to Jim Sherwin who is in the pool.' Looking remarkably dry for a man supposed to be in an Olympic pool, Sherwin drowned O'Toole out with commentary about Smith's new diet.

I was one who went along with the Michelle Smith hype, and I was prepared to dismiss credible people as just typical Irish knockers, be-grudging the success of one of our own. I joined the mob.

Like the coming unbelievable boom, the unbelievable Michelle Smith touched something deeper in me.

I was living in London in 1996 and when the British papers got involved in the whispering campaign against Michelle, my inner Republican was offended. I became all 'tiochfaidh ár lá' over the swimmer. The fact that she spoke Irish compounded my sense of national pride. As far as I was concerned, this time it *was* different. Performance-enhancing drugs didn't come into it.

I remember getting into pub rows with old English friends over Michelle Smith. It was OK for me to level suspicion at Linford Christie, but I refused to accept any criticism of Michelle Smith.

In my mind, Michelle Smith could have turned all physical evidence on its head and for me, and thousands of others, she could do this without drugs. She could have improved more dramatically than any athlete in human history. I believed the stuff about her diet and her new training methods in the same way as many believed the stuff about Ireland's unique demographics, education system and the reservoir of

Poles who would keep renting our houses until the 22nd century.

Maybe when we remember our faith in the boom, a forgiving way to look at that belief is to consider the Michelle Smith test. People accepted the hype and believed that our economy could have broken all the rules and grown as if it were on steroids. We convinced ourselves that Ireland could have done this without the performance-enhancing drug that is cheap credit.

Most of us respond badly to criticism, as if it is a personal attack. We invited the sceptics to come and see for themselves. When foreigners started to express concern, they were dismissed as not understanding the Irish model or, worse still, we adopted the default position of the victim and accused these knockers of being jealous. We were, the expression went, 'the envy of Europe'.

Had I not been involved in the economics game and worked in a variety of different countries that had experienced similar cycles, I would probably have been unquestioning too.

But if you look around the world, the rules of economics are simple, as simple as the rules of sport. Freaks do not appear very often and if an economy begins to behave like a freak, then there are likely to be problems. If you win the equivalent of three Olympic golds from nowhere, something dodgy is going on.

Ireland was the Michelle Smith of modern economics, and cheap credit was our drug. It was sold, packaged and marketed by the banking Mafia with the help of the likes of Shylock, the Merchant of Ennis and others who took their cut.

It was hyped by the propagandists, who used and abused economics. The message was disseminated by the advertising industry, who trousered three-quarters of a billion euros for their efforts.

In the end, a country of credit junkies thought the trip would never end. Now the comedown is truly miserable. Cold turkey is ripping us apart.

But remember who got us into this mess in the first place. If the blueprint for recovery is being drafted by them, which it is, let's be careful.

To be led up the garden path once is a tragic mistake. To allow ourselves to be taken there again would be unforgiveable.

| THE BENT COPS

Through our drugs analogy, we have seen how the banks pushed easy credit onto the people, in practically every way imaginable. This was highly profitable at every stage in the distribution pyramid, from the very top where the Godfather reigned, right down to the sofa salesman selling expensive money to people who could not afford it.

The single most important mechanism in Ireland for pushing this money into the economy was the housing and property market. Without the property boom, the banks would have remained important but not such overwhelmingly huge players in the Irish economy. With the property mania and the attendant lending, the banks managed to create a system whereby the domestic banks became four times bigger than our national income.

With so much money (and power) at stake, it would have been impossible for the banks to achieve their position at the top of the pyramid without the complicity of the State—in the person of our politicians. Perhaps it is a bad reflection on our elected representatives that they could be purchased so cheaply.

We ended up in a situation whereby the interests of the banks and property developers were seen as the same as the interests of the people. What was good for property was good for us and this was reinforced, rhetorically and legislatively. The Dons and the developers couldn't lose and, as we will see, the people charged with regulating the system not only didn't regulate to protect the people, but on retirement took high profile, highly paid positions within the Mafia.

Going back to our drugs analogy, this would be like the Garda Commissioner not only turning a blind eye to the crimes of John Gilligan, but taking a job from Gilligan when he retired.

George Bernard Shaw said 'a government that robs Peter to pay Paul can always depend on the support of Paul'. The Peter who the government robbed was the Juggler Generation, the first-time buyers and all those below the top tiers of the financial pyramid. This being Ireland, Paul was the usual suspects, the banks, the brokers, the developers and their mates, the estate agents.

THE FIRM

But it is not enough for the cops to turn a blind eye. A Godfather needs legislation to help make his fortune. And once he has made his pile, he needs more legislation to help him avoid taxes.

Of course, this taxation relief is dressed up to make the whole operation look legit. What better way of doing this than by giving this helpful little law a sterile, official and opaque name like 'section 23' or 'section 28'? And let's announce these schemes under the banner of 'Urban Regeneration'. Who could argue with that? 'Regeneration' sounds good. No one in their right mind could be against something progressive like regeneration. The people were led to believe that such laws were passed for their benefit, but they weren't.

The developers and estate agents—enormous recipients of the fruits of the boom—were certainly in favour of such legislation. Anyone wanting to find out more about these schemes might look up the website www.section23.ie. If you try it, you will find yourself on a website run by Hooke and MacDonald, the estate agents. The website is devoted to flogging apartments under the tagline 'Pay Tax . . . or Acquire Appreciating Assets . . . the Choice is yours'. They even provide helpful links to some well-known mid-level credit dealers—the type of outfit where Shylock learned his trade.

All your money can be squirrelled away; not away from the prying eyes of the taxman, but with the taxman's blessing. There is no need to pretend to live offshore any more.

The banks needed to be able to expand at will and so, helpfully, the State spent the best part of 20 years removing the legislative and regulatory glass ceilings to bank expansion and bank lending. In 1980, Ireland was a different country for the banks. The loans they could make were strictly controlled, especially the loans they could make to what the regulators called 'non-productive sectors' such as the financial, property and personal sectors.

They were further hamstrung by a requirement to maintain a primary liquidity ratio of 10 per cent. This means they had to keep some of their money in cash. Counter-intuitively, cash on deposit is no good to banks. If they can't lend it out and make interest on it, it's a cost to the banks. So, all this was, understandably, very inconvenient for the Dons.

Between 1980 and 2000, they managed to get most inconvenient legislation rescinded, and so were poised, on Ireland's entry into the euro, to unleash a flood of credit on the Irish consumer.[1]

But the ability to lend is not enough to grow a bank. It needs people who want to borrow, so it has to give them something to borrow for. That's where the little issue of stamping comes in.

QUALITY CONTROL
You remember in the drugs trade, the dealers would only buy drugs that were 'stamped'. Their authenticity had to be verified by an outside source before they would be accepted by the middlemen.

Likewise in the easy credit racket, the banks and their Dons needed to know that the State would allow as many valuers as possible to work freely and the State could in no way question the validity of these valuations. So if an estate agent who was working with a mortgage broker, who in turn was working for a bank, put a valuation of €300,000 on a property, even though the cost of building it was only €150,000, the State had to be counted on not to interfere or question anything.

The price of houses and property was put down to the free market. And the answer to any critic or to the people who had to pay these prices was that they didn't understand supply and demand. But they did, and they also understood that the market was rigged.

This was a complex operation, one that demanded lots of favours, bribes and, most importantly, lots of tacit acceptance that what was clearly wrong and in the interest of a small few over and above the majority was not only normal but good for all.

The State had to be prepared to bring the entire power of the office of Taoiseach down on dissenters and the government had to publicly denounce anyone who dared to question the Dons and their easy credit racket.

All the way up to the very top, the government ridiculed and denigrated anyone who might risk exposing the pyramid. There was simply too much money at stake. Had the government not been prepared to do these things, the whole sorry mess might have been avoided.

A mantra was needed to protect the interests of the Dons and the Godfather, the Merchants and the Shylocks. It needed to be short and snappy and paint the sceptic in a harsh, quasi-traitorous light. Something like 'talking down the economy'. Yes, that sounded good.

It was crucial that the victims of this pyramid scheme, the borrowers—in particular, the Juggling Generation—who were paying the price for all this, thought that it was progress to take on such debts. It was essential that they took their very misery to be a sign of success. This conceit was a stroke of Orwellian genius.

To be pulled off, it needed a perverse ideology to be planted and cultivated based on the new idea that what was good for the few was also good for the many.

So far we have seen how the government had relaxed banking regulation and, through taxation changes, incentivised property speculation. Their policies had proved successful for the Dons and the Merchants, so successful that not long into the new millennium, the Irish economy was starting to reach boiling point.

If there is too much money sloshing around in a country and it is driving up prices, Leaving Cert economics tells us that the State should raise taxes, take the heat out of the economy and use the money to do something productive, for example build a new railway network. The government should have realised that no one would ever criticise them for spending taxpayers' money on real things like roads, railways and hospitals because infrastructural investments raise the potential of the country and make it a better place to live.

But instead of infrastructural investment, we got the SSIAS which could only have been conceived by someone with the banks' interests in mind. This was probably the silliest initiative announced during the boom. The SSIAS were supposed to take money out of the overheating economy, with the government paying savers to encourage them to join the scheme. On the face of it, it seems logical, until we remember that money deposited with the banks is quickly turned into credit and pumped back into the economy. The government top-ups, added to the savings accounts, just increased the amount of credit (and profit) the banks could lend out.

For the SSIA idea to successfully cool the economy, the money in the SSIA accounts would have had to be ring-fenced so that it could not have reappeared in the economy as credit nearly as quickly as it left. But, of course, such an idea would not have been in the banks' interest.

The SSIA story reveals that the banks and the property sector had not just influenced politicians excessively but had been adopted by the real power: the top civil servants who run the country.

If you doubt that the top civil servants are in the banks' pockets, consider the DIRT scandal of a few years back. The Central Bank and the Department of Finance knew that millions of pounds was being squirrelled away to avoid DIRT tax in bogus non-resident accounts. But they said nothing. So they facilitated law-breaking. In fact, this could never have happened without the Central Bank's connivance because we had exchange controls, which were broken by all this cash flooding abroad.

So we have the bizarre situation where the two top economic agencies in the State are breaking the law and thus reducing the tax take of the Department of Revenue in order to boost the profits of the banks. You couldn't make it up!

Until of course you understand that this was all part of the plan. At its core, the interests of the banks and their property friends were the key anchors of economic policy.

THE UNTOUCHABLES
There is nothing new in the financial Mafia trying to take over an economy for its own ends. It is a universally recognised threat. So too is the risk that we are, or at least can be turned into, credit junkies. The finance industry cannot be trusted on its own to run itself for the good of the nation. The temptations are simply too great.

The similarities between the financial industry's easy credit and criminality are so strong that every civilised country institutes a powerful Financial Regulator to police the game.

Ultimately, on the basis that 'the best way to rob a bank is to run one', these financial cops are supposed to keep an eye on the dealers. The Regulator is supposed to keep the Dons and the smaller fish who supply credit on the straight and narrow. The Regulator's job is to protect us from our own banking system.

Think of the movie *The Untouchables*. The hero of the movie is the straight cop Elliot Ness, who goes after the Mob, and Al Capone in particular. Up to then, the cops who went after the Mob in Chicago in the 1920s and 1930s were paid off by them.

Of course, the Mob ran the place but the perception was that the authorities were doing something when in fact they were doing nothing, bar massaging the optics.

Similarly, merely putting a Regulator in place is worth nothing unless the Regulator does his job, which is to protect the public.

In a modern trading economy, there is a second reason for the Regulator to be strong and focused. Ireland has gambled that the IFSC will become a major international financial centre and many good people have worked very hard to make that happen. One of the attributes we are selling is that a foreign company's money is safe here and Ireland will keep an eye on what is going on. We are in the business of attracting legitimate money. The reputation of the company or the bank that sets up in Ireland will be enhanced by its association with us.

If only.

DUNNER'S WEDDING

The wedding odyssey was in its fourth day. It was a marathon of heroic Irish drinking and carousing. Lounging by the enormous infinity pool, the guests could see the Tuscan Hills which rolled out beyond to the bizarre medieval skyscrapers of San Gimignano. These huge phallic towers jutting out in the Tuscan countryside were the fourteenth-century equivalent of the Jurys Tower in Ballsbridge, the U2 Tower and Harry Crosbie's Point Village.

During the Renaissance, the merchants in this town tried to outdo each other by building these huge towers. Clearly, the man who erected the biggest tower also had the biggest you-know-what. Interestingly, the decline of San Gimignano was put down to the huge fortunes the merchants spent on these ludicrous ego trips. While the merchants of Florence were using their cash to build and expand their businesses, the boys of San Gimignano got involved in a pointless and extremely expensive race to build the tallest tower in Tuscany. In the end, they blew all their money on these useless pillars and the city, which was the richest in Tuscany, if not in all Italy, started its steady decline.

Maybe this lesson from history went over the heads of the guests but, given that most of the oligarchs of the Irish property binge were there, a wee bit of history might have warned them off making that call to the celebrity architect to build the biggest tower in Dublin.

Financial history tells us something else about these monuments to hubris. In property circles it's called the 'hard on' indicator. The hard on indicator notes the relationship between the size of the skyscrapers built and the property crash. The bigger the building and the more outlandish the plans, the closer the crash.

The Empire State Building was started just before the 1929 crash. It was such a white elephant that it was known as the Empty State Building until the Second World War, when its offices finally began to fill up. The world's tallest building, the Petronas Towers in Malaysia, was completed months before the Asian crisis, while the first blocks of Canary Wharf in London were laid just weeks before the city's property crash of the late 1980s.

Similarly, the Ballsbridge Jurys Tower and all the other great symbols of the boom that were unveiled in the past two years were planned and financed just when the market in Dublin peaked. Interestingly, if you talk to bankers now, with their after-the-event wisdom many say, 'we knew this Jurys deal was a deal too far'. Who are they trying to kid? If you look at the evidence, you'll see that, like the failed merchants of San Gimignano, all the big Irish builders and their banker mates bid for the Jurys site.

Far from being a bridge too far, the Ballsbridge Jurys deal was hailed as a triumph. It was even nominated for Capital Markets' 'Deal of the Year 2006'.

(According to the *Irish Times* of 28 July 2005, there were 13 under-bidders for the site. Rumoured to have come closest to Dunner's bid are Alanis Ltd. (owned by the McCormack Brothers and private clients of Anglo Irish Bank), Glenkerrin Group (owned by Ray Grehan) and Taggart Homes (owned by the Taggart Brothers from Northern Ireland —who went into administration owing €150 million in October 2008).[2])

Dublin 4 was the place to spend money if you were a developer. Ray Grehan may have failed on the Jurys site, but he managed to spend €171.5 million for the former UCD Veterinary College site. Bernard McNamara was there too, as he owns sites across the road from Jurys.[3]

The wedding party was in full swing. They'd be up all night and rightly so. Then off to the *Christiana O*, the boat on which Grace Kelly and Prince Rainier honeymooned. Nothing less for the Prince and Princess of Jurys.

The phone rang. It was Charlie McCreevy. 'Put Charlie on the loudspeaker,' shouted the groom, wiping the sweat from a jeroboam of vintage champagne off his brow. What's the point in having mates like that if no one knows? The finance minister with a true grasp of economics who once said, 'when I have money I spend it, and when I don't I don't' wished everyone well. Up ya boy ya, Charlie.

Twenty minutes later the phone rang again. It was Bertie Ahern.

You might be familiar with this great socialist from reading works like *Das Kapital* or *The Communist Manifesto*. Remember that bit where Karl Marx advocates blowing smoke up the arse of landlords as the true path to a socialist future?

According to the subsequent *Sunday Independent* gossip on Sean Dunne's wedding, Bertie announced to all and sundry, 'Dunner, you and I go back a long way. I wish I could be there. I'm sorry I couldn't come but I would have been more trouble to you than I'd be worth.'[4]

Uproar! Bertie was before the Mahon Tribunal at the time, facing questions about Paddy the Plasterer, a few bungs and how he'd won it all on the gee-gees.

The following week, on official business, Bertie dropped in on the bridal couple and their guests at the Splendido in Portofino. Ah, the halcyon days.

Of course there's nothing wrong with people having a good time, but the fact that our politicians were so close to the big developers ensured that the government was incapable of making any decisions that might inconvenience the builders and their financiers, the bankers, in any way.

Remember, our politicians are there to represent the people—all the people—but if they are in the pocket of one huge lobby—which is actively making a fortune by charging huge sums for bad houses, thus turning a generation into serious debtors, then the politicians are accountable.

And what's the easiest way of getting someone into your pocket? You line their pockets with donations and cash and the promise of more of the same lovely stuff if they will do your bidding. It couldn't be simpler.

And it doesn't matter if you are at the top of the tree like Sean Dunne and Bertie Ahern or if you are further down the pecking order. Once a politician is indebted to a developer, builder or banker, objectivity goes out the window. Why do you think they give money to politicians? For favours, of course!

And as any lover of gangster movies knows, if the cops are in bed with the drug lords, if they are not prepared to protect the addicts but are on the side of the dealers, all hell will break loose on the streets. It's a recipe for chaos—which in Ireland is just what we have now.

SMALL-TIME BRIAN

If Bertie was rocking with the high rollers, small-time Brian was at the same carry-on with smaller players but people who nonetheless needed favours done. And the present Taoiseach's attitude to politicians accepting donations? When asked about his boss's difficulties and his opinion of Bertie's regular 'whip rounds', Mr Cowen described such behaviour as 'not incorrect'.

What exactly does that mean? Well, maybe it can all be explained if we take ourselves off to north Dublin in the same week as Bertie was testifying at the Tribunal.

While Bertie Ahern was facing questions about those events which he had observed might get his mate Sean Dunne into trouble, Brian Cowen, the current boss of the family firm that is known as Fianna Fáil, was shuffling around Hollystown golf course just beyond Dublin Airport at a golf classic.[4]

It was an event to raise money for the good, humanitarian cause that is Brian Cowen, then Minister for Finance. Just to keep him ticking over, one supposes.

As I'm not a golfer, I am not too sure what was 'classic' about this particular golf classic but what is interesting for our investigation is that almost everyone who gave money to our dear leader, famous for his loyalty, was in the building game in some way. And even if they weren't, they were about to get some payback for their largesse.

A man who gave €1,000 to the Brian Cowen benevolent fund that day was a chap called Hugh Cooney. He is an accountant and a friend of the Taoiseach's. Following his donation, this man was made the head of Enterprise Ireland. Enterprise Ireland is an organisation charged with finding and cultivating Irish companies that will have the ability to compete abroad. It is arguably the most important state agency of all because in the course of the next few years, Ireland needs to build its own world-beating companies. You would expect the man appointed to run this to be someone with international experience of seeding and commercialising companies. You would expect someone who has a track record in international strategy, identifying crucial areas and bringing ideas to commercial reality using both networks and financial savvy. It might be helpful if the person had experience of start-up companies, venture capital and international finance.

This chap now at the top of Enterprise Ireland had been a partner in BDO Simpson Xavier, a middle-ranking financial company which specialises in putting together tax avoidance strategies for syndicates of Irish investors in—yes, you've guessed it—property.[6] (Or perhaps we shouldn't be so surprised after all. We do have a Minister for Enterprise whose only experience, outside the family business of politics, is as a social worker.)

The second donation of €1,000 to the Brian Cowen kitty came from developers McDermott & Farrell Ltd., who are involved in apartment building down in Dublin's Docklands.[7] This area was at the time controlled by the Dublin Docklands Development Authority whose boss was a director of Anglo, while Anglo's boss was a director of DDDA. All these directorships and appointments to the body that has fast-track planning powers in the Docklands are State sanctioned.

Another grand came from Kevin Kelly of Market Holdings Ltd.[8] This is an abbreviation of Castle Market Holdings, a subsidiary of Treasury Holdings, one of Ireland's biggest developers and again a major player down in the DDDA. Kevin Kelly is chairman and non-executive director of the company which also happens to be one of Anglo's biggest clients. From 1997 to 2007, Treasury Holdings donated €98,408 to the Fianna Fáil party and its representatives and €69,302 to the PDS.[9]

The next €1,000 came from Annette McDonnell of Ballymore Projects Services Ltd.[10] This is the commercial vehicle of Seán Mulryan, one of the massive developers who was financed almost exclusively by Anglo Irish and whose assets will now probably end up in NAMA with the taxpayer footing the bill. By the way, just to go a little deeper, a former director of Ballymore, Dr Peter Bacon, was architect of the NAMA bad bank plan. The spin is that Mr Bacon was only involved in

Ballymore's European ventures. This is not true. Mr Bacon's involvement with Ballymore is deeper than many have admitted thus far and not just Ballymore but Ballymore and one of our most disgraced Dons, Michael Fingleton aka Fingers of Irish Nationwide. Ballymore and Irish Nationwide have a joint venture company registered in Oxford called Clearstorm, which was set up to finance Ballymore's investments in the UK. Mr Bacon was appointed a director of this venture in 2003.[11] Incidentally, Ballymore Properties happens to have donated €29,580 in the run up to the 2007 General Election, just when Bertie's own funding was beginning to raise eyebrows.

So the man charged with designing the government 'financial skip', which is set up to bail out the developers and save the banks, is actually one of the gang. And these people who we are now bailing out are the very bankers and developers who got us into the mess in the first place!

And worse still, they were giving donations to Brian Cowen.

One wonders what the present Taoiseach's guests were discussing that afternoon.

Yet another grand was donated by Ken MacDonald, the top man at Hooke & MacDonald estate agents—the biggest seller of apartments in the country. You might remember him from the section 23 website earlier and from his comments in 2007, such as:

As one who has been involved in the Irish property market for 40 years and has experienced every type of market scenario, I am totally convinced that the market is currently in good shape and that anyone buying now will do extremely well in the years ahead. There is no better investment than Irish property at present, and I believe that I will be proved right in this conviction.[12]

Why do we allow scaremongers and doomsayers with unfounded pessimism and unbridled negativity dictate our thinking and blunt consumer confidence? The Irish economy is the envy of the world.[13]

Next up with his hand in his pocket was John O'Loughlin of Qualceram Ltd., the bathroom products firm, which has a huge interest in the construction boom.

He was followed by developer Eugene Larkin, who donated the same amount. Larkin established Twinlite Developments in 1997. In 2001,

Twinlite launched Tyrrelstown Town Centre in west Dublin, its flagship development, with 2,220 homes. In May 2006, it invested €40 million in the new 155-bedroom Park Plaza Hotel in Tyrrelstown,[14] and Larkin opened a new retail park there in 2007.

Just to round off the picture of the men and women at the golf classic in Dublin that day in September 2006 when the concerns of the country were on Bertie Ahern and the identity of Paddy the Plasterer, another €1,000 came from Peter Cosgrave, boss of Cosgrave Developments.[15] In that same year, Cosgrave Developments was given the go-ahead by Dun Laoghaire-Rathdown County Council to build 856 residential units on Dun Laoghaire Golf Club, despite objections from almost 450 local people.[16]

Perhaps it's unfair to single out our glorious leader—what he was doing was considered completely normal in the culture of the Fianna Fáil party. Between 1997 and 2007, Fianna Fáil received €599,990 in disclosed donations from developers and construction-related donors—this is 40 per cent of their overall take for the period, a proportion that increased significantly as the property sector gained power.[17] This is not unique to the gene pool of Fianna Fáil. In the run up to the 2007 General Election, 71 per cent of donations to political parties came from businesses whose primary interest was property development.[18]

It is difficult in the light of what has emerged in the past year to even write this, let alone reread it, without wincing.

The present and former Taoisigh were being bankrolled by the construction industry that in turn was being bankrolled by the banks who were in the business of dealing easy credit to the entire nation.

THE VIRTUOUS CIRCLE

The main reason the politicians wanted to keep the vested interests happy was that they were basking in the short-term glory of a balloon economy that looked as if it was booming. So when it came to ticking short-term boxes, tax was up because of all this borrowed money washing over us, employment was up because were we building houses that no one really wanted but this was employing lads on sites, the prices went up the more the Dons threw money at the economy and the more the place looked like a miracle.

The trifling little issue that we were impoverishing our young people and creating an economy that would implode seemed to matter not a jot. The mantra was 'the rising tide will lift all boats'—a mantra that would soon be replaced by 'an economic tsunami'.

The bankers were paying themselves a fortune in the process and were happy, the profits were increasing so the shareholders were happy and, since the Irish pension funds had invested heavily in the Irish banks, the pensioners were happy too as they were getting better and better returns every year. But these returns were ultimately a mirage, as many hundreds of thousands of people have now discovered. The tax revenue that was a reflection of all the borrowed cash was allowing the politicians to dole out favours and create quangos for their mates, and they could swan around taking credit for a boom when all they were doing was the bidding of their masters, the bankers and developers.

WHERE WAS ELLIOT NESS?

So, where were the accountants in all this? That noble profession charged with maintaining integrity in the dirty world of money-lending. You'd think that the various accountancy bodies would have had something to say about the strange goings-on in Anglo.

Indeed, the Institute of Chartered Accountants in Ireland, the country's biggest accountancy body, set up its own regulator (CARB) in 2007 to look out for such things. The first chairman of CARB was Liam O'Reilly,[19] former chief executive of the Financial Regulator, who presided over the AIB overcharging fiasco of 2004/2005. He is also a member of the board of Irish Life and Permanent Plc. This is the bank that tried to hoodwink its shareholders and those of Anglo Irish Bank by lending Anglo Irish €7 billion in October to pretend that Anglo's deposit base was more secure than it actually was. A safe pair of hands there.

In 2009, CARB appointed John Purcell as its 'Special Investigator into additional matters involving Anglo Irish Bank'.[20] What was special about this appointment was that Purcell was (and still is, in 2009) a director of Fingers' outfit Irish Nationwide, which gave millions of euro in loans to Fitzpatrick, again in order to deceive Anglo's shareholders. Who says accountants don't have a sense of humour?

Of course Sean Fitzpatrick, a celebrated council member of the same accounting institute, was laughing all the way to the bank. It's a measure of how progressive an institution it is that the Institute of Chartered Accountants in Ireland can embrace someone who makes such strides in pushing the boundaries of creative accounting. Then again, this is the same venerable institute that made Charlie Haughey an honorary life member and which also has former Anglo directors David Drumm and William McAteer on its members' list. Far from 'belts and braces' regulation, this is going commando!

Former Minister for Finance, Charlie McCreevy, famous for his 'less-is-more' approach to regulation, is also a member of the institute. In fact, he and Sean Fitzpatrick articled together as trainee accountants in what was later to become Ernst & Young, the firm that signed off Anglo's accounts.[21]

Maybe this is the type of regulation we were getting. Nod and wink regulation, where whatever a bank did was justified.

But this was just a professional body. What about the government? What was the Financial Regulator doing? Where was the Elliot Ness who was supposed to be protecting the addicts from the dealers?

A charitable interpretation of events suggests that the Regulator was bought off and didn't seem to have a clue what was going on. This is bad enough but doesn't stack up. What actually happened was that the Regulator was afraid of asking any questions of the banks when it was clear that the banks—both the local shower and the new international banks that showed up—were breaking every rule in the book.

But the Regulator was not concerned about rules. It was a kind of Bord Fáilte for the banking sector, part of an effort to build a business and foster an industry. Therefore, 'let the industry regulate itself' seemed to be the approach, no matter what the consequences.

But the consequences were shocking, as the Minister for Finance learned when he picked up the phone the morning after announcing the guarantee last autumn.

A tired but giddy Brian Lenihan told his Chief of Staff to put the German caller through.

Angela Merkel, who was about to write a check for €64 billion to cover Depfa's losses, had questions about the regulation of Irish banks even if the Irish Regulator did not.

Chapter 15 ∿

| DOWN ON THE STREET

BERTIE THE SOCIALIST

Not long after he declared himself a 'socialist', Bertie Ahern, a great man for opening shops, nightclubs and sports centres, opened the new offices of HSBC bank in Dublin. Through its subsidiary HFC, this large bank's presence in Ireland was significant but well disguised. However, you are likely to have come across it. In fact, you may well be a customer without actually knowing it.

HFC financed one of the most conspicuous developments of the tail end of the boom which was the emergence of places that could only be described as 'Little Britain' on the outskirts of our towns and cities. You know the places, the out of town retail parks home to M&S, Topshop, Tesco, River Island, B&Q, Currys and Oasis.

HFC provided the 'unbelievable' finance deals for Reid, Currys, Argos, Dixons and PC World. So one of the Irish banks financed the developer to build the retail park initially. Then another one of the banks lent the Little Britain outlets themselves the working capital to open up and finally, at the end, HFC made sure that the customers got tied up in seductive finance deals to keep them addicted to easy money.

These finance deals are the bottom of the credit barrel, the financial equivalent of scoring drugs on O'Connell Bridge off a bloke in a hoodie.

But none of this was on the mind of our great socialist leader on the day. Bertie, a man who was following in the footsteps of great Irish socialists like Countess Markievicz, James Connolly and Dick Spring, turned to the chairman of HSBC, John Bond, and bellowed triumphantly, 'I hope you make a fortune here' as he cut the ribbon.[1]

Let that sink in for a minute.

HFC bank's leaflet drop that day gushed that it was a 'member of the HSBC Group with 100 million customers worldwide and provides retail finance loans, unsecured personal loans and insurance—helping people realise their short-term and medium-term aspirations so that they can live their lives the way they want to'. What could be less threatening?

Think about what it was saying. First, by indicating that it was part of a global team, HFC reinforced subliminally the message that it was 'too big to fail'. *You can trust us, everyone else does. If you want money, 100 million people can't be wrong.*

This was one of the key driving forces of the banking world during the boom years. Everyone wanted distribution channels to be close to the poor addict so that they could push more and more easy credit in a variety of different ways at the misfortunate aspirant. They would convince him that a sofa could really change his life and then get him on the hook.

Therefore, we saw a spate of large investment banks taking over small specialist ones. HSBC obviously wanted the sales force of PC World and was prepared to pay through the nose when it bought HFC. This is exactly what the drugs gangs of Ireland do as well. They merge with other outfits that might have better distribution. Rather than fight turf wars, which are only for the small lads and attract far too much attention from the cops, the most effective way for a drugs gang to extend its reach and gain market share is by doing deals at the top.

Just for the record, Bertie's mate that day, John Bond, resigned as chairman of HSBC in 2006, trousering an annual salary of €6.56 million.[2] On his retirement, 'Sir John' (because the Brits seem to give those titles out to any old geezer, a bit like miraculous medals at Knock) also got a pension of over €750,000 per year.[3] One shareholder commented angrily that his salary had gone up by 597 per cent in six years while shareholder return had gone up by only 37 per cent in the same period.[4] It was a complaint that echoed the anxieties of ordinary shareholders right across the banking and financial sector when the big bust hit. Just for the record, so that you can be assured we are in good hands for the future, HSBC has just been appointed advisor to the new National Asset Management Agency that is supposed to save Ireland.

But why pick on HFC which was involved at the bottom, extending credit to our addicts at extortionate prices? There were many more glorified moneylenders in Prada, such as ACC Asset Finance, CIT Group Finance, Caterpillar Financial Services, and Clydesdale Financial Services which was described by the *Financial Times* as Barclays' 'sub-prime store card business'.

Even the ESB—a semi-state company with very powerful unions that claim to be on the side of the ordinary working man—is at the loan sharking racket. I suppose if Bertie can be a socialist and can cheerlead the moneylenders, the trade unions at ESB have nothing to be ashamed of. Leadership comes from the top, so they say. ESB Retail, under the euphemistic title of the Easy Pay option, advertises a great value interest rate of 22 per cent and it reassuringly assuages the fears of the most delinquent credit addict by confirming that it performs 'no external credit checks'.

THE MORNING AFTER

Fin Boy checks himself in the long mirror that stands between the sea of unsold couches at Harvey Norman. Good job the Aussie head office is keeping the faith in Ireland, otherwise he'd be back in the mam's box room, watching 'The All Ireland Talent Show' with the family on a Sunday night. Last week's show featured his cousin's daughter—*What does that make her?*, he wonders. *Third cousin, that's it.* He didn't watch it, but the aul' one said she sounded like a little Mariah Carey. Da told Ma to cop on out of it. He said that was a noise only whales can make out—the sort of racket that makes dogs howl.

Ma went off to the kitchen in a huff, but he could see she was trying not to laugh, her face all red like a tomato. The aul' lad was right, though. He saw it later on the DVR—the sound of the young one!

They got on well, the aul' pair. There was always chatting and joking, although Da's roofing business was all going a bit Pete Tong at the minute. The new Ducato with his name in signwriting hadn't moved from the front for a few weeks. Course, Da wasn't hassled, as usual. He said not to worry: with Torres in this form, something would turn up. The Da always looked at everything like it was a Liverpool FC match. The scousers hadn't won so much as a cup of piss in years, never mind a trophy. You'd never catch Fin Boy supporting that crowd.

But the aul' fella was not for turning. He'd found a new word lately: 'stoic'. He was always coming up with new ones after an afternoon with the *Sunday World* crossword. Now everything was 'stoic'. The other week Fin Boy was saying that another of his mates got the P45 and the Da came out with it again. Fin Boy almost lamped him.

Fin Boy liked going over to the aul' pair on a Sunday. Get the shirts ironed for the week, bit of the roast, maybe a couple of jars after. But he was always ready to head by seven. Quick hug for his little sister. If he wasn't in a mad rush he'd take her for a blem in the motor around the block before heading for the flat in Skerries, with the washing in the boot, all smelling of the ma.

He could still pay the rent, thank God. Not like some. So he was still in the flat with the lads. Even so, the three of them were feeling the squeeze, like. Sometimes he'd thought of moving back to the box room and stashing the rent for a rainy day. But he needed the gaff now. His luck had just changed. Into something that looked pretty fucking sweet in a thong, as it happened.

'No point worrying about the future. Just go for it, man,' he says to himself, winking at the mirror. In Fuengirola they said he looked like an Irish Enrique Iglesias. Good enough for him. Made up, so he was.

Today the fin is perfection. It leans slightly to the left like a follicular Leaning Tower of Pisa. He has half a tub of extra firm hold gel and other random gunk maintaining the miracle resting on his narrow head. At the back, the 2007 bushy mullet is growing out a bit but is still sculpted. He looks like Luke Fitzgerald from the front and Garret FitzGerald from the back.

It's exquisite. He can't take his own eyes off it. Sure why would he? That fin helped him pull Miss Modified Motors in Fairview's Barcode. He took her on to the Academy in Abbey Street and then back to her place. Result.

I mean, he knew he was looking the business at the RDS Modified Motors Show. He was top to toe Top Man. Standard issue frayed jeans. Shiny shoes. Checked shirt. He was the business, bud. But, man, was she hot.

He'd been to the premiere of *The Fast and the Furious 4* on Saturday, courtesy of tickets he'd won on a phone-in on Spin 103.8. He wouldn't have paid for them what with things getting tighter. He'd been watching the pennies. His floor manager—that wagon from Cavan—warned him that things were getting worse. His targets were way down and the next few weeks were crucial.

But it'll all pass, he thought. All the lads were saying that. One thing bothered him, though. If that was going to pass, how come so many of them were laid off in the past few months? Unemployment in Ireland amongst the 18–34 age group has increased 15 times faster than any other demographic and Fin Boy sat right in the middle of it.

He'd just splashed out six grand on the jam jar. But in fairness, it looked deadly. And you have to walk the walk. When Fin Boy sat in the Nissan, the uber-wide Havoc kit by Ibherdesign gave her that hard as nails look. The Big Bremo branded callipers peeked out from behind the spokes and clamped down on the 330 mm discs. It looked whopper, like.

He had managed to get it featured in January's 'Nutts Corner', in *Modified Motors*. He'd texted in a photo of him and the motor on his new iPhone to the 083 number and bang, there it was the next week. His mate Jude gave him the shout out. Deadly.

So, Miss Modified Motors. Jacqui, apparently. In fact, she was a runner up in that competition but she should have won; in Fin Boy's eyes, she would always be the real Miss Modified Motors. He was with the lads, necking a Corona, when yer one comes over, all San Tropezed and push up bra. Then she started with the hair flicking. He'd already had a few—he was going to stay with the Ma and Da last night (they live down the road from Barcode)—so he's leaning over, all chatty, like. He still reckons, *No way, man, not tonight, she must be havin' a laugh.* But she's giving it socks. They go out for a smoke and she's there, necking the breezer like she means it.

But fuck it, he thinks. You've got to go for it. I mean, Miss Modified Motors? She doesn't come around every day. Game on.

He was the man last night. Jacqui's ma was away in Blackpool, ballroom dancing, so she had a free gaff. He was up all night. A few sneaky lines helped the pair of them. Jaysus, she was down to business again this morning, before he had to buzz for work. Rockin', man.

He revved the motor out of her estate at half-seven because he had to get home to change for work. She waved at him from the porch, like a missus would. If a missus had platinum blonde hair extensions and wore a teddy, then he might be on for it, he thought.

He swaggered into the flat—the dog with two dicks and the lads there, wide to the whole thing, having to eat humble. Bragging rights to the Fin.

He can't wait for the five-a-side tonight in Santry. His team, Brayzil—'coz one of the lads is from out there—is doing well. Tonight's the semi-final. It's against a group of spacers called 'LSD Mindwoven'. They're aul' fellas from the over-35s who are quite handy, but. They can 'play a bit', these lads.

Brayzil will be in the trademark Boca Juniors strip, taking the sting out of the aul' lads in the first 10, making them chase the game. No Man U strips for Brayzil. Real fans have moved on from the Premiership dross years ago. It's River Plate, Kaizer Chiefs, Dinamo Zagreb or Flamingos kit for these boys. In the same way that you have to scour the globe for the best gear for your motor—places like Finland and Tennessee are hot now—you have to open wide to the world when looking for proper 'ball. The Premiership is for kids who don't know any better and for aul' lads like his da who think the Intertoto Cup is exotic.

But no matter who wins, in the dressing room tonight there will be only one man who nailed Miss Modified Motors. He won't let the lads forget that. He shoots. He scores.

THE GOLDEN AGE

Shower, shave, sculpt, then away to work.

She'd texted him twice already and it was only half-ten. Jaysus, she was filthy as well as gorgeous. He showed the lads in the store room and they thought he was pulling the piss. 'Seriously, boys, straight up, I wouldn't shit yez.'

What did he care if there was no business? Sure the whole place was a ghost town this morning. He was made up anyway.

He flicked through *Nuts* magazine absent-mindedly. He waited for customers. No one came. Last year it was so different.

He used to be run off his feet, signing people up to deals, flogging settees, three-piece suites, complete kitchens, the lot. People, particularly young brides with the 'just done' French manicure, came through the door by the dozen with that demented 'I've gotta have it' look in their eyes.

The routine was simple. He'd flirt away, complimenting them and, above all, listening patiently, which was difficult as some of them had that high-pitched nasal tone that only bats could figure out. Usually he only got half the conversation, but it didn't matter because he knew what they wanted: the most expensive thing in the shop, on the best credit lines, preferably nothing down, so the house out in Kells could be perfect before they moved in.

He wanted their signature so he'd put on his best 'Adrian Kennedy Phone Show' voice, all concern and sympathy. The flirting helped of course, but that came naturally to him and flattery worked to close the deal.

The patter was down to a fine art now. Zero rate finance, no docs required, walk away and don't worry about a thing. The whole house could be kitted out on tick so that on the night of the hen, when you were just starting out, the place would look like a double platinum rapper's crib, all top of the range, gleaming and brand new. Proper class, man.

Once he got the signature, they were bagged. It worked on a very simple basis. Every time he got a new customer signed up to any credit deal—no matter how big or small—he got €5 added to his pay packet. In the Golden Age, this could stretch up to €200 a day, particularly in spring, ahead of the wedding season in May and June, and of course after Halloween when the Christmas thing kicked off and he just sat back in his River Island suit and coined it.

The commission helped him move out of his ma's. Up to then, all his extra cash was ploughed into his wheels. Now he had both—wheels and a gaff—and he was on the way up. D'ya think Miss Modified Motors would've touched him with Wayne Rooney's if he was still living in the box room?

The commission was flowing. If he could get them over the line on the insurance deal, he got another €10 per customer. The insurance was harder back then because, first, there is that sort of person who never cares about tomorrow and couldn't be arsed getting it. Second, he noticed that people were so cocky. No one told them they might have a problem paying off the debts. After all, weren't they making more money than they'd ever imagined? Third, Fin Boy realised that some of those coming through the door—the sofa addicts—were already in way over their head and the extra €200 a year to insure everything against the calamity around the corner would have sunk them.

This is how the low level dealing in credit exploded in Ireland, down here where money is expensive and the penalties are huge. Dealers like Fin Boy were given a big incentive through their commission to flog more and more easy credit.

Fin Boy rarely looked at the terms. His company was like everyone else's. The banks, which were lending them the money before they took their cut and passed it on to the credit junkie, set more or less the same terms for everyone. He was offering zero per cent finance and a fixed repayment rate for the first 17 months of the deal.

Then what is called a 'balloon payment' kicks in. This is where the customer has to pay a significant amount of the principal on the eighteenth month. Many people can't pay this on the day, so the nice people at Harvey Norman offer you a deal where the sofa can be refinanced for 48 months at an interest rate of 26 per cent. European Central Bank rates are now just over 1 per cent. So it is easy to see how the banks are borrowing at close to 1 per cent, yet, when the credit gets down to the low-level dealers like Fin Boy, after everyone has taken their cut, the same money costs 26 times more to people at the end of the chain.

The deal is the same whether you are at Dixons, DID Electrical, PC World, Woodies, ESB or Reid. The addicts want stuff they can't afford. The seller wants to sign them up to as many deals on LCD TVs, Smeg fridges or three in-one-sofa suites as possible. In the middle is the finance package.

As with small-time drug dealers, the proposition is always more or less the same. The addict is offered a zero interest option for 12 to 18 months. They get the LCD and forget about the terms. They pay a fixed amount each month by direct debit. Everything seems fine. Then, after 18 months, the balloon payment falls due, which is a big chunk of the principal. If they pay this, the payment until the deal ends in (say) four years is smaller. If they make every payment on time, the TV costs the same as it would have in cash had they stumped up the money straightaway.

But people rarely make the payments, because if they could have done so at the start they would have. Some take out protection, which Fin Boy gets paid a tenner for signing people up to, but usually they don't bother, which is when they get into trouble.

So they end up paying 26 per cent APR and giving the banks and the retailer, who are both taking a cut, a fortune.

When we had full employment and house values were moving upwards, the country could just about afford all these never-nevers, but now, with people defaulting all over the place, the mood in Fin Boy's sales office is getting rawer every day.

FIN BOY'S DILEMMA
He'd always thought it was a bit dodgy. When he told his da, the aul' lad called them 'poxy crooks'.

'No better than them little toerags that do be shooting each other all over the city.'

Fin Boy didn't like it but apparently a new bank was giving them the money to continue lending to the desperate housewives of Meath and Kildare. The new deal was called the 'Bite-Sized Way to Pay'. The poor addict would come in, strung out before a wedding or a Communion or a Debs, needing something new in the house to show to the neighbours who would be coming round.

Fin Boy was all over them. They'd sign up. He got his commission and, on the eighteenth month, the addict would have to come up with a huge whack or else the rest of the payments, for months on end, would be charged at 26 per cent. Previously, they'd contact the customer a month or two in advance and warn them that the payments were changing.

But this time it was different. They didn't contact the customer. And the poor addict had so much going on with kids and work and other stuff that she never noticed. Suddenly, without warning, the day passed and she was hooked on a 26 per cent interest rate penalty for the rest of the loan's term. No one told Fin Boy about this, so the first he heard of it was when people started ringing up complaining.

This week they'd told him and the lads that this might start happening. They were all given a few hours' training in customer service by a fat man with lots of gold jewellery who looked and sounded like Terry Venables. He kept repeating, 'Refer them to customer service in Croydon.'

That's all very fuckin' well for you to say, thought Fin Boy, *but I know these heads. Do you not remember the course you sent us all on about network selling? The same slimy bollix had gone on and on about how easy it was to sell to people you knew or your family knew. What about all that other shite you spouted on about? 'The six degrees of separation'; how we all had huge networks of mates who had networks of mates and if we could tap into them we'd sell all day and all night.*

He said our commission would go through the roof and the punters would love us for it.

Fin Boy had taken this to heart. He was actively converting his mates to his shop like some sort of Jehovah's Witness. And they were being shafted.

The whole house of cards was falling down around him. In the Golden Age, he had been the King. Month after month he was the top salesman. His commission had rocketed. The punters thanked him for the deals. Now he realised he'd been had. He wasn't the King any more.

Half the dressing room had been conned too. Lads were losing their jobs. He'd sold beds to their missuses, which were now kicking into penalty interest rates without them knowing. How could he face his mates? That was the lowest thing you could do. Sure, you could have borrowed the money from the bank to clear it off and save a fortune, but the banks weren't lending now.

What was he going to do? He'd betrayed his own. Miss Modified Motors certainly wouldn't hang around with a lad who had shafted his own. He was going to be a leper.

He checked himself in the mirror again. The fin was wilting.

Chapter 16 ∽

| THE JUNKIE

THE MANIA

When we think of the boom years, why don't we call our collective experience the 'Mania'? The word 'mania' carries so much more meaning. A boom is a sterile expression located in the unemotional world of economics and finance, whereas a mania comes from somewhere deep within us. It is a character flaw, an urge and an irrational desire to have, to hold, to be. The word 'mania' transports us to an extraordinary landscape where reality is distorted and we cease to be ourselves.

During the Mania, we experienced compulsive highs and we were emotional, grandiose, self-absorbed and belligerent in equal measure. It was as if we experienced a national personality disorder. But the Mania was real. Hard as it is to believe now, we did buy the most expensive houses in Europe; our banks did gamble our future on one monumental bet on property; our government did cheerlead from the sidelines. We are experiencing a depression, not a recession and, yes, we will be paying off the national credit card bill for a generation. This all happened. We experienced in five years what most normal countries experience in a generation.

We got high on the drug of cheap credit that the Dons, the Godfather and the Shylocks doled out like Smarties. We became a nation of credit junkies prone to highs and lows, dominated by the effervescence of the trip and deep, deep depression and self-loathing of the comedown.

The most distasteful realisation is that, like the simple relationship between the dealer and the junkie, the whole thing was orchestrated from the top.

As with the story of every addict, there is the constant denial. You are always looking for someone in worse shape than yourself to make you feel better.

All drug users—including the easy credit addicts—quickly form a bond with each other. They feel that they have the inside track and if you are not going for it, well, obviously there is something wrong with you.

The dealer understands the group psychology and knows that the junkies hang out together in certain places, certain haunts. He knows that the junkies have their own networks and their own gossip. He knows the junkie patois. Why wouldn't he? They are dependent on each other, after all—the junkie and the dealer. Sometimes the dealers can't believe that it is all so easy but in many cases, at least down the chain, the dealers are addicted too. So it all becomes a blur.

LONDON CALLING THE NEW CONVERTS

It's half-eight on Friday night and the last plane out of Shannon is evacuating a new force, deploying this battle-hardened crew to where it is most needed. An army is on the move and the Merchant of Ennis, his missus and 20 others are its brigadiers. If Jack's Army characterised the emerging hope of the late 1980s and early 1990s, comically enthusiastic but not quite believing that we were where we were, defeat was always expected. It was the era of the 'nil all' Irish victory. In contrast, the Munster Army represented the Mania. This was the New Ireland, tough, no nonsense, taking no prisoners. Victory was expected. Defeat was not an option.

Many plausible reasons have been offered to explain why Munster GAA embraced Munster Rugby. It wasn't always like this.

I have cousins who are Munster devotees today, yet when they were young they didn't know one end of the rugby ball from the other. In fact, when I was sent down to Cork for the ritual slapping that jackeen cousins have to endure when staying with family in the country, my cousins accused me of playing a 'poof's game'. Or worse still, as another cousin remarked, 'Sure that game's only for English people or Protestants or both.'

Back then, nothing marked you out as a potential informer as much as an appreciation of rugby. Rugby was foreign and posh. In west Cork, football or hurling—but mainly football—was the game. In 1983, as a boy, when I mentioned to the family that Ireland had won the Triple Crown, I was told in no uncertain terms to 'go back to your fecking croquet, ye West Brit. There'll be no crowns celebrated down here, triple or otherwise'!

In the past 10 years, there has been a dramatic transformation. These mountainy men, latter day 'Boys of Kilmichael', for whom the assassination of Michael Collins was a momentous day in our country's glorious calendar, have embraced rugby—a garrison sport if ever there was one.

They are Munster devotees. Men who lived through the entire twentieth century without knowing their 'line outs' from their 'drop goals' are now versed in the bizarre lexicon of rugby, adopting the rituals with the gusto of converts.

And it is the lexicon of rugby that acts as a barrier to the uninitiated. Rugby, above all sports, has its own patois. So the new convert has to learn the intricate language that distinguishes soft hands from quick hands, hard yards from gain lines, forward momentum from collapsed maul, offside from crossing, drift defence from zonal defence and his scrum back from his against the head. That's before he comes to terms with the idea that the fly half, the 10 and the out half, are the same bloke who might put snow on it if he's in the mood. The convert has to nonchalantly know that the back three involves a wing three-quarters as well as a full back. The wing forward is also a flanker and the lock is also the second row and that's before you've decided whether the prop's head is tight or loose. Never mind the front five, which is different from the engine room, but both are integral to the pack that together with the halfbacks can play 10-man rugby if the conditions demand it. Then there is lifting, burrowing, throwing, rucking, mauling or gouging, all of which we do just to set up the danger man, who may well be an impact player, who has come off the bench because of a blood substitution. At least we have the satisfaction of knowing that he will put it up his jumper and go for a walk.

All this is, as they say in rugby circles, a 'big ask' for a novice or a convert.

The Merchant of Ennis is a convert to the Munster creed. When they beat the All Blacks on that famous night depicted in *Alone It Stands*, he couldn't have told you who the All Blacks were. One thing was clear: they weren't the Cats, the Deise, the Kingdom or the Rebels. The Merchant was a Banner Man and hurling was his sport. The Munster final was his Nirvana.

When he first met Elaine while he was the man—'97 Kevin—in his hurling pomp and doing construction studies in LIT, he didn't know one end of a rugby ball from the other. But Elaine was a good Limerick girl, and she set about educating him. She took him to Thomond Park, just around the corner from the college, to watch Shannon play. Mick Galwey was the captain then, and sure hadn't he won an All-Ireland playing football for Kerry? Maybe this rugby craic wasn't so British, after all.

Nothing succeeds like success and he made the switch when he knew it would be good for business. All sorts of pop-psychology has been cited to account for the mass conversion to rugby in Munster but the best explanation I heard came from a friend from Kerry who summed it up succinctly when he noted, 'It allowed us to go on the lash in a foreign country for the first time ever. Actually, it was like Munster Final weekend in Inter Cert French!'

You can't argue with that. During the Mania, we all converted. The personality disorder was so widespread that former GAA rule 21 stalwarts found themselves in Twickenham. And didn't feel out of place.

The Merchant had a season ticket at the new Thomond.

The Merchant was off to blow someone else's money watching Munster while Elaine and the girls were off to blow someone else's money in Westfield. They were on a strict timetable as they were being flown back by a builder friend that night so as to be in Limerick for the last pints.

MECCA

Elaine and the other girls from Laurel Hill headed straight for the holy of holies, the biggest shopping centre in the world. They'd been on a similar trip to New York last year where the travel agent also found Elaine a shopping planner. It was a hoot. The planner was amazing. Not only did she organise tours of the great shopping Mecca that is New York City, she organised the essential limos, special spa, nail and wax treatments and booked restaurants for after a hard day's spending in the Big Apple.

The whole thing was planned like an assault. With military precision, the Limerick girls took Manhattan. First, there was a financially high-risk, quick incursion uptown to Bergdorf Goodman and Tiffany, followed by a thrust down Fifth to Macy's. Having successfully accomplished this mission, our well-armed, elite shopping troop fanned out in Bloomingdale's on Lexington, to regroup at Fitzpatrick's Hotel—the base camp—at around lunchtime. There was a late brunch on Third Avenue before they headed downtown to the boutique territory of SoHo, Chelsea and the meatpacking district.

By the time she was on the plane home, Elaine was knackered. She couldn't face the children. She needed a holiday. At least London this year wouldn't be so manic.

Elaine sat in Starbucks in the world's largest shopping centre, taking it all in. It is Wembley for girls with a Manolo Blahnik fetish.

The place is vast. Westfield in Shepherd's Bush, west London, opened in October 2008. With 300 shops and 50 restaurants, it makes Dundrum Town Centre look like a 1950s Londis in Cavan. It is so huge, you are given a map so that you don't get lost. Most shoppers are studying these coordinates closely for fear that they take a wrong turn and are never seen again. This is a GPS system for people on the way to maxing out their credit cards.

Westfield is the Victoria Beckham of shopping centres: it is loud, brash, pushy and, most of all, brandtastic. The people behind Westfield have obviously got into the heads of the people who are shopping there. The owners' aim is quite simple: you can read their manifesto in the huge lifestyle ad at the entrance, which states boldly that Westfield is a 'fabulous place, for fabulous people'. Because it is the incarnation of global high-end shopping, it is a wonderfully rich savannah in which to watch the various different shopping tribes roam, many trying desperately to look and be different but ending up crushingly similar.

And the interesting thing is, you could be anywhere. The only thing that makes this feel like London is the red buses, chugging around the revamped Shepherd's Bush. Close your eyes and the place is eerily familiar. This could be Grafton Street, Lincoln Drive in Miami, Fifth Avenue or any of the British-themed retail parks that have sprung up all over our country.

Back at Westfield, we have the Joseph tribe, the Habitat tribe, the Armani tribe and the Calvin Klein tribe all brushing up against each other, professing their affinity with each brand. When they head into Miu Miu, for example, they are not saying, 'Oh I like that,' rather they are stating, 'I am like that. This is my church and these are my people.' This is the retail equivalent of the Orange Order and the bank holiday sales are this tribe's 12th of July. You put on your flyest gear and off you go, plumes on display.

What makes this tribal issue interesting is that the appeal of the brand supersedes or at least coexists with all sorts of other tribal touchstones.

Elaine sips her tall skinny latte as she remarks how the Saudi women in full burkas can happily entertain both Allah and Accessorize, while their less observant sisters are tottering on six-inch Manolo Blahniks, dolled up with thick suggestive eyeliner which is all the more alluring because their dark eyes are accentuated by their black hijabs.

The black teenagers with their bleached white trainers roll around the place looking menacing and snarl like caged dogs at the authority of the State. Yet they behave like little lambs, whimpering and bleating with subservience, when faced with the authority of Tommy Hilfiger.

The first floor is full of skinny stick insects who can barely be seen from the side. This, as the *Sunday Times* observes, is the '1666 Club'— women in skinny jeans who look 16 from the back and 66 from the front. They look as if they haven't eaten since Christmas. They are obsessed with the natural world and so eschew processed food. Yet they crowd around the cosmetics stand and are happy to spend fortunes here on face cream. Maybe when they are not focusing on opening their chakras at the One World Yoga centre they should be reminded that L'Oréal has protested against the EU's ban on animal testing by lodging a case at the European Court of Justice in Luxembourg.

Elaine may be a little self-conscious as she wolfs down an almond Danish, and sees lots of unathletic people—who've just driven up to the nearest exits in the labyrinthine car park so that they don't have to walk too far—waddling around in fitness tracksuits. These people— who probably haven't broken sweat since their own birth—are knocking back energy sports drinks as if they've just finished a triathlon. Meanwhile, others—who clearly have never been up a hill as modest as the Sugarloaf and get that scrunched up, fed up 'rain face' in an April shower—are busy grappling with which extreme weather Matterhorn mountaineering gear to stock up on at a shop called the North Face.

And then of course there is the Apple shop, the tabernacle of the most informed addicts on earth. The distinctive powering up sound of the Apple Mac screeches an expensive education. You are now close to the top of the shopping hierarchy where the Apple tribe roams. These are the Spartans of shoppers, brave, chiselled and, most of all, knowing. They look down their technically sophisticated nose at the rest of the laptop-buying world as they swarm round the Apple store, marvelling at the phenomenal capacity and graphics capability of the new MacBook. In reality, all they use it for is Googling cheap Ryanair flights and downloading CDs from iTunes onto their new iPod shuffle. Yet these people are proselytisers, always on the lookout for yet another convert to the Church of Steve Jobs. Have you ever met an Apple Mac user who doesn't try to convert you? No, me neither. If L. Ron Hubbard did laptops, he'd do Apple.

In Ireland the picture is the same. Hundreds of thousands became credit addicts and our own creatures are no less exotic than those in Westfield. We had freckly Sinn Féin voters with faded Saor Éire tattoos and crew cuts waving their two fingers at Brian Lenihan's appeal to patriotism as they crossed the border in their droves to what they might call the 'occupied six counties' to get a bargain in B&Q. We had muffin-topped tanorexics in their 'going out' tracksuits maxing out in A wear. Everything was on tick, everyone could pay later and, more to the point, no one could abandon the habits of the past few years, even as the clouds came in.

The worst thing is that when the music stopped and the credit taps were turned off, we had nothing to show for it.

THE COMEDOWN

Initially, like all addicts, we thought that we could handle the drug. We dabbled here and there, putting a few things on the credit card, taking out a large loan to build the essential Veluxed kitchen extension or buy the new car that we simply had to have.

But gradually we became addicted. We decided that we could live in this junkie never-never land, spending the rest of the world's money. All we needed was someone to keep us topped up.

Elaine started to notice things getting out of hand in late 2007. Until then, she'd been able to keep everything more or less under control. But a few years ago, she started getting new credit cards, the ones that were advertised in the papers. There seemed to be so many of them. The country had opened itself up to all sorts of dealers. And they didn't seem to ask any questions.

First, it was clothes and things for the kids, something from the Petit Bateau catalogue. Then it was a few small items for the house and the new kitchen. Obviously the pilgrimages were expensive, but everyone else was doing it. Anyway, all their husbands were in property and things were going very well.

The new car didn't seem like an extravagance. But soon her sense of self became wrapped up in the lifestyle they had acquired. The house in Roundstone in August, the share in the Galway hooker and the fully stocked wine cellar didn't seem so over the top. The dinner parties and the Christian Louboutins and the children's sports camp, the place they had in the Algarve and the second xc90 in two years—these were all things that lots of people had. How had they got so carried away?

Anyway, her husband was always being reported doing deals in the local newspaper. There was nothing to worry about.

When the bills and the credit card statements came in she was shocked. She used to always clear the card every month. This is what kept her within limits. But then she started to pay just the interest. This gave her a huge breathing space. She was moving towards her limits. When everyone was talking about millions this and millions that, what difference would a few cards with a €14,000 limit on them make?

But the spending just spiralled. There were a few more charity balls a month. But they were a well-known couple in the town and her husband had clients who had to be entertained and anyway, everyone was becoming a philanthropist now.

That was the new thing. The Merchant of Ennis had been over to New York too and he had noticed that the very rich gave their money away. To be a real business person in the us, you needed to adopt a charity and donate to it. This involved raising more cash and having evenings where you raffled certain things and tapped your friends for cash. Elaine took over the running of these events.

They never seemed to break even and, although the charity was worthy, they couldn't get money out of people. She was always out of pocket for these nights.

Then the banks started calling in the debts and refused to allow her to roll all the credit card debts into one with a term loan as it had done last year. Without credit, her lifestyle was gone. She'd never felt extravagant. She always thought she could manage everything.

But when the crunch came, her outgoings were twice as much as her income. That was all it took to push her over the brink. She was an addict and she'd never noticed it. Without her credit, she was nothing but a pathetic debt junkie going through cold turkey 2009-style. Elaine

Flannery, seven honours in her Leaving Cert, head of her class at Laurel Hill, UCC Comm graduate, former advertising executive, career woman taking a break for her children, was now hiding bills and making up excuses. How did it come to this? And how could she ever tell him? She looked over at him, sitting there in the back of Clohessy's in his Munster jersey, apparently without a care in the world. The Merchant of Ennis—a man going places.

PART III

Chapter 17

IRELAND—EUROPE'S VIETNAM

D eep down, everyone knows that reunions are not about meeting *them*—the other people you pretend to be interested in. Frankly, if you were that interested, why would you leave it 20 years before seeing them again?

My class reunion is for the College of Europe in Bruges—from which I and eight other Irish students graduated in the summer of 1989—just before the Wall came down. In July of that year, thousands of East Germans rocked the world by bolting in their Trabants through a gap in the Iron Curtain in Hungary. The system was tottering.

The College of Europe is to the European Union what WestPoint is to the US military or Sandhurst is to the British Army. It trains the officer class of the European Commission, Council and Parliament. True to form, 20 years later, the majority of my former classmates are well up in the European bureaucracy.

They have become the new European breed that Schuman and Monet—the intellectual founders of the EU—wanted to create. As they have been cocooned in Brussels for the past two decades, they see the world differently from the rest of us. They've married other bilingual people from different countries and now have trilingual children in multinational schools, and benefit from tax-free incomes and very, very long public sector holidays.

Many wear those funny Germanic glasses that make them look as if someone's garden gate is grafted onto their head, and they can't understand, in any language, why people would vote no to Lisbon.

This is the cosmopolitan elite that the *Daily Mail* and Libertas ranted about. Their very aloofness is their Achilles' heel.

In reality, they are very nice people who believe in a project that has ensured peace in Europe for over half a century. While some may feather their own nests first, they've also introduced a way of looking at the EU that is both humane and progressive. When you meet them, they are not the caricatures of devious, faceless, committee members intent on world domination who are depicted in the British press.

Granted, they're not too hot on democracy and, if pushed, can't see the point in plebiscites. If they have a weakness, it is that they tend to pigeonhole those who might disagree with them as racist, nationalist and antediluvian. Because they have embedded themselves in the mandarin ways of Brussels, there is an intolerance of dissent even when referendum after referendum (in those countries brave enough to have them) reveals that the people of Europe are not that enamoured with everything that comes out of the EU. Old allegiances like race, tribe and locality remain strong and are, for many, more attractive that the United Colours of Benetton European ideal.

This public dissent has forced the elite to accept that it is not all one-way traffic, that there are other opinions, however debased, which must be taken into account. The cosmopolitans are learning to cope with these minor irritants. As someone who has voted pro-Europe in all our referenda, I could forgive them their elite foibles if they could learn to forgive mine.

However, late at night, at the 20-year reunion of the College of Europe, after more than a few glasses of white, many senior officers of the EU reveal their true colours.

When you mention Ireland, our risk of default and our banks, it is like talking to the Moonies or, more accurately, military strategists from a bygone era. It is like listening to Dwight Eisenhower speaking of Korea or Henry Kissinger talking about Cambodia. This explains a lot.

THE DOMINO THEORY

After the Second World War, the American military top brass were obsessed with stopping the spread of communism. Central to their strategy was what they called the domino theory. It held that communist success in one country would lead to a domino effect, therefore movements and rebellions had to be snuffed out everywhere, no matter how remote or inconsequential. The Americans' policy was to do everything in their power to fight communist movements wherever they emerged. This is why the Americans got involved in Vietnam. They believed that with communist North Korea already in existence, the

Chinese and Russians would use success in Vietnam to help communist movements in Thailand and Cambodia. In no time, the entire sub-continent would be overrun.

Having lost Cuba to that upstart Castro, they drew a line in the sand in Ho Chi Minh in Vietnam, the move that summed up the Americans' domino theory approach to international relations. Initially, the residents of Saigon must have welcomed the huge power of the USA coming in on the side of their army much as the residents of Seoul had done less than two decades earlier. But as the last desperate US chopper airlifted US embassy staff out of Saigon in 1975, the average man on the street there must have been left reassessing the wisdom of siding with Uncle Sam.

The military lesson of Vietnam is that the strongest power in the world can be defeated if it is faced with an organised, disciplined and more popular local force. Sometimes, defending the indefensible for the wrong reasons, half-heartedly and with the wrong policies, leads to defeat. And this defeat leads to huge costs in terms of both the prestige of the superpower that is defeated and the people it purported to be helping.

For the Americans, Vietnam could have been anywhere. It could have been Burma, Thailand, Malaysia or Borneo. It just happened to be Vietnam because the domino doctrine decreed it.

Now with this idea fresh in our heads, let's look at what the European Central Bank is doing with Ireland. Ireland is the ECB's Vietnam.

THE ECB'S VIETNAM

Like the Americans, my friends in the European elite believe in the domino doctrine. They think in terms of big supra-state ideas whereby the State is a building block to a great political edifice. They believe in 'spheres of influence', and Ireland certainly falls within theirs.

They have invested so much political capital in the euro that a default or even questioning the wisdom of the currency in one country could lead to a chain reaction in others, undermining the entire monetary union. Europe's interests are put before the interests of individual nations. With Ireland only accounting for one-fiftieth of euro zone GDP, any other reaction would be a clear case of the tail wagging the dog.

So like the Americans flinging every bit of military hardware at the South Vietnamese in their bid to halt the spread of communism in the

1960s, the European elite, through the ECB, is doing everything in its power to keep the failing Irish banking system afloat. It knows what the cost of failure is. If the Irish banks fail, the next domino to quickly fall (because of the guarantee) will be the Irish State. And if one state within the currency union falls, then others might follow.

This may seem like a great leap—from a bank default to widespread sovereign default—but it is important to remember that the entire financial system runs on trust. Investors are willing to buy Irish debt because they understand that the ECB would not allow an Irish default. To investors, it is like a parent signing as guarantor for a young person without a credit rating. The investors don't calculate the risk based on the young person's record; they calculate it based on the parent's record. Now imagine what the investors would think if the young person stopped paying their debts and the parent decided not to cover the loan. The young person's credit rating would be ruined, but the parent's credit rating would also be brought into question.

But this generous parent has 15 children, and has signed as guarantor for all of them. All these guarantees now become worthless, so investors will be much less willing to give loans to any of their children. As the children find they can't borrow more money to fund their lavish lifestyle, they too go into default. And so the dominoes tumble.

Preventing the 'trust' in the system breaking down like this is the ECB's Tet Offensive.

Let's examine what this means for our financial balance sheet in Ireland. We have huge debts, which are far bigger than our ability to pay. If left to their own devices and the vagaries of private money moving in and out of the country, the Irish banks would go bust. They should be bust now.

There is a significant likelihood that money would've been pulled out of the Irish banks already if they hadn't been guaranteed. If this had not happened, there would have been a run on the banks. I remember my mother calling me last September when I was in China and asking me whether she should take her savings out of Bank of Ireland and put them into a foreign bank like Rabo, which didn't seem to have problems. She is not the only person who called me. People were concerned and they had every right to be.

Our savings are our own money. They are not 'invested' in the bank. We deposit them with the bank for safekeeping and it would be remiss of us to leave them with a bank whose security was questionable. The fact that the banks view our savings as their money is their problem, not ours. The miserly interest rates they pay us certainly do not compensate us for taking any risk.

We have seen in Chapter 11 how the Irish banks endangered us and our savings by their mad rush for profits, and how the rest of Europe—the people lending money to the Irish banks—became uncomfortable with us in September 2007, a full year before the crisis. We also now know that the Central Bank was aware that funding was drying up, but rather than warn the ordinary people that their savings might be in danger, the Bank's Governor only tried to reassure the markets that the Irish banks were not exposed to the exotic 'subprime CDOs' that, he claimed, were causing the problems. He failed to mention that the Irish banks didn't need to be exposed to American subprime borrowers. We had our own toxic brew here—development loans—that would lead to much greater problems than over-borrowed underpaid Americans ever could.

Today, the risk of bank failure has not gone away. But it is risk that is far too great for the ECB to allow because of its belief in the domino theory. So, amazingly, the same bunch of cronies who managed to inflate the boom and bankrupt the country are being bailed out by the ECB. The cronies have managed to achieve the exalted status of 'too big to fail'. For Ireland, they have become 'too big to bail' so the country should be bankrupt, but they are being bailed by the ECB, not because the ECB is worried about the people of Ireland but because it wants to protect the euro. I hope that you, the reader, are starting to see how little your interests are being addressed in this entire mess.

Every day, every minute as you read this, billions of euros are being pumped into the Irish banks to keep them afloat. The ECB is giving them as much money as they want to survive.

Look at the figures. In autumn 2008 when the crisis began, the ECB was providing about €20–€30 billion in short-term financing to the Irish banks.[1] It is 'normal' in international banking for the ECB to go into the market and supply funds to banks, smoothing out any temporary cash shortages. Like the rest of us, a bank needs an overdraft and some access to cash to make sure that all its bills can be paid. Sometimes it has loads of cash; at other times, it's a few days late bringing money in, so it needs the ECB to smooth over the bumps.

The ECB complements other sources of financing, particularly what the banks lend to each other. That's how the system works in 'normal times'. But while the ECB is happy to be a supplementary source of cash, it never wants to be the only source for a banking system. In fact, it is debarred from being that 'lender of last resort' on a permanent basis because then you just have a Central Bank that legitimises and encourages bad practice.

Using the US military analogy, this normal additional support is like the US Army providing the South Vietnamese Army with CIA advisors, additional logistics and air support. The US never wanted to get bogged down on the ground in the jungle and similarly, the ECB was hoping that, after a bit of support, the financial markets would come back and support the Irish banks. But that has not happened, because the markets are worried that the Irish banks are in such a perilous state that any money they lend to an Irish bank will just disappear into the black hole of huge property-related debts.

Like the US in Vietnam, the ECB has become increasingly bogged down in Ireland. As of September 2009 the ECB is providing the Irish banking system with some €180 billion of financing on an ongoing basis.[2]

But don't be fooled into thinking that this is a cheap way out of the crisis. This cash is just more Irish borrowing with a different name on it. The ECB is now our only source of finance. No one else will touch us.

Here is the next twist in the story. The Irish government, which is running an enormous budget deficit, has to issue bonds to cover its running costs. We have to borrow to stay afloat. But who will lend to us? The rest of the world will only lend to us if we are prepared to pay them an interest rate that is 70 per cent above the rate that Germany has to pay. Why should this be? Are we not both part of the same monetary union with the same exchange rate?

Either Irish government bonds are the buy of the century or they are a harbinger of default.

But as we said before, the EU will not countenance a default because of the domino theory. So investors are betting on the fact that the Irish people will permanently pay more for their money despite the fact that we are supposedly in the same monetary union.

It's easy to understand once you realise that these bond investors think that the Irish government will side with them and turn Ireland into a large debt-servicing machine, paying over the odds to people who are already loaded. These investors believe that the Irish government, together with its friends at the ECB, will put the interests of foreign bondholders before the interests of Irish taxpayers! We will commit ourselves to paying the debt, even if it means cutting back on budgets for stuff that people really need. If you wonder why, in the coming years, you can't get good medical care, or why you have to pay to put your child through college, remember it is because the government has decided it is more important to pay foreign investors over the odds for money than invest in the future of Ireland's citizens.

And the worst thing about this is that the foreign investors are right. As we will see a bit later, the current cornerstone of Irish financial policy is 'no bondholder is left behind'. But bondholders are grown-ups and they never expected to be given a free lunch by the Irish State when they took a gamble on Irish banks. The Irish banks were a risk, offering double-digit interest rates on bonds at one stage during the crisis. The bondholder—who is a large billion-dollar financial institution—is getting this money without any risk. It is getting the returns associated with a place like Bolivia in exchange for the economic security of Germany. And guess what? You are paying for it.

This is not economics, it is politics and, worse still, it is ideology. I'd say in strategy meetings in the City of London, the bondholders can't believe their luck.

There is no way the European empire will indulge chaos on the borders so its leaders have indicated to our mandarins that whatever it takes, they will support us in our efforts to pay back all this debt, even if we are only paying back the old debt with new debt borrowed from the ECB. Ireland is being encouraged to pay old debt with new debt. There are two guaranteed outcomes from this tactic. First, our debt will grow larger (as we are also borrowing to fund current spending, as well as to recycle old debt). Second, a tipping point will be reached where our debt will become so large that it will cripple the economy. All the earnings of the economy will go towards servicing the debt rather than towards providing for the citizens of the State.

In case you are thinking that this is little more than scaremongering, look at the debt we are currently issuing. The NTMA issued €15.5 billion worth of short-term debt between March and July 2009 (incidentally, this is also the total value of the pension reserve fund—the national piggy bank). This is debt that will have to be repaid in less than a year. The government will not be in a position to repay this debt, so the next time it borrows, it will have to borrow to repay this debt *and* continue to fund the running of the State. When push comes to shove (as it will), the government will repay the debt before it pays for the running of the State.

FAULTLINES

Can this last indefinitely? There are three pressure points. The first is the tolerance of German savers to keep pumping in cash. In military terms, a German pullout would be the equivalent of the US pulling out of Vietnam way before defeat under enormous domestic political pressure.

The second is the tolerance of the Irish unemployed to put up with this carry-on, which will run out once what is happening becomes apparent. When it becomes obvious to people like Miss Pencil Skirt, in the dole office in Kilbarrack, that the banks are still pulling the strings, they will react. After years of high taxes, high unemployment and emigration, people will say, *Enough of this nonsense!*

In military terms, this would be like the South Vietnamese realising that they were simply pawns in America's Great Game. If the South Vietnamese had realised that their casualties and their suffering didn't matter a jot to the likes of Henry Kissinger, who still saw the world as a collection of toy soldiers on battlefield maps spread out in a Cabinet War Room, they'd have made peace in the mid-1960s. But they didn't and they had to suffer for another decade, pointlessly. The same is very likely to happen here, in economic terms at least, before we wake up.

The third scenario is that we will end up with a default. We will experience the economic equivalent of the last Americans being airlifted out of Saigon, their domino theory in tatters because the whole strategy was based on an idea in Washington rather than the facts on the ground in Vietnam. Similarly, trying to prevent the Irish banks defaulting only to protect the euro, but ignoring the financial facts on the ground, doesn't seem very sound. The very cost of keeping all the Irish banks open is precisely why there is still a risk of default. The financial markets are still not convinced.

THE FACTS ON THE GROUND

In the same way that there were only so many troops the Americans could lose in Vietnam, there are only so many euros the German taxpayer will lend to us before someone over there spots what is going on.

The politics of this has become all the more complicated because the Irish State is now using the Irish banks to recycle new Irish government debt that couldn't be financed any other way.

Here's what's going on. We need money to pay the ever-increasing dole bill every week. The government issues IOUs. The Irish banks buy the IOUs, some of which they pay for with money the government already gave them through the national pension fund when it 'recapitalised' them. So already you can see that the State is using the money that is supposed to look after us in our dotage to finance spending today. It would be more honest (and less costly) if it just raided the fund for current spending.

The banks then take the government IOUs and pledge them as security to the ECB. The ECB lends the banks money and the new cash goes into the banks' balance sheets.

However, the ECB's huge bailout of the Irish banks is not tackling the underlying problem, which is that the Irish banks face—at the minimum—a €77 billion hole in their balance sheets from bad property loans, which are unlikely to be repaid. No matter how much the ECB lends to us, we can't get away from this fact.

The strategy of the Irish State and the ECB is to buy time in order to avoid liquidating our land holdings now in this frozen market. If we were to try to sell now, it would surely mean that all the banks in Ireland would collapse or have to be nationalised.

However, the success of the present policy rests on the long-term assumption that Ireland needs to experience another land boom in the not too distant future. Is this what we want? I don't believe so. We've had enough of the Merchant of Ennis and Shylock.

Let us examine what the government is up to. In the next few paragraphs we will stitch a thread between the ECB's ongoing bailout of the Irish banks and our government's policy on the ground and how Miss Pencil Skirt's job prospects are going to be affected by it.

At the moment, because there is so much recrimination and hostility towards the banks and the government, it is understandable that many of us are in danger of turning into taxi drivers at the back of the rank, ranting. Let's try to gain a bit of altitude to see the overall picture rather than focusing on just the bits that annoy us.

VIETNAMA

The government guarantee, which provides a blanket government promise to underwrite all loans made by the Irish banking system, was announced in September 2008. As someone who championed it and was involved closely with the Minister for Finance, I saw it as the only viable alternative to the total collapse of our banking system. I have little doubt that would have happened in the first week of October last year.

The guarantee has worked in the sense that it was designed as a short-term solution to prevent a mass movement of deposits out of the banking system. It was a containment policy.

However, in the past few months the government seems to have moved from the logical position of hoping to save what possibly looked like a good banking system to trying to save at all costs what we now know is a bad banking system.

At the time, the few people who were involved in the decision were aware that the guarantee, if abused, could lead to a situation where bad behaviour was rewarded. More problematically, by keeping bad banks alive, we could create a financial version of Frankenstein's monster. These Frankenbanks would turn into a black hole for the State's diminishing financial resources and, as in Mary Shelley's novel, our financial Frankenbanks could break free of their creator's control.

So it is crucial that the guarantee tail doesn't wag the banking dog. It should not be used—as I fear it is—to keep rotten banks open at all costs. Or, furthermore, it should not be used as a shield behind which investors in the bonds of these banks are bailed out.

We are in a catch-22 situation because as long as the guarantee remains in place, a bank default is technically an Irish government default by proxy. So the choice would appear to be very simple: either the guarantee elapses in September 2010 and is not extended as was the original intention or the ordinary Irish taxpayer pays for the past sins of the banking Mafia.

This was as clear in September 2008 as it is now. The original aim of the guarantee was to give the banks time to sort out their own balance sheets. Those banks that can't deal with their own mistakes should be placed in well-organised examinership. The guarantee should have been used to ensure that this happened in an orderly fashion without panic, allowing time for a new bank to be set up which would attract deposits and buy the assets of the old banks, such as a branch network. Who wouldn't put their deposits into such a new bank? Instead of this logical approach, where deposits are guaranteed and the creditors of the banks pay for their own mistakes, the Mafia got to the politicians again.

In the months following the granting of the guarantee, the debate focused on the idea of a financial skip into which we would throw all the bad loans and dreadful mistakes of the past decade. Either we could have announced a fire-sale or got the banks to pay for the cost of the skip from their income. Crucially, the taxpayer was to be placed as far away from the skip as possible.

Suddenly this perfectly plausible plan was replaced by a bizarre initiative to lumber the ordinary man on the street with the sins of our bankers and developers. The very poor were instructed to bail out the very rich.

No country has ever done anything like this—this is not the Swedish model, the Swiss model, the US approach or the Asian or Latin American approach. It is a unique Irish model, conceived in Dublin to protect the vested interests and, as it happens, the ECB.

This Orwellian creation—NAMA—is designed to take the bad assets away from the Irish banks so that they can survive this crisis without suffering the ramifications of their own stupidity or greed. That's it in a nutshell.

This is the second pillar of the ECB's Vietnamese strategy. The Irish banks have admitted that €77 billion of loans to developers are now underwater. Remember the ghost estates and the empty retail park from Chapter 4? These are what we are talking about when we say development loans. And worse still, think about all the land, now fit only for grazing cattle, that was bought for millions and millions of euros by developers who were going to build new estates for the growing population. These estates will never be built. The debt still stands, but the land is almost worthless.

Think of the 'portfolio' of the Merchant of Ennis. All the property he bought on behalf of his clients back home, all financed by Shylock, will end up in the financial skip that is NAMA.

The State—that means you and me—will buy this toxic waste from the banks and, in return, the Irish government will issue them with Irish government bonds. The most important thing here is the price which the State pays for this crud. This is called the 'haircut' in the vernacular. The 'haircut' is the difference between what the State is prepared to pay for this trash and what the banks paid for it in the first place.

The government has invented another Orwellian concept called the 'long-term economic value' of land and has decided that we will pay somewhere between the current market value and the projected long-term value of land. This is based on the twin assumptions that we are now at the bottom so that today's price constitutes the floor and that the price of land always goes up. But neither of these is guaranteed; in fact, the floor could still be a long way down and the recovery could be anaemic. Your money will plug the gap.

We, the taxpayers, are getting a bad deal. The more we pay, the less the banks will pay for their stupidity. The Irish government seems to think that there are only two options: either the old discredited Irish banks continue as private banks or the old discredited Irish banks continue as nationalised banks. But why should they exist at all?

What is really odd is that the Minister for Finance appears to have allied the interests of the Irish State with the interests of the Irish banks and the financial institutions that gambled on them. Why?

CUI BONO?

Let us plough on with the logic of NAMA to show you the hand of the ECB in this initiative and how it is all part of the domino theory. And more crucially, how very powerful interests both at the top of the banks and the top of the Civil Service are beneficiaries of NAMA. We also have to appreciate that the powerful vested interests have managed to transfer all the risk and all the repercussions of their smash-and-grab property escapade onto the average Joe.

Having used the State as a money-recycling operation, the Irish financial elite has just pulled another monumental stroke.

Let's examine how it intends to get away with this.

Given our precarious financial position, very few investors would be prepared to buy Irish government bonds that were simply backed by the hope that Irish land might go up in value over the next 10 years. So for NAMA to fly and for the Irish banks to have a chance of surviving, the government has gone to the ECB for more credit. The ECB obliged, not surprisingly.

NAMA is the sweet spot where the short-term interests of the Irish government, the financial oligarchy and the top of the civil service overlap with the long-term interests of the ECB.

Once we see NAMA as a vehicle for the preservation of the banks and the financial oligarchy that still, despite the mess they have got us into, have a huge influence on how the country is run, things become much clearer.

So this is how the next chapter of Europe's Vietnam will work: The State buys the land portfolio of the banks. In return it gives the banks Irish government bonds which no one in their right mind would touch. So the banks rock up to the ECB and change these bonds into money.

This is supposed to recapitalise the banks without the government injecting more capital into them. This is a crucial part of the plan because if the government was to inject more money into the banks in return for shares, the State would then become the majority share-holder and then the banks would be nationalised. The State is against this for ideological reasons, believing that once you nationalise your banking system, you join the great unwashed of failed financial entities.

It might also have something to do with the fact that the financial oligarchy don't want this to happen, because the Irish pension funds would lose money and the Irish stock market would disappear as a business since the banks are a huge part of the index. So it is not in the oligarchy's best interests.

16 SEPTEMBER 2009

On Thursday, 9 September 2009—the day the Green Party leadership announced that they would back NAMA with some minor amendm-ents—the share price of Bank of Ireland rose by 10 per cent. The shares rose again by 9 per cent on Friday, 10 September. What more evidence did we need that this travesty will result in a direct transfer of wealth from the taxpayers of Ireland to the shareholders of Bank of Ireland?

The markets knew straightaway, once the Greens were on-side, that the banks, the Dons and the Shylocks had been given their 'get out of jail' card. This is why the share price was rising. The taxpayers would take the rotten stuff and the shareholders, who in every other banking rescue plan—particularly the Swedish plan—had been wiped out, were getting a free lunch. For many small shareholders who had seen their life's savings wiped out by the reckless activity of the Dons and the

Godfather, it might not seem that way. But unfortunately it is. It must be cold comfort to know that in any other country, such a banking investment would have disappeared in total.

On Wednesday, 16 September a defiant Minister stood up in the Dáil to mortgage the future of the Pope's Children. This was precisely a year to the day since a traumatised Brian Lenihan knocked on my door in the dead of night clutching a copy of the *Irish Independent*. That night, neither of us knew it would come to this. In fact, the bank guarantee was supposed to avoid this outcome. But the Establishment had got to the politicians yet again.

The government will buy up €77 billion of property loans, for which it will pay €54 billion but even the Minister admitted that the value of the loans now was only €47 billion. The haircut was 21 per cent, as widely expected, even though in previous boom/bust scenarios, such as in Japan in the 1990s, commercial land prices fell by over 70 per cent from peak to trough. This implies that the government is already paying over the odds for the assets because the market hasn't reached anywhere near the bottom.

Immediately, stockbrokers in Dublin scribbled congratulatory notes to clients and the financial establishment knew that they were off the hook and we, the people, were up the swanney. If you were in any doubt about who is going to win from this, the share prices of Bank of Ireland and AIB rose by over 25 per cent in New York on the night NAMA was announced.

So the Pope's Children, people like Miss Pencil Skirt, our golden generation that was supposed to inherit the country, have been lumbered with the greatest debt legacy of any people in Europe.

As a result of NAMA, they have been shafted four times. First, they were railroaded into paying huge prices for houses and in the process they transferred vast wealth to developers and bankers. This monumental transfer of money was supported in every way possible by the same politicians who are now bailing out the banks. Now these houses are in negative equity. And, there is no NAMA for ordinary people, just for the big guys.

Second, the taxes of the Pope's Children will be increased, not to pay for hospitals and schools for their children, but to pay for the burgeoning national debt that will result from NAMA and cleaning up the mess made by the Dons in their turf war with the Godfather.

Third, they will pay for the bank levy. The government say that at the end of NAMA when the 'ghost estates' and development land is still on the books of NAMA, the banks will pay for these remaining debts via a levy. But who do they think will pay for this levy? The banks' customers—people like Fin Boy and Miss Pencil Skirt—of course, in the form of higher banking charges. And of course, part of the NAMA subtext is to have just two big banks standing at the end of all this. Therefore, without competition in the sector, there will be nowhere to hide from these charges.

Fourth, as the NAMA plan hinges on reflating the property market, the Pope's Children will not even have the comfort of lower land costs in the future which might make their generation more competitive in the international market in the years ahead.

Extraordinary.

BADLANDS

So when you examine who pays for this complicated arrangement, it becomes clear that the Irish taxpayer is on the hook. The government's plan is based on the idea that if it holds the bad land long enough, it will become good. Maybe now, rather than just trust the people who presided over this mess, we should have a stab at what the future Irish housing market might look like.

If the government is so sure that if it holds the land long enough it will go back up in value, what financial models is it working from? Equally, if the State through NAMA is starting to buy land now, it must be sure that we are at the bottom, or at least close to it.

Before we do a little calculation, it might be worth considering that when people get burned on houses, when the apartment we bought as an investment becomes loss-making, we tend to operate on the 'once bitten, twice shy' basis. Like the Japanese, we tend to become 'homophobic'. When we've lost money, for a while at least, we say never again. We'll invest in anything but houses. This phenomenon tends to make the recession in the housing market more drawn out than it might otherwise be.

But let's just see how low, in the context of rising unemployment, rising taxes and a credit crunch, Irish house prices will go. To establish this, we need to figure out what a house is worth.

As well as a place to live, a house is also a simple investment and should be valued according to some financial benchmark. A way to value a house as an investment is to look at the rate of return you get from the rent as a rate of interest or a dividend. So let's say you can get an interest rate of 4 per cent for a decent deposit in AIB or, more to the point, you can borrow money from Bank of Ireland at 5 per cent, then you'd only invest in something like a house with all the hassle it incurs if the interest rate you get is at least 7 per cent a year. Many would suggest a return of 10 per cent is necessary to cover the trouble and the risk but, for the sake of charity, let's stick with a minimum interest rate of 7 per cent.

In America—where they have had booms and busts in every generation—the way houses are valued is based on this 7 per cent yield idea. The long-term price of a house is considered to be equal to 14 times the annual rent the place can generate (100 divided by 7 = 14). Using this valuation, what is the right price for Irish houses?

So, let's go back to Chapter 4 and our ghost estates. Pick a typical ghost estate area such as Oranmore in Galway. If you go on Daft.ie you will find all the answers. If you want to buy a three-bed semi in Oranmore, it will set you back €335,000. However, you can rent the same place for €800 a month. What's more, there are 75 vacant three-bed semis in Oranmore advertised on Daft.ie alone.

Using the above valuation method, it implies that the house generates rent of €9,600 for the owner and so the house is worth 14 times that, which gives us a value of €134,400. Yet the seller is asking €335,000 for it!

In other words, to make it worth your while buying the house, the price would need to be about half of what it is now. We have to assume that the days of large capital gains on houses are over. Therefore, the average Irish house in these estates is likely to fall by anywhere between 50 per cent and 60 per cent in the next few years. And even that is assuming that prices don't undershoot on the downside the way they overshot on the upside.

This is a tragedy for the people who own the properties, and for us, because, ultimately, many of these shells will find their way into NAMA.

So you see why we should be worried about the ability of NAMA to get the price right. We are still a long way from the bottom of the property market and the State thinks it should be using today's price as a floor.

As for the presumption that house prices will inevitably rise, we have many examples from history where house prices simply didn't recover. This is important because NAMA is based entirely on land price reflation. We would be wise to consider the fate of Mountjoy Square in Dublin. When the square was built, it was the height of Georgian chic and the elegant townhouses sold for £8,000 in 1791. After the Act of Union in 1801, their price had fallen to £2,500. By 1850, these houses were lucky to sell for £500.

The obvious counter to this example is that the Famine drove prices down but, over the survey period, the population of Dublin actually doubled between 1800 (200,000) and 1852 (405,000). It even showed an increase during the Famine (probably the only part of the country to do so) from 372,000 in 1841 to 405,000 in 1851.

So we can't even claim that the so-called 'fundamentals' such as demography were going against house prices. The lesson from Mountjoy Square is straightforward: house and land prices can fall for a long, long time as well as rise.

But the State, in an effort to protect the usual suspects, thinks that house prices will rise again and we'll have, if not quite another boom, house price inflation over and above the rate of wage growth and the rate of interest.

If this NAMA—which is really a State-owned land company—holds the land long enough and we have another land boom, the taxpayer will sell the bad land back to ourselves.

So in other words, rather then learn from the mistakes of the past 10 years, we are setting up a solution which is based on repeating exactly the same travesty. To do this, the ordinary taxpayer will be hijacked again to keep the Mafia in business. NAMA guarantees that a new generation of the likes of the Merchant of Ennis and Shylock hoodwink a new generation of Miss Pencil Skirts.

Surely this is precisely what we want to avoid? We should be saying never again rather than predicating our solution on a bigger version of the problem that got us into the crisis.

The Mafia stays in charge, the top civil servants don't have to worry about the ignominy of being regarded as an embarrassment in Europe and it's all paid for by the taxpayer, yet again.

It's a nice stroke and, in the process, the opportunity it lost. Instead of using the crisis to turn our country into a vibrant economy with hope for the future, we succeed in creating a debt-servicing machine where taxes are raised to pay the interest on debts to keep our banks open and our masters happy.

There must be an alternative.

Chapter 18 ∿

IRELAND AND THE WORLD

IRELAND AND THE WORLD

In trying to understand what happens next in Ireland, it is not enough to say that all the bankers are crooks or that all politicians are in their pockets or the Regulator was the worst public servant visited on Ireland since Trevelyan. All three might be true but that won't get us back on track.

To understand how we are going to get out of this mess, we need to put our story in an international context. Ireland is not the first country to have got itself into a bind like this, nor will it be the last. However, it is crucial that we get out of this as quickly as possible without any unnecessarily prolonged suffering. It is also essential that we change Ireland in such a way that this lamentable episode never happens again. This means changing the way we think and changing the people who believe they do our thinking for us. Do we have the guts to change our thinking and do something we've never done before?

Let's see what the road map for recovery looks like in Ireland. What are the chances that Ireland can recover reasonably quickly without defaulting on our debts internationally? As the most indebted people in the world, this will be difficult. Can we, as one society, pull through this together, without one section of our people feeling left behind? There is much more to this than finance and economics. Up until now, the people have been very tolerant, in spite of unemployment moving way into double digits.

The last thing we need to see is unemployed young lads in 'Celtic shirts' on the streets rioting with the Guards or large swathes of our suburbs becoming lawless as people give up hope and turn to violence. But equally the last thing we need is to have a society that feels this way because of a perception that the lads at the top got away with it again.

Another risk—which we've never had before—is that the immigrant population becomes the target of disaffection, as has happened in many continental countries. What about young people—a percentage of the first-time buyers who are now in negative equity—simply walking away from their debts and their homes and deciding that there is no point in paying for a house that will never be worth what they paid for it, particularly when they can rent more cheaply down the road?

There is a direct link between all these risks, because as unemployment rises so too will social welfare bills. To square this the State will have to raise taxes, which makes employing people more expensive and causes more layoffs. This means the cycle starts again at a higher level of joblessness.

In addition, the more layoffs, the more defaults we will experience as the national loan book unravels and defaults move from the developers' loan books to private houses, credit card bills, car finance and right across the board.

Ireland has always had the safety valve of emigration. This is now not a viable option for the thousands of people who are lining up every week in dole offices all around the country. The USA is experiencing 9 per cent unemployment,[1] likewise the UK, and although Australia has missed out on much of the worst of the downturn there is only so much it can take.

On an individual and emotional level, we are flirting with a national catastrophe because the boom created an expectation amongst many people about what Ireland could deliver. It was a place of hope, of achievement. For the first time in our history, Irish people could stay at home and live the sort of life that in the past we could have lived only in Connecticut or Massachusetts. OK, so Dollymount was never quite Hyannis Port, but you get the picture.

Significantly, for the past 10 years, Ireland and the Irish lived in the future rather than the past. In many ways we became more American, trying things out and being less hung up about failure and more optimistic about our lives and those of the people around us. The boom was infectious. It is very fashionable now to talk about how we blew the boom, but there will be some lasting positive legacies.

For example, the Left can point to an unemployment benefit system that is far more generous than almost anywhere in Europe. The Right can point to labour flexibility and tax support for investment. Conservatives still have the protection of the family in the Constitution, while Liberals have gay rights. Conservationists have An Taisce, and developers—those that are left—have fast-tracking systems. There are more people in education than ever before. But there are still lamentable deficiencies. Drive past Mountrath and see the roads for yourself.

The problem is that when you have soared so high, to fall can be difficult to come to terms with. We are already seeing a marked increase in the use of anti-depressants and the worst thing for the nation would be to lose hope.

Nations do lose hope. Sometimes the trauma of the comedown is so significant that people just give up. Anyone who has travelled in certain parts of Eastern Europe has seen what it is like when a country becomes dysfunctional, when people are disenfranchised and isolated.

Although the money seems to have evaporated overnight, foreign investors will come back. They always do. They'll be back once they see that Ireland has changed and changed for good. If the road to recovery is based on protecting those who got us into this mess, no new money will materialise. This very lack of change at the top and lack of a new direction is precisely why the present policy of protecting the banks through NAMA and shafting the taxpayer is not the right thing to do. The financial markets understand this. The market has no interest in Ireland failing. In fact, the opposite is the case. The foreign investors want to see a policy that maximises Ireland's strength, because this is how they will make money here. So let's get inside the head of a trader to see what he thinks. Once we understand this, we can start to piece the new jigsaw together.

INSIDE THE HEAD OF A TRADER

I was first really made aware of a trader's way of looking at the world in 1997 when I attended the annual IMF jamboree in Hong Kong. Back then, Hong Kong was on the precipice, with both the good and the bad sides of globalisation on display. There was also the little issue of the island being handed back to China and the memories of Tiananmen Square were still fresh in the minds of the locals. So to say the place was a little tense would be an understatement.

This was the era of the three 't's—the things you couldn't talk about publicly in China—Tiananmen, Tibet and Taiwan. (Now there is a fourth 't' that is unmentionable in China—Treasury bills.)

There was a palpable fear on the part of many people that they would be smothered by mainland communism—a fear that wasn't without justification at the time. Although Deng Xiaoping had said that he wanted two systems in one country and indeed had gone so far a decade earlier as saying that 'to be rich is glorious', the collective memory in Hong Kong of students being crushed by tanks and, a decade or so earlier, the Cultural Revolution, more than outweighed soothing words from Beijing.

The second issue on the minds of the IMF delegates was the Asian Crisis that was swirling like a tempest around the region. Hong Kong was in the eye of the storm that had already brought down the Tiger economies of Korea, Thailand, Malaysia and Indonesia.

While there was the feeling that Asia would be the clear beneficiary of globalisation largely because of its manufacturing potential, its abundant supply of cheap labour and the fact that the IMF was presiding over the spread of globalisation all over the world, this was the era of Clinton's apparently unbeatable America. It was the world's only superpower. Alan Greenspan bestrode the globe lecturing on the need for less and less regulation. He was at the top table with Bill and Hillary, and the Wall Street takeover of Washington's politics was complete when the consummate Wall Street insider Bob Rubin was installed as Treasury Secretary.

This triumphalist American swagger dominated the meeting, so much so that the Asian economies that were being battered by the financial markets were regarded by the Americans as 'crony capitalists', who were being found out by the laserlike purity of free capital movements. That story was an easy one to tell but it was not wholly accurate.

No one reminded those who were chastising the Thais, Koreans and Malaysians that two years previously the same people were holding up the Asian Tigers as a model of how to do things.

The interesting thing for us Irish observers of Hong Kong is that it is our role model now. It is the only country to have ever been successful in dealing with a massive property bust and a decrepit banking system without devaluing its currency.

If our government's policy is to have a sliver of a chance of working, we have to out-Hong Kong Hong Kong.

In this forgetful world, the Russian delegation was the most over the top. I was there to talk to the Russians who, in typical Russian oligarch style, travelled over in private jets and stayed at the finest hotels. One of the stockbrokers even brought a live bear and paraded it round their outrageous party at the China Club. Not until the Irish developers and their banker backers invaded Cheltenham in 2006, in a display of helicopter firepower that matched the opening scene of *Apocalypse Now*, was so much opulence splashed around so carelessly again.

The Russians, full of self-confident bravado, had no idea what was in store for them less than 10 months later. Nor did I, even though I was supposed to be the expert on Russia for Banque Nationale de Paris.

But one man I met understood and enlightened me. He is still a very successful fund manager based in Hong Kong. We were in a bar, late at night. Ken Clarke, the former British Chancellor, was regaling the table with hilarious stories about Black Wednesday and the chaos at the top of the British political system that day. Most notably, he painted a picture of just how out of touch the Cabinet was with events in the financial markets.

Clarke explained how he, then Home Secretary, John Major, the Prime Minister, and Norman Lamont, the Chancellor—the three most important politicians in the UK—had to resort to a transistor radio tuned into BBC Radio 4 in the kitchen of Number 10 for information on what was happening to sterling on a minute-by-minute basis. The picture of the three of them huddled around the wireless while, outside, the entire cornerstone of British economic policy was collapsing is a wonderfully poignant vignette.

Clarke, of course, was putting his finger, in his jocular, accessible style, on the nub of the issue. Politicians and the power of national institutions count for nothing when money is allowed to flow freely all around the world. Events in far-off places have massive ramifications for people and countries that appear to be totally unrelated.

Ultimately in a crisis, the end game is always the same: massive capital flight and the destruction of the national balance sheet as all the borrowings that made the country look so strong can no longer be rolled over.

The fund manager understood what was going on during the Asian Crisis and also twigged that Russia would be the next to go. He explained to me in very simple terms why he was going to sell his Russian assets to cover the losses he had suffered in Thailand. The fact that Thailand and Russia had nothing to do with each other economically, which is what all the experts on CNN were saying to assuage people's fears about the viability of Russia, didn't matter to him.

He not only thought like a trader but his balance sheet dictated his moves. He needed cash every time he faced a loss somewhere because he had bought everything on what is called 'margin'.

This means that he borrowed the cash to buy all his assets. If the price of the assets fell below a certain level, he was penalised by what was termed a 'margin call'. This means the banks that lent him the money to buy the assets wanted more security as, obviously, the riskiness of the loan increased. If the banks were taking the stocks he owns as collateral, he needed to provide them with either more collateral or more cash.

And when financial markets panic, the only asset that everyone wants is cash. Therefore, the trader needs to sell what he can to cover the margin call or he will be in default. So he sells what he can.

In the boom the opposite applies. When the markets are going up, all the collateral looks brilliant. It more than covers the money lent against it. In good times, if the banks were to ask the trader to sell the asset there would be more than enough cash to pay the banks, give the trader a healthy profit and cover the bar bill at the Four Seasons. In the Mania, the banks lend more and more and the trader takes bigger and bigger bets with someone else's money.

When the tipping point comes, the trader and the banks panic and all loans are withdrawn. This has a knock-on effect because the banks also lend to each other. So the banks become worried about the creditworthiness of other banks and they stop trusting each other. In fact, the worldwide boom became so crazy that banks no longer trusted themselves—one department of a bank mistrusted another. In Ireland, the credit departments that keep an eye on loans ceased to trust the sales departments that made the loans in the first place.

By then it is too late. The damage is already done.

This is when a crisis turns into a rout because the banks stop lending to each other. They are all scared that the collateral the other banks claim they have to cover the loans is contaminated. This is when banks begin the painful process of going bust.

Once the banks get into difficulties, the country gets into difficulty. Investors think, *Wait a second, if the banks can't pay back their loan, then the next stop is a country wobble.* Money leaves the country. Both local investors and foreign investors flee.

All financial crises follow the same pattern, more or less. One similarity between Ireland and emerging nations in Asia and Latin America is the proximity of the oligarch class to the government. In many ways, although part of the European Union, Ireland behaves more like an emerging market. There is no shame in this; when you look at the similarities between the crises in Mexico in 1994, Asia in 1997, Russia in 1998 and Argentina in 2001, there are many parallels with Ireland.

But this doesn't mean that we are a backward nation. In fact, many observers have said that the US is experiencing something like a Latin American style emerging markets crisis. By this they mean the banking industry holds enormous power in the American government. They highlight the Washington–Wall Street corridor as the real power nexus in the US. The way in which even the left-leaning Obama administration moved to prop up the banking system bears this out.

In what are termed 'banana republics' of Central America, the power brokers are the banana producers. In the US, the brokers are the Wall Street establishment. In Russia, the oligarchs are the oil barons, and in Ireland, we know who they were—the property/banking cabal.

Because of their proximity to the political parties, these interests tend to get legislation changed so that it advances their interests, which they dress up as the national interest or some other phoney ideology.

Every boom starts with an event that changes the way investors perceive a country. This can be political, as it was with us when we joined the EMU, or the deregulation of the financial industry in the US or the rise in oil prices in Russia.

Once a country opens itself up to free movement of capital, a virtuous but ultimately unstable cycle kicks off. Because of the event change, the returns in a certain sector begin to look very attractive. Take the tax shelters for car parks in Ireland. The change in legislation resulted in funds being channelled into that particular sector. Tax changes do that sort of thing.

So money floods into the country. This pushes up the return on the assets that are in favour. If the country has its own exchange rate, this usually rises. In all cases, inflation rises and this should be an early warning sign to everyone. When, for example, did Irish people start to have conversations about how cheap it is on the Continent, particularly in Spain? A few years ago, maybe around 2000.

These conversations are the most obvious manifestation of our inflation rate rising way above that of our neighbours. If you can get fed and sloshed in Spain for a third of the price you would in Cork, then Cork has a competitiveness problem.

But as the cash flows in, you don't see it. The local oligarchs become arrogant. As the saying on Wall Street warns, 'don't confuse brains with a bull market'. In other emerging markets, the local banking system organises huge amounts of foreign currency loans. Take the example of Iceland, which I visited a few months back. The taxi driver who picked me up at the station, as well as having an encyclopaedic knowledge of Michael Collins, had a mortgage that was denominated in yen of all currencies! He said that so huge was the interest rate difference between the Japanese yen and the local currency, the Icelandic krona (one of the few currencies that Thomas Cook refused to take from me at Heathrow), that it was worth taking out his mortgage in Reykjavik in a currency of a country he knew nothing about. But he didn't worry, because everyone told him there was no serious exchange rate risk and that which existed could be hedged by taking out an insurance policy with one of the local banks.

Iceland behaved the way most emerging markets do. The Thais, the Koreans and the Malays were all at the same game. They borrowed huge amounts in foreign currency to chase the boom at home.

As someone who arranged these loans to be made to Russia at around the same time, labouring away in the dream world that is investment banking, I know the process is pretty straightforward. The country that begins to boom becomes flavour of the month. *The Economist* writes nice things about it. The local oligarchs see a potential wall of money ready to come into the country. This means everything they own will suddenly go up massively in value, so they arrange a huge loan either for their companies or their banks or they agitate for the State to do likewise to fund a toll bridge which they will build. The investment bank places all the IOUs with pensions funds and investors around the world, and we're off.

In the Irish case, as we've seen from our gangster analogy, we borrowed from everyone everywhere using the cloak of the euro to make legitimate what was a roll of the dice on a crowded roulette table.

Normally things fly along for a while, but typically what happens is that the very profitable aspects of the initial part of the boom, such as productivity, ebb away as we all start going out too late, heading to our favourite sushi restaurant and using the borrowed money to snap up the latest Christian Louboutin red-soled killer heels.

But all is well, because liquidity is plentiful. During this period, in Russia for example, Moscow became the most expensive city in Europe, possibly in the world. In Hong Kong, everyone invested wildly in property all the way up to the crash of 1997. Malaysia completed the tallest building in the world and in Dublin an acre of land was going for €70 million. What is already frenetic becomes a Mania as the banks get into leverage, lending to anyone for anything. All the while, the oligarchs are closer and closer to the government and the assumption is that if something goes wrong, they will be too big to fail, too politically important to be let go.

This insidious process takes time and in most countries it comes with its own idiosyncratic national frills. In Ireland our own peculiarity was the tent at the Galway Races; in Russia it was the national football team that bonded the top brass together. In fact, some sport or other is always bound up in the cosy cartel. In Ireland, as well as the races, golf seemed to host an inordinate number of business meetings and discussions.

But when things start to get a little tricky, money begins to leave. In most countries with exchange rates, there is pressure on the exchange rate. The financial markets—with the attention span of a gnat—go from loving the country or the company to believing nothing that comes out of the mouth of anyone in the place. We saw this type of behaviour with, for example, the Irish banks, the Russian commodities companies and the Icelandic and Thai currencies. Whatever can be sold is sold. This becomes a self-reinforcing downward spiral as everyone panics and goes to cash.

Then the technology kicks in. Because everyone is on Bloomberg, the internet and even Twitter, there is nowhere for the misfortunate country or company to hide. Rumours beget rumours and the herd begins to stampede, driven by the cacophony of 24/7 instant communication.

Think back to our trader and his leverage dilemma. You'll remember that when he sold, it was not because he wanted to but because he needed the cash.

This is how the financial world that we live in works. And like it or not, we now have to do something to make this money come back to Ireland. We have to be open for business but that means doing something to encourage investors to invest here. This means doing something that makes the economy grow as quickly as possible in a way that employs the most people but also makes the economy stronger.

Successful countries that have weathered the storms of recession have tended to tear up the script and start again. This liberates people but also sends a signal to the rest of the world that the country is on the move again and going in the right direction.

If we go back to the old policies, the financial markets will see through us and we will suffer a longer recession than we have to. The way out is not to turn in on ourselves but to be open and regard the financial markets as our allies, not our enemies in this crusade. There is always new money looking for a home. Sometimes it is the same money that left the country, sometimes it is different, but it is always available to us, if we do the right thing.

The trader, sitting in cash, who wants to reinvest in Ireland, needs a sign that the cowboys like the Shylocks of this world are gone and the real Ireland, the country with an open, enthusiastic, young educated population like Miss Pencil Skirt, is firmly back in control.

Why wouldn't he want to back this country? Why wouldn't he want to share in our reinvention and success? We've got to make it easy for ourselves by making it easy for him. The choice is ours.

Chapter 19 ～

THE ALTERNATIVE

The little boy cycled as fast as he could. He couldn't wait to tell his dad that he had saved the penalty and now Cabinteely Boys would be in the under-10s final against Cherry Orchard. He didn't really know how he did it. He just dived to the left and the ball seemed to hit his hand. It was really sore, because the big lad from the other team had blasted it and his fingers were frozen as he had left his gloves at home. Later on, the lads said he looked like Paddy Roche who played for Man Utd. The little boy remembered the team running to him and hugging him.

He was nearly home now. He was past Baker's Corner in the rain and his trousers were soaked but it was all downhill from here, down Abbey Road, past TEK and on home. His dad always told him to be careful at the roundabout and, if the tinkers had their caravans on it, which they did every spring, to keep away from them.

He looked down at the speedometer. It was straining to touch 16 miles an hour. He pedalled furiously and wondered at this speed how long it would take him to cycle to Granny's. A day? Two days? He'd take the dog with him. He never went anywhere without the dog. They could sleep in a tent or a caravan like the tinkers somewhere down the country.

This was the first game his dad had missed all season, but Mum said that his dad had an important meeting with someone special. The little boy thought that he was probably going to that strange place in town again—the place with the funny women and their prams piled high with clothes and all the hundreds of skinny children. His dad went there every week to give a parcel to his friend who had lots of friends and they all queued up to give him something. He must have lots of things by now, the man at the top of the queue whom they all went to see.

He started talking as soon as his mother opened the door, telling her how he'd saved the penalty and how the team hugged him and he didn't really see the ball at all but he didn't let on to anyone, just her. She smiled at him as he gasped for breath to get out the next bit of the story as if he feared that if he stopped, he'd lose her attention. He didn't know that would never happen.

When he finally looked up at her in the kitchen, she seemed very happy. Why wouldn't she be? He had saved the penalty after all! She was laughing. She didn't laugh much lately. She said that his dad had some special news, really, really good news. His dad was in the back garden feeding the dog who was supposed to be called Johan after Johan Cruyff but, as no one on the road could pronounce Johan correctly, the dog was called Bruno.

The father waved to the boy who started to tell him about the penalty and the dive and how he'd play Cherry Orchard in the final and how his team had already beaten them in the league.

He told the boy he was sorry he missed the game. He was laughing too and as they came into the kitchen he said that he had got a new job, a real one. The boy was disappointed because he wouldn't drive behind him to school in the mornings any more and he had forgotten what it was like before his dad went to school with him. It must've been ages ago, even before Liverpool started winning everything and Leeds started losing everything.

His dad said he would be going to some place called Sutton, which was miles away but you could see it from the end of Dun Laoghaire pier and that he would have to work very hard. They were both delighted and so was the boy after his dad promised that he could still drive behind him to school for another few weeks.

It was nice to see my mother laughing again.

THE WAY OUT

Unemployment changes families. It is far more than an economic problem; it affects everything. Today, all over our country, people who have just been laid off are stressed out, depressed and losing hope. They don't know what to do and realise that the piles of rejection letters will get higher and higher as the recession gets deeper and deeper.

The extraordinary thing is that much of this suffering can be ameliorated. There is an obvious way out of this economic downturn, which is based on sound economic theory and empirical evidence from all over the world. It ensures a rapid return to growth and is the most likely path to reduced unemployment. Like all policy changes, it is not painless and there will be risks and some losers, but it has worked time and again throughout the world.

In contrast, the government's current approach to getting out of the depression will definitely make things worse. We are told there is no alternative to slashing government spending, raising taxes and injecting billions into bankrupt banks. We are also told that there is no alternative to mortgaging the next generation via NAMA to clean up the mess made by a tiny minority of the present generation.

How do I put this politely? The present government's policy is as perverted now as it was in the boom. These are the people who got us into this mess and they are intent on saving their own skins and those of their friends in the banks.

Our government's policy is not based on any economic theory at all. Worse still, it is not based on any successful empirical evidence from any comparable economy anywhere in the world. Tellingly, many of the mainstream economists and commentators—who now broadly support the government's policy of spending billions to keep the banks afloat and cutting back spending on schools and hospitals to balance the books—are the very same people who told you two years ago that Ireland would experience a 'soft landing'. These people didn't have the foresight to see the crash coming back then and they don't have the foresight to realise that now we must dramatically change policy.

The only thing that will save us is a rapid return to economic growth and this has to be the aim of policy. We have to do everything we can to make sure that people stay in jobs, that there is opportunity for the next generation and that Ireland recovers its hope and our belief in the future.

INSIDERS AND OUTSIDERS

In thinking about alternatives and what we can do in Ireland in the next two years to get the economy moving again, we have to start with a blank sheet of paper. What do we want to achieve, how can we do it and what would it entail? It's not good enough to say we can't do this or we can't do that because of prior commitments. We need to entertain, as T. K. Whitaker did in 1959, tearing up the script and starting afresh.

We have to be proactive. It is not good enough just to sit tight and wait for a global upswing as appears to be the default position of many of our Establishment. You will have heard the spin over the past few months about how the world is in a mess and we will just have to wait to be dragged out by the global upswing. Let us remind ourselves that we are perfectly capable of languishing while the rest of the world recovers. In the 1980s, when the world was booming, Ireland, due to its own appalling economic management, stayed in the doldrums. In the 1950s, when the world experienced a post-war boom, Ireland imploded with over half a million people emigrating to Britain alone.

We should also note that it was after these two crises that we saw dramatic policy changes in Ireland. These changes, particularly the T. K. Whitaker blueprint written in the depth of the 1950s crisis, reveal that all crises are opportunities. This one is no different. Let's not blow the bust as well as blowing the boom.

As an economy that faces bankruptcy, meaning our financial system could not survive on its own if it had to tomorrow, we have to ask ourselves if we want a short sharp shock, which is traumatic but not prolonged. We would all take a hit to our living standards, but we could be out the far side and competitive, creating jobs for the likes of Miss Pencil Skirt and Fin Boy again in a few months. Alternatively, we can do this the hard way and prolong the downturn by trying to keep the old banks, the old system and, ultimately, the old Establishment alive. This means postponing the day of reckoning and lumbering the next generation with the sins of the present one. It also implies that we will not seize the opportunity for real change, which this crisis presents.

Traditionally in Ireland, crises tend to play out in a predictable way. The country splits between insiders and outsiders. The insiders are the Establishment, the professional classes, the broad public sector and those who work for large secure corporations. They include the media, marketing and the professional service sectors. In a crisis, like the 1980s, they become poor versions of the European middle classes, taxed heavily but ultimately still with a stake in our society. They have a decent network and the old Irish gelling agent of 'pull' and 'who you know' prevents them from slipping precipitously downwards in the recession.

In contrast, the outsiders include the poorly educated, the un-connected small business people, startup entrepreneurs, the young and the unemployed. These people tend not to have a strong foothold in society and many tens of thousands emigrate. The insider/outsider dilemma in Ireland is not solely a class issue and it would be wrong to see it as this. For example, many of Ireland's emigrants in the 1980s were considerably more educated than those who stayed behind. Emigration amongst graduates, as a proportion of total, was actually higher than among the general population.

Insiders have too much to lose by leaving. Outsiders are the opposite; they have nothing to lose by heading off and not much to gain from hanging around. The poorer outsiders become the long-term unemployed. The insider/outsider phenomenon comes down to how significant your stake is in our society.

We saw in the 1950s and again in the 1980s the way society splits. The insiders protect what they have on the basis that it's better to have a bit of a shrinking pie than have no pie at all. Typically, the way they protect their position is by keeping the outsiders out.

As the recession gets worse, this insider/outsider divide will become more obvious.

The insider/outsider concept also explains why there is rarely the same urgency in Irish policy making that we see elsewhere. At all costs the aim of policy is to postpone the problem and buy time, hoping something will turn up. Many years ago, when I worked in the Central Bank, it was referred to as the 'don't frighten the horses' approach to decision making. The politicians and the circus around them of mates and quangos have too much to lose by confronting problems head on. Someone they know might get hurt in the collision.

This is the reason so many 'serious' people in Ireland, be they commentators, bankers, advisors or politicians, eschew tackling big problems immediately. They are too protected by the status quo. So Ireland is paralysed, dazzled in the face of a challenge.

However, countries that are serious about sorting out their problems tend to move swiftly. For example, in Sweden's banking crisis of 1992, it issued a blanket guarantee, devalued its currency and nationalised its banks—all in five months. In these type of countries, the State acts with all the power a sovereign government has, to do what is best for all the people, not just those on the inside. This sometimes leads to organised bank receiverships, currency changes and unpalatable consequences for insiders. But ultimately, such bold moves benefit the whole society.

THE TWO-HANDED POLICY MAKER

Economic policy in most sovereign countries has two arms. One arm is fiscal or budgetary policy. The first thing a government can do in a crisis like this is increase spending to cushion the blow internally. The second arm is what is called monetary policy. This involves printing money, issuing currency to kick life back into the economy. There are few economic dilemmas that can't be solved by new money. And especially if people are afraid to spend because they feel prices are falling and will be lower again tomorrow, the State can create inflation by printing money. This will push up prices and prompt people to spend, because they'll believe that prices are on the way back up again so you'll get a bargain by spending today rather than waiting till tomorrow. Externally, printing money at home pushes down the exchange rate, which makes exports cheaper and imports dearer. This is a shot in the arm for the exporting sector, raising the returns in the exporting sector and causing investment in the exporting sector to increase dramatically. Of course, Ireland has no monetary policy, being a member of the euro.

Without exchange rate freedom, a country's government becomes a one-handed policy maker, which—like a boxer entering the ring with one hand tied behind his back— means the country will always suffer more than it has to.

Having the latitude to print your own money in a crisis also allows a country to soften the blow of letting a bankrupt bank go to the wall, because it can print more money to make sure there is no negative credit knock-on effect from the bank disappearing. People might worry about inflation resulting from such a policy but in Ireland prices are falling, not rising and with such a recession ongoing and with such attendant unemployment, inflation is the least of our worries.

And if we have to let a bank go, so what? New banks will come in and replace them as has happened time and again all over the world. If that means changing our currency, again what is the problem? Dozens of countries have given us a road map for this, but they have all made decisions based on hard thinking rather than mantras. It is time for Ireland to do the same.

The economic alternative to the present policy is not some radical, untested option. Nor is it the preserve of a small 'way-out' economic sect. This alternative is what every country that has got itself into this mess has done. It is the mainstream, rational response to economic depression. Far from being radical, the alternative is exactly what every economic textbook advocates, what every financial market lesson instructs and what every piece of hard data supports. The big lesson from the 1930s depression is that when a country faces a prolonged downturn and a very high level of unemployment, the currency has to fall or the government has to spend its way out of the downturn or a bit of both. When the country is facing falling prices because people are afraid to spend today, postponing spending until tomorrow, the obvious remedy is to do something that would get them to bring forward spending. What we need is inflation, whereby people think prices will rise tomorrow, not more deflation whereby people think prices will fall more tomorrow. This problem is made all the more urgent because we have huge debts and our incomes are falling. Economists refer to what we are facing now as 'debt deflation', which means that the cost of servicing our debts is still going up every year—or is at best constant—but our ability to pay is falling because we are losing our jobs or taking pay cuts. This means that the proportion of today's now reduced income we need just to pay off yesterday's debts is exploding. So if we are to pay our debts, we must stop spending on something else. But the less all of us spend, the more the rate of unemployment goes up and the downward spiral reinforces itself.

This is basic stuff. But we are not following this obvious economic remedy, which has worked all over the world again and again. Ireland and Irish economic policy has been hijacked (yet again) by a small group of powerful people, supported by their cheerleaders who are intent on executing a policy that is neither fair (because the poor will pay for the mistakes of the rich) nor efficient (because it will only deepen the crisis). We are yet again pretending that we are different. It was the same in the boom when our politicians, banks, top civil servants and much of the economics profession said that Ireland was the exception, that our strong fundamentals meant that house prices would continue to rise and we could escape the realities of basic economics. They were wrong then and they are wrong again now.

Today, in the bust we are adopting policies that will only make things worse for the ordinary man on the street while saving bankers at the top of the tree. People like the Dons and Shylock are smiling, having been bailed out yet again by the likes of Miss Pencil Skirt.

THE EVIDENCE

It is time to stop gazing at our own navels and look around a bit. In recent global economic history many countries have emerged from similar depressions, which were also caused by too much debt, too much credit, housing booms, irresponsible banks and second-rate politicians.

Obviously, we should look at the blueprint of those countries that successfully managed to get out of recession quickly and to start again with the least pain. These successful countries have significantly different economic characteristics. Some have everything going for them, others don't; some are European, others are Asian; some are countries clearly on the way up, others are formerly rich countries on their way down. Countries like Sweden have a brilliant welfare state, cradle to the grave care and its people have impressive longevity. In contrast, countries like Korea have hardly any welfare system, families look after each other and infant mortality is relatively high. Some countries such as Argentina are places that were once rich; others like Thailand are countries that were always poor. Some are vast like Russia and some are tiny like Taiwan.

However, what binds them all together is that when faced with a bust, they all tore up the rule book and changed the way they did business. More importantly, some used the crises to change fundamentally the way in which their countries were run.

All the booms began the same way, with huge amounts of money flooding into the country, and ended the same way, with a local credit crunch, where money just disappeared.

Take the Scandinavians. When Sweden and Finland faced a banking crisis in the early 1990s, the first reaction was to protect the banks, make sure the currency remained strong, cut public spending and raise taxes. Quickly, both countries realised that this wouldn't work. So—having told the world they would keep their currencies pegged to the German mark and would not devalue—they did a u-turn. They both allowed their currencies to fall. Both economies recovered rapidly, money flowed back in to avail of the now cheaper Swedish and Finnish workforces and both countries emerged speedily from what looked at first like a deep depression. By cutting the currencies loose, they exported their way out of the problem. They also printed their own money, allowing some appreciation in land prices, which meant that their solution to the banking crisis, the bad bank, worked. The competitive gains from the weaker currencies were much more significant and lasting that anyone had expected.

Both countries set up a 'bad bank' to deal with the property-related debts of the banking system but, unlike our NAMA, the State bought the land at rock bottom prices, profiting from the banks' stupidity. If buying the land at fire-sale prices caused a bank that had lent foolishly in the boom to go under, the Swedes nationalised it. The Swedes also let banks go bust. They liquidated banks which, in their eyes, were beyond redemption. Crucially, the Swedes and the Fins wrote down the land rapidly. There was no prolonged NAMA-type nonsense and because of this the total cost of the banking crisis in the Swedish case was limited to 4 per cent of GDP. (The IMF forecast that the Irish bank bailout would be the most expensive in financial history and it could cost us close to 30 per cent of GDP.)

It is noteworthy that when both countries broke their promises to creditors and allowed the exchange rates to fall, their exporters thrived. There was no flood of money out of Scandinavia after they announced huge devaluation. In fact, the opposite occurred—money flooded back in.

The reason is simple: investors realised that trying to hold the currency would not work. They realised that trying to regain competitiveness via grinding prices and wages downward would not work. The people would not accept a 30 per cent wage cut nor would they tolerate being out of work for long, nor indeed would they accept that their children's hospital wards needed to be shut down in order to save money which could then be given to foreign speculators who had gambled on the Swedish financial markets in the boom. As long as their economic policy had these big question marks over it, money stayed away because investors were waiting for a significant change. Then once the devaluation happened, the air was clear again. In the eyes of investors, 'the event' had happened and it was time to avail of a highly educated Scandinavian workforce at half the price.

The Swedes and Fins showed that you can save your banks but to do this you have to devalue your currency. It simply isn't possible for a sovereign State to save its banks and remain in a currency union where the single currency is considerably stronger than the currency would be if the beleaguered country had its own currency. The reason for this is that for the country to emerge from a debt splurge and thus save its banks, someone has to pay. If you ease the banks' financing problems by injecting new cheaper money into the balance sheet to replace the older more expensive debt, the bank has a chance of surviving and the cost will be modest. This is what the Fins and Swedes did. They inflated away the old debt with piles of new money.

This is also the reason that the US banks go bust frequently. If a region like New England experiences a boom-bust cycle, because the region can't devalue and replace the old debt with new money, the banks go bust because the cost of keeping them open is simply too high.

Countries facing a banking crisis, like ours, have to make a choice. It's the banks or the currency.

The Asian Tigers got into difficulties in the late 1990s. Like Ireland, their banks had borrowed heavily from abroad and gambled the cash on local property. In the bust, all of them (except Hong Kong) copied the Swedish and Finnish example and allowed their currencies to devalue. In so doing, the Asian Tigers burned the investors who had originally thought that the currencies would be stable. Some, like Korea, allowed banks to fail and devalued their currencies. Korea emerged from the 1997 crisis faster and stronger than any other country. Thailand and Indonesia also allowed banks to fail, but guaranteed deposits so that the average saver simply transferred their savings to a new bank.

The moral of the story is that economics is all about flexibility, countries must remain open to change and nothing is sacred. For example, in the US in the past year, over 300 banks and financial institutions have failed with material impact on the economy. Banks go bust. It's not that cataclysmic unless of course it is as a disorganised rout, in which case everyone loses.

And a disorganised rout is just what happened in Argentina in 2001 and 2002. Argentina is possibly one of the best examples of how not to do things in economics. A common expression in Victorian England was to be 'as rich as an Argentine'. Since then the country has experienced more economic calamities than any other and, having been very wealthy, it is now poor by our standards. In the mid-1990s, Argentina constructed a monetary union with the US whereby the dollar was pegged to the peso and both currencies were interchangeable in Argentina. This has the same effect on the economy as our single currency has on Ireland. In the good times money floods in and in bad times it floods out. But when money floods out, if the country can't change its currency, the local recession is much, much deeper than would otherwise be the case.

After the Asian crisis in 1997 and the Russian crisis of 1998, all the countries commonly referred to in financial jargon as 'emerging markets' by financial markets devalued their currencies; all that is, except Argentina. But this made Argentina very expensive and companies started to go to the wall. Unemployment rose progressively and money began to leave the country. Still the authorities in Argentina insisted that their currency was as strong as the US dollar despite the fact that the local economy was enfeebled and the US economy had never been stronger than under Clinton. This is the same conceit that we are trying to get away with in Ireland because our badly weakened economy has a monetary union with a much stronger neighbour, Germany. Eventually, as will happen in Ireland, the local economy in Argentina continued to contract and, ultimately, the policy imploded overnight. In 2001, investors clambered to get out of Argentina as quickly as they could. The entire economy seized to a halt and, in the chaos, the Argentineans cancelled their currency peg with the US. They obviously could have taken this decision in 1998—like the rest of the emerging world had done—but they tried to be the tough guys and in the end it was the ordinary people who suffered.

Having had five years of stagnant growth and rising unemployment, within a year of the currency's fall the Argentinean economy started to grow again. The country needn't have had the 2001 crisis at all.

The lesson from recent economic history is that banks go bust and currencies change. It is not the end of the world. It's a matter of guaranteeing savers' deposits in the new currency, setting up a new bank and starting again. It is not the Irish people's fault that bond investors took a gamble on the Irish banks. They are professional investors. They know the risks and so what if they get burned? That's the free market. Our State has no business lumbering the ordinary Irish taxpayer with the bad bets of international gamblers.

Now the spin is that if we allow one of our banks to fail there will be a black mark against us for years and money will not return to Ireland. This is their mantra, but it has no empirical basis in financial history. Investors have no emotion nor should they have. This is why the same people who lost money on the Irish banks last year are possibly the same people buying Irish bank shares now. You win some, you lose some, but you move on.

When Sweden devalued overnight and wiped out the return of investors, did they stop investing in Sweden? Of course not; they did the opposite. They invested more after the devaluation! Likewise the Asian Tigers. When the Koreans renegotiated with creditors, did the Korean economy go into a tailspin? No. In fact, it got stronger because investors, even those who lost money, took this renegotiation as a sign that the worst was now over and it was time to re-invest. When Israel, another small country, devalued its currency, the brains of the Israeli tech industry suddenly became available to investors for a song. Now Israel is the world's best example of a 'smart economy'.

In all the above examples, the key lesson is that economic growth solves most problems. And in order to get the economy moving again, with unemployment falling, the State has to do something radical. Once the boil has been lanced, once the pressure is released, the country can get down to the business of recovery.

Contrast this approach with the lesson of Japan in the 1990s. Japan tried to keep sick banks open by throwing good money after bad, and the economy got stuck in what economists call a 'deflationary spiral' where huge debts weighed down the economy. Prices fell and fell again and the more they fell the less people bought because they expected prices to fall yet more tomorrow. The economy stalled for over 10 years in what became known as the 'lost decade'.

DOING A DEAL
To get us out of the crisis and to get people back to work, we need a new bank or a series of new banks that will begin where the old ones left off. The creditors of the old banks lose out. Only new banks will have an unambiguous incentive to lend because they will be trying to increase their market share from day one, whereas the old banks will just be trying to protect existing business and clients.

The government's obsession with keeping delinquent banks afloat and its NAMA idea will prevent new banks from starting up. All they are doing is making sure that some foreign bank comes in and buys all the nice bits of the Irish banking system while the toxic bits are picked up by us, the taxpayer.

The financial world does not believe that we can or should buy up all this land for an inflated price because, while it may clean the bank's balance sheet, it lumbers the average person with the bill. This is why no one except the ECB is prepared to buy the bonds that NAMA will issue and why Ireland is becoming Europe's Vietnam.

The State should instead renegotiate with creditors. Many years ago I worked on a distressed debt trading team in London. We were involved in trying to trade the distressed debt of countries, debts that had been renegotiated due largely to bank collapses. Contrary to our government's spin, there is always a market for distressed debt as long as there is some hope of redemption. For example, during the Russian banking crisis of 1998, the Russians, like good chess players, decided that the debts of Russia, like the debts that we have wracked up in Ireland, could not be paid. Did they do a NAMA and place the burden on the Russian taxpayer for the debts of the Russian oligarchs?

The Russians calculated that they were in a corner and the way out was to minimise the cost to the average Russian citizen. So they defaulted on their internal rouble-denominated debts—knowing that these were held by foreign investors looking for yield. They chose not to default on foreign debt, knowing that Russians held the dollar-denominated stuff. In so doing they minimised, not neutralised, the cost to the average Russian. In a game of who blinks first, the Russians took the view that the foreign lenders to Russia's banks were at least as culpable as the Russian borrowers themselves. They therefore shared the pain with the lenders, having made the calculation that it would be better to allow some of its banks to go under and start again than lumber the people with the bill.

In a similar vein, given that the Irish government is prepared to write down 50 per cent of the value of assets in NAMA, then, rather than go to us, the taxpayer, and say, 'You might have to make up some of the difference between the price the banks lent for the land in the first place and the price we are now buying it for,' why not renegotiate with the people who lent the banks the money in the first place, the creditors?

Before we might broach this subject with the creditors, we would have to go to the ECB to make sure that the ECB would continue to provide liquidity to the Irish system. Why wouldn't it? It's our Central Bank, after all, and that is what Central Banks do.

The State should go into a room with the bondholders and say, 'Listen, we are in two minds about the bank guarantee.' The State could make the legitimate argument that the taxpayer has no business buying land, which is of no value to us and might be too expensive at today's prices anyway.

The State could then set out the details to the creditors of, say, Bank of Ireland. It could say something like, 'Listen, lads, today you will get one hundred per cent of your money back as long as the guarantee is in place, but on 1 October 2010, if we allow the guarantee to lapse, you will get zero. There are many ways we can do this but obviously you need to think about where you want to do a deal. Do you want to be closer to zero or one hundred per cent? You make up your minds, because after 1 October next year, it's got nothing to do with us. You took a bet on Bank of Ireland, not the State of Ireland, and we'd just like to make that clear to you.'

This approach, which is totally normal in business, would focus the minds of bond investors because they would know that there is no longer a one-way bet in Ireland underwritten by the taxpayers. A deal would be done and as the clock ticked down towards October 2010, the creditors would be screaming for a resolution to the Irish banking crisis.

Given that we would now be in control of the process rather than the process controlling us, the examinership of Bank of Ireland, or AIB for that matter, would be done in an orderly fashion. The assets, like the branch network, would be sold off and the depositors covered by a new State guarantee, which could be underwritten by a deposit guarantee insurance policy.

It's not that difficult and we'd save ourselves the tens of billions that the big banks' brutal balance sheets are likely to cost us. You can build a lot of hospitals with that sort of cash. And as has been the case in every country that has had a bank failure, money comes back in reasonably quickly. Obviously, the terms will be different and there will be a premium demanded initially. But if we gave the old bondholders equity in the new bank that we would create, they'd have an interest in the new bank flourishing. Very quickly the premium on Irish financial assets would fall back into line. Land prices would fall rapidly. The developers would go bust and we'd start again.

Even a child on a second-hand bike cycling home from a football match would realise this is the obvious thing to do.

Chapter 20

DAYLIGHT SAVING

Ireland must become cheap if we are to trade our way out of this recession. We can do this the easy way or the hard way. Our government is doing it the hard way by driving wages and prices down in a long recession, and massive pay cuts and deep cuts in essential public spending. (I'm not too sure what economic model advocates reducing spending on learning support for children as a route to sustained economic growth.)

This deflation will be almost impossible to achieve politically as the unions will refuse to accept the pay cuts. The more we squeeze prices downwards, the more people will hoard their cash and the more prices will fall. Therefore we will accelerate the downward spiral. In addition, the cuts to public spending will simply reinforce, rightly, in the public mind that the poor are being targeted to benefit the rich.

The other much less painful way to become competitive again is to suspend our membership of the euro, reinstate the Irish punt and allow it to find its own level. Overnight we would become competitive without all the hassle of cutting wages. More importantly, as all the empirical evidence shows, when a country devalues to get out of a mess like ours, money flows back in. In short, devaluations work. This is what Britain is doing at the moment, as is the US, as did Switzerland when it had its banking crisis in the early 1990s, as well as Sweden, Finland, Israel, Thailand, Indonesia, Korea, Malaysia and Taiwan.

Many argue that one of the big costs of a devaluation would be that it reduces the value of people's savings because the savings will now be in the new currency—the Irish punt—which will initially fall against the euro. This is true. But like many arguments, this one is circular.

While it is true that savers will lose out now, it was savers who gained by joining the euro in the first place. In the same way as going back to the Irish punt would devalue savings, joining the euro revalued the same savings in 2000. Savers in Ireland received a one-off increase in their wealth when we joined the euro because their savings were generated in a weak currency—the Irish punt—and now were crystallised in a strong currency, the euro. So for savers, the Irish experience with the euro has been brilliant, getting paid in hard currency for money they originally saved in a soft currency. There was a massive wealth transfer to savers when we joined the euro, ultimately funded by borrowers.

Naturally, for Irish borrowers, the opposite has been the case. Borrowers have had to generate a surplus in a hard currency—the euro—to pay for our debts. Now that we know the legacy of the euro has been a mad splurge with other peoples' money, the lasting legacy is generations of debt in a hard currency.

And for the country as a whole, the euro has changed the balance of the economy. It has been a boom for those on salaries in sectors of the economy that do not export. This is because, at the moment, those who work in the exporting sector need to generate the hard currency in euros in order to pay the salaries of those who don't export. If we can't generate enough hard currency, we have to borrow to stay afloat—which is what we have been doing almost from the day we joined the euro.

There is also a generational dilemma to this. Put simply, the young subsidise the middle-aged in an environment like EMU because there is a demographic divide between the profiles of savers and borrowers. There is a theory in economics called the 'life-cycle theory of consumption'. Like most things in economics, this is a difficult-sounding name given to something that is surprisingly simple. This idea is the notion that we spend when we are younger, save when we are middle-aged and spend again when we are old. It is based on the fact that we earn and save most in middle age.

So the present euro policy, which involves a massive wealth transfer from borrowers to savers, implies a massive transfer of wealth from the young to the middle-aged as well as a massive transfer from the exporting sector to those sectors that do not export. This is precisely the opposite policy demanded for Europe's youngest country, which needs to export in order to prosper.

While devaluation self-evidently makes economic sense for a small exporting economy, in fact so much so that it is difficult to name a small manufacturing country that has become wealthy without devaluing its exchange rate, there are huge technical challenges that need to be overcome during a transition from the euro to a new Irish punt.

The minute people hear that we might leave the euro, they will naturally take money out of Ireland and put it in euro deposits elsewhere. Therefore, the announcement would have to be coincident with the move. This would be difficult to achieve, but not impossible. The key in the run up would be to avoid a freezing of the payments system as people are confused about just how much the new currency will be worth. Capital flight will be necessary, in fact, as you'd want the currency to fall substantially, so that we could lock in the competitive gain.

We would have to negotiate a new source of financing, probably from the IMF rather than the ECB although, if we negotiated in advance with the ECB, we might get short-term financing from it as other non-euro European countries, such as Denmark, Poland, Hungary and the Baltic countries, have done in recent months. Once we have covered the risk of a freezing of the payments system in the country, by ensuring that we have provided enough liquidity, we could proceed calmly.

Remember, one of the major arguments against devaluation is the Establishment's one that says 'proper' countries can't contemplate such things. In other words, for those of who are not persuaded by shibboleths, once you have covered the management risk in the transition, there is nothing to fear. However, as a devaluation would transfer wealth and opportunity to the outsiders in our society and away from the insiders, opposition to it would be a combination of self-preservation and indignation rather than hard economics. In short, as in so many cases where we fail to do the right thing in Ireland, it would be mantras versus hard thinking yet again.

Devaluations are not without costs, but the costs would be significantly less than what would be experienced by a long recession. Unfortunately, no political party in Ireland seems capable of advocating the obvious. Across the mainstream political parties there seems to be consensus that we should keep our old delinquent banks afloat—in some shape or form—at all costs and so to do this we make ordinary people buy land that we don't want. There is no economic logic for this and it is based exclusively on keeping the banking Mafia, the builders and their political friends in power. As for mentioning suspending our euro membership, anyone who might advocate this is regarded, just as I was when I said the housing market would definitely crash, as a pariah.

In fact, suggesting that we entertain changes to our exchange rate arrangement makes you worse than a pariah in the eyes of many. But it is interesting to note that many who bristle at the idea of reducing your costs by devaluation are not offering any alternative to the economics of deflation which contend that a long recession is better that a short one. In fact, they proffer more of the same for Ireland, the same basic policies, the same people and the same system.

This aversion is possibly because reinstating an Irish punt, although economically sensible, tends to have implications for politics, for the Establishment and of course for perceptions of Ireland in Europe. It also involves a transfer of wealth and opportunity from the insiders in Irish society to the outsiders. This type of policy change is almost revolutionary in the context of what we have become used to.

Thus the reasonably cosy mainstream in Ireland might dismiss such a gearshift as being too revolutionary. Rather than see that this is what the rest of the world has done time and again in a crisis, they are paralysed by fear of the crisis itself. The Irish policy-making fraternity is afraid of the day when everything changes and whether they would be able to control events. As such, they are afraid of the event itself rather than the consequences. We have to look beyond the event and think about what the country is going to look like afterwards.

The mainstream in Irish history has always been the same, innately conservative, constantly afraid to rock the boat. That's all very well when the boat is in calm waters, but now this little economic boat is sinking and we must do something.

It is interesting to think back to 1916 when most of mainstream nationalism believed the revolutionaries were mad and their ideas crazy and highly dangerous. Yet today, there are few people in the Republic who would choose to be back under British rule. So something that can appear radical at the time is ultimately adopted by everyone because the prize is so enormous that the event—although difficult—is actually incidental.

We are in a similar place with the exchange rate discussion. This is the short, sharp shock option and maybe it is just the thing we need to jolt the insiders out of their slumber. The costs of doing nothing are just too great.

CUCKOO CLOCK ECONOMICS

Let me explain why devaluations are the easy way to achieve competitiveness while the present policy of grinding down wages and prices is much more destructive. Let's look at the logic of a devaluation over deflation by reference to daylight saving and moving the clock back every year. Sometimes the simple ideas are the best ones. And sometimes, just by looking at a problem differently, an obvious solution will present itself.

Take time, for example. Standardised time came into existence only about 150 years ago, with the expansion of railway networks. For trains to run to a schedule, the same time needed to be kept in all parts of the network. This 'standard time' proved very successful and was quickly adopted.

And later standard time was tweaked with the introduction of summer time. While out walking one summer morning, an Englishman, William Willett, noted that most of his countrymen were sleeping through a large part of the morning, wasting daylight. The obvious solution to this waste would be for everyone to get up an hour or so earlier to make the most of the day. But then, as now, nobody was particularly keen on getting up at 6am, so Mr Willett came up with a different solution. Instead of changing the habits of millions of his fellow Englishmen, he advocated changing the clock. By moving the measure of what part of the day it is, he could very quickly (literally, overnight) change the habits of an entire nation. They would be getting up at the same time, by the clock, as the day before, but it would just happen to be an hour earlier.

When it was introduced to the British Parliament in 1907, it was defeated. (Interestingly, the proposal was opposed mostly by intellectuals such as the Astronomer Royal as well as the Meteorological Office.) In fact, the idea was originally implemented by Britain's enemies in the First World War, Germany and her allies (in order to reduce consumption of coal and oil). But once it was introduced in one country, it caught on across the world.

Now let's go back to the economy for a moment, because a devaluation works just like changing the clock. Consider the arguments for staying with the single currency through the prism of the debate on changing the time.

Can you imagine a political regime that advocated getting up an hour earlier instead of the clock going back every year by one hour?

Also imagine that the key advisors to this regime were people who made clocks that you could not change, because they came without the knob necessary to change the hour. So the advisors had a vested interest in the clock not going back.

Imagine the chaos in the country on the morning the whole nation was supposed to get up an hour earlier. (In fact, this was tried in Washington DC in 1922 when Daylight Saving Time was abandoned by President Harding, who ordered all Federal employees to come to work an hour early during the summer. Needless to say, the idea was a failure.)

Now consider the notion that an ideology was created which supported this fixed stance and had believers at the highest levels of society. The ideology regarded any change in the clock as heresy. People who believed this creed also believed that putting the clock back would undermine the integrity of the entire day, and not only the day but the hours of work we put into the day. Who were we trying to fool by changing the clock?

By changing the clock we would be cheating, they would say. These cuckoo clock economists would say that if we wanted to get an extra hour of light, we would have to do this the hard way, by hauling our lazy asses out of bed an hour earlier.

The true believers argue that people who want to change the clock are only fooling themselves by taking the easy option. The sluggards are undermining the real value of the extra hour of light. The real value is the pain of getting up earlier, rather than the light itself. The pain is the acid test. Without pain, there can be no good.

Of course you would think these people were members of a bonkers sect. Why get up earlier when you can just change the clock?

Yet this same type of ideology now governs Ireland because either we devalue and reinstate our old currency (change the clock) or we grind the economy to a pulp with unemployment, so wages will fall over a five-year to ten-year period (get up an hour earlier).

To make ourselves more competitive, we can just change our exchange rate. This means that overnight we would change the price of goods produced here.

Implementing this obvious strategy, which has been followed by practically every country that has ever found itself in difficulties like ours, would involve a national effort and a mindset change at the top.

BOSTON OR BERLIN?

The first thing we would have to do is go to Brussels and Frankfurt and say that we want to be like the other good Europeans who don't have the euro. We'd like to be good members of the EU with our own currency, like Sweden, the UK, Denmark, Estonia, Latvia, Lithuania, Poland, the Czech Republic and Hungary. We would ask the Commission whether these countries are any less European for not having the same currency as Germany and France.

We should argue that we will rejoin the euro when the European Union becomes a full political union like the United States of America—where there are full budgetary and tax powers and an elected government—with a President of Europe. And we will fully support treaties like the Lisbon Treaty and future political treaties to make political union more likely.

Let's digress a little here to flesh out this point about why having a single currency (which I think in principle is a good idea) will only work properly if there is full European political integration. Let's go back to the 1980s and early 1990s. You might be one of the thousands of us who emigrated to the US in those years. I headed to Boston in the late 1980s.

Back then, Boston was like Ireland last year and the preceding decade. We could get as many jobs as we wanted but it was impossible to find anywhere to live. So, like immigrants the world over, we slept four to a room. Boston was the centre of the New England property and banking boom, which was known as the Massachusetts Miracle. People came from all over the US and abroad to work there, bars and restaurants were full, property prices were soaring and new landmark buildings were being erected every day.

But like all booms, it eventually crashed. Prices started to fall and banks got into trouble. Just ask Bank of Ireland about this because their subsidiary, the Bank of New Hampshire, went bust and nearly brought down its parent in Dublin. (Do these bankers ever learn?)

Anyway, the crucial point is that when an American State like Massachusetts gets into trouble, the US political system reacts because it is one country. If Massachusetts is in trouble, unemployment rises, property prices fall and taxes fall. Its budget deficit explodes. It mirrors exactly what is happening in Ireland at the moment, except for two crucial aspects which explain why America is a real monetary union, and Europe is only a pretend one.

First, the rest of the US pays the dole of Massachusetts. The tax of the rest of the US goes to the State that is in trouble and bails it out. So taxpayers in Chicago pay some of the unemployment benefit of people who have lost their jobs in Boston. This acts as a cushion for Boston.

Second, when Americans in Boston lose their jobs, they up sticks and go to California to find work. Mobility in the US helps the State in crisis in two ways: fewer unemployed people means less spending on social welfare payments and also allows the property market to adjust faster because prices fall quicker and the State can start again soon.

None of this happens in Europe, yet. So to have a properly functioning Europe with our own currency, we need a proper political union. At the moment we have a 'back to front' Europe with a single currency but no single government.

The implication of all this for Ireland is that we are being held hostage to an unusual ideology, which is what we might call the 'myth of the euro'. The big lie underpinning the euro is its advocates think that just by having the single currency, Europe acts as a single political union. They want us to live in a make-believe world where we think that having the same money means we have the same government. But it doesn't. Maybe it will some day, but at the moment we are far from that. So the currency is missing its most important element, the full political union. This is why it doesn't work fully and it is why the euro exacerbates the upswing and the downturn. And when we think about our present downturn, what will happen when Germany and France— already in recovery mode—decide to raise European interest rates? What happens to all those Irish people on the brink of default, who have lost their jobs in the past few months? Are we supposed to tolerate rising interest rates in the middle of the deepest recession this country has ever experienced?

This is the conundrum we find ourselves in. The euro, in the boom, meant too much money flowed into the country. In the bust, when we should be printing money to get the system going again, the euro prevents us from doing this.

There is also a cultural dimension to the euro and it may explain why it is not suited to us as a currency arrangement. Had you turned on your telly in Ireland, the UK or the USA over the past few years, it would have been practically impossible to have avoided a property programme focusing on interior makeovers, buying homes abroad like

'Househunters in the Sun' and the like. This was part of the culture of the English-speaking world—the world of floating currencies. It was not part of the continental world—the world of EMU and fixed currencies. In the major euro economies there is no real tradition of house price booms or busts and, therefore, the structure of the economies and the nature of their challenges are entirely different.

So when the bust happens, the UK and the US allow their currencies to fall to absorb the shock, but the Irish, who displayed the most virulent form of the housing disease, are uniquely joined to the euro, with a currency that is appreciating, not depreciating, in the downturn.

Even when it is obvious to the most basic economics student that we are in the wrong currency regime and that being in the euro is a mistake, the spin continues unabated.

The cost of being in the wrong currency regime is significant. Our joining the euro was an entirely political move with little attention given to the obvious differences between the aspirations of the political elite and the realities of the Irish economy.

While it is easy to understand the politics behind our decision to join, EMU came out of the blue and for Ireland it posed an enormous dilemma, which at the time was not fully debated.

THE BERLIN WALL COMES TO MERRION STREET

In Europe, there have always been two schools of thought about how the European economy might integrate. Maybe a little detail of this divergence might help us to understand how we ended up joining the euro. In the ascendancy for many years in the European Commission was the 'economist' school of thought. The 'economists' believed that gradually the economy of the European Community would, via trade and capital flows, become so integrated that political unity would become logical. We'd end up trading so much with each other that, ultimately, the European economy would become one large trading area—a single economy in all but name. It could be called organic integration. This was the logic behind the single market initiative in 1992.

There was another more aggressive path to economic and political integration espoused by the 'monetarists'. They believed that the EU could accelerate economic integration by having one currency because this would force the economies together. If integration was going too slowly, a single currency would speed it up. We had tied ourselves to the deutschemark in the 1980s, in what was a foretaste of monetary union.

So there were two schools of political thought about how to achieve integration running concurrently, the 'easy does it' economist side and the 'full on' single currency merchant side. In 1989, the monetarists still held a minority view in the politics of the European Union.

That was until the shock unification of Germany. Up to then, the incremental, piece-by-piece integration model of the economists was in the ascendancy. Europe's politicians, even the more federally minded, were happy with the pace of integration. Then, 20 years ago this November, when the Berlin Wall came down, the French civil service panicked. They were horrified by the prospect of an eastward-looking unified Germany. They retreated into Second World War thinking and feared that the new Germany would turn its back on the European Community. As a result, federalists in Europe (particularly in the European Commission), threatened by the perceived resurgence of nationalism, decided to accelerate European political integration. France needed to lock Germany into the European project; it was terrified by German reunification but realised that it couldn't stop it. So rather than try to halt Germany, the French proposed a trade off— Germany could reunify if the quid pro quo was a single currency. Germany would give up its currency, lock itself into the EU and continue to be the anchor tenant of the European Union rather than the Greater Germany of old.

That's how it all came about so quickly. It posed a dilemma for Ireland because by the time we realised what was going on, we had already devalued three times against the deutschemark. We couldn't keep up with the Germans. But we were now faced with a dilemma: were we real Europeans or not?

There was a perception that we could truly be in the EU if we signed up. The argument was that there were many new member states wanting to join the EU and it would be good for our European credentials if we stayed within the inner core. Deep down there was a feeling that we could never properly break away from sterling if we remained an independent currency, even though Denmark and Britain—the two countries that joined the EEC with us in 1973—were opting to stay out of the euro, as was Sweden. But one of the major reasons, which was never questioned (and I saw this at first hand while working as an economist in the Central Bank during the Maastricht Treaty negotiation in the early 1990s), was that the euro was simply considered an article of faith. It was seen as part of the European deal and to opt out would have undermined our commitment to the European project. While it made sense for the French, the consequences for Ireland were never fully explained or questioned.

We didn't have the self-confidence of the Danes to say, 'We are fully paid up members of the EU, but we don't think the currency suits us.' The Swedes did likewise, as did the new member states albeit for different reasons. Britain's reasons for staying out are of course determined by its general Eurosceptical view and the fact that Britain understood that its economy was not sufficiently integrated with the EU to make the marriage work.

Maybe it's because we have been, understandably, using the EU to escape the gravitational pull of London that we didn't have the confidence to properly analyse the economic situation like the Danes or Swedes did. Whatever the reasons for our membership, the experience has been quite disastrous.

We got an unsustainable housing boom, facilitated by cheap money from Germany which allowed the Dons to blow the national balance sheet using reckless borrowing from eurozone banks. This deluge of cash—not demographics or supply and demand—inspired the Merchant of Ennis to build wherever he could. And ultimately, as prices rose and rose, our membership of the euro and the greed of our bankers, which it encouraged, has resulted in a generation of Miss Pencil Skirts being lumbered with huge debts and negative equity.

The euro made the crazy Irish boom possible and now that we are in the bust, our membership of the euro is making any recovery virtually impossible.

'MARRY ME NOW, THE LOVE WILL COME LATER'

In economic theory there is a significant amount of study on what is termed 'the optimal currency area'. This is a highfalutin term for the study of whether countries should join currencies. One way of looking at the wisdom of a monetary union is to regard economic theory as being like a marriage guidance course, which tries to figure out if the couple is suited, before they get married. It's the Lisdoonvarna matchmaker of monetary economics.

A monetary union between two countries is a bit like an arranged marriage. The financial matchmaker should be called in to see whether these two countries are compatible with each other and, on the basis of suitability, the likelihood of long-term stability. If the two countries are wildly different, the matchmaker will predict trouble down the road, when the honeymoon is but a fond memory.

This optimal currency area theory is such a matchmaker. It argues that the basis for a monetary union should be that both economies are complementary. A country should join a monetary union with a region that has a similar tax system. It should join a union with countries that it does most trade with and with those countries where its workers migrate to and from. The idea behind this is that the more similar and integrated the economies, the more appropriate a marriage would be.

If the economies of the monetary union move in natural tandem, then there is much less risk in the marriage. However, if the countries have very different economies, there will be problems and what is appropriate for the region might not be appropriate for the outlying country. Like a bad marriage, the country will find itself locked in a loveless union where it is constantly compromised. Ultimately, if there is no divorce, the country suffers until the day it either walks out or gets the dominant partner to change its ways.

The problem for Ireland is that we never consulted the matchmaker. We fell in love quickly and after the currency crisis of 1993 (which terrified our mandarin class), our joining the euro was probably more of a shotgun wedding than a happy ever after fairytale.

Our economy trades considerably more with the UK and the US than mainland Europe, our workers migrate to the UK and the US in a recession and our tax system and philosophy up to now has been Anglo-American rather than continental European.

Unfortunately, these are the facts that can't be wished away. Now maybe in a few decades, we will become more German in the way we run our economy and society, but we are not there yet.

I was in Berlin a few months ago and, like a typical Irishman in a restaurant, I tried to pay with a credit card. The restaurant, a pretty decent establishment, didn't accept cards, only cash. This experience was repeated a few times during the weekend. The Germans don't do cards in the same way we do. They deal in cash not credit, in the present not the future. Maybe it's a legacy of their past but, for whatever reason, reasonably swanky restaurants expect to be paid in cash. In Ireland, the opposite is the case.

And this explains something more about the differences between Ireland and continental Europe. In Ireland, we borrow using short-term interest rates. So for example your mortgage will change if short-term interest rates change, even though the term of your mortgage is 20 years. We also finance the majority of our mortgages at flexible, not fixed, rates of interest. So when the short-term interest rate changes, it changes the amount of money in our pockets. In Germany, the opposite is the case. If the average German borrows for something big like a house (which they don't in the majority), they do so at a fixed longer-term rate. This means that when the ECB raises rates, the average German, or Frenchman for that matter, hardly notices and short-term interest rates do not have a big effect on personal spending.

And within the next two years, or as soon as the German and French economies recover, the ECB will ratchet up interest rates and we—with our huge mortgages and credit card bills—will suffer more than any other European citizens.

This is the reason the IMF's forecast for Ireland is of a prolonged recession with a real threat of deflation, persistently high unemployment and a bank bailout that will be the most expensive in the world.

Having our own currency would protect us from bad policy and bad economic management. If the financial markets see a country that is borrowing far too much, the markets will simply sell the currency, signalling displeasure with our profligate politicians. Therefore, we would be compelled to act quicker to get our house in order. And the quicker we act, the better for all of us.

The lesson from history, and just about every country that has got into a mess like ours, is that having your own currency forces you to wake up to reality and take hard decisions. Far from 'protecting' Ireland, the euro is prolonging our misery and, by forcing us to be Europe's Vietnam, the ideology that underpins the euro (the domino theory) will cause us to suffer unnecessarily. It is simply drawing out the downturn and allowing politicians and the banking Mafia to stitch up the people with their idiotic ideas like NAMA. We will end up living in a weak economy with a strong currency—highly uncompetitive and about as bad a combination in a recession as you can get.

While we still have our sovereignty, Ireland should be putting in place policies to help the Irish people rather than genuflect to an ideology which is not yet fully formed. When we have full political integration in Europe, we should by all means become a member of the single currency but, until that day, it makes no sense for Ireland—whose main trading partners are the us and the uk—to have a currency union with Germany.

We are deliberately setting ourselves up for a deep, deep depression whereby thousands of people will lose their jobs unnecessarily and where the people who will directly benefit are the bondholders of bust Irish banks. We are going to preside over many individual cases of depression, divorce and emotional trauma to pay off grown up investors who have already made provisions for their losses in Ireland. And we are doing all this to suit an ideology and a political aspiration that is so far away from full fruition that it could be two lifetimes before we see it.

Chapter 21

DO THE RIGHT THING

W hen it became obvious that an economic policy was hollowing out the marrow of the country, our greatest civil servant, T. K. Whitaker, made a strategy choice for the nation. He saw the old regime with its closed economy mentality as being part of the problem for Ireland in the 1950s.

His economic move was contrary to the huge vested interests of the time. Protectionism was good for many powerful people. Companies built up under protectionism did well, as did semi-states. More importantly, Whitaker had to change the mindset of the old revolutionaries at the top who equated nationalism with economic nationalism.

But he did it and, crucially, Lemass, an old soldier, backed him. They had the courage to change, realising that the 1950s crisis was too good an opportunity to miss. This was the time for change, when the people were restless and wanted a new economic alternative.

We are in similar times now.

The need for a currency change will become more obvious when we face huge industrial unrest as the government tries to reduce costs in the economy. Reducing costs in a shrinking economy will be virtually impossible. We are soon to see the mother and father of all struggles, what could be termed the 'war for the last tax euro'.

On one side we have the business community and on the other we have the workers. But this is a false dichotomy because in many cases they are one and the same thing. Thousands of Irish families include a small business owner, a Garda, a teacher, a nurse, a manager at a multinational or an unemployed graduate. The idea that there are two clearly delineated Irelands is not accurate. So we are limbering up for a scrap with ourselves.

Someone has to lose in the stalemate we are setting ourselves up for. It doesn't have to be like this. Remember the State is doing this to keep delinquent banks afloat and to pay creditors who took a gamble in the boom. There is a better way.

YEAR ZERO

Our government's objective should be to get as many people into jobs as quickly as possible. To do this we have to announce a clear break with the past and its practices. We can then draw a line in the sand, announce a year zero and begin again, with the youngest population in Europe, the most educated workforce aged under 40 in the developed world, the cheapest costs in the rich world, and away we go!

Yes, of course there will be difficulties. Initially, the world will be sceptical because a country that goes through a boom and bust might do it again. But financial history tells us a totally different story to the one articulated by the cuckoo economics of cloud cuckoo land. Remember the clock and putting the hour back? We are dealing with a sect that has taken over the running of the country and is advocating a plan that not only exists to protect itself, but is actually a perversion of mainstream economics.

Economics is the art of the possible, not the impossible. And there are ways out of our mess that are not only well-versed in economic theory but, more importantly, have worked time and again in practically every country that has got into the type of difficulties we face.

By looking at what the rest of the world has done, we can abandon this pointless self-flagellation and get on with living.

Overnight, Ireland would become highly competitive with little pain. Exports would be cheap and imports expensive and we could resume our role as an exporting country. Can you imagine the US multinationals' reaction if they heard that Ireland's highly productive workforce was suddenly 30 per cent cheaper? Their return on investment would go through the roof and investment would flood in.

Why not stay cheap by making sure that land and house prices never get out of control again? At the same time as we devalue, we could instigate a simple rule which would outlaw a return to the housing price bubble that has caused us so much pain. The best way to do this is to insist that the value of the collateral used to lend against a house is the average price of this house over the last 30 years. This means that no more than the average price of the last 30 years could be lent out against the house. This would eliminate any booms and busts in housing prices immediately. Remember, as we've established, it's not the houses that drive the bubble but the amount of money lent against them. We could have much cheaper workers and much cheaper land, giving us a permanent comparative advantage.

All this will be watched by the financial markets. Once they see that the event they have been waiting for has occurred, money will flood back into Ireland to take advantage of the real wealth here: our people, our skills, the fact that we are the most open economy in Europe and the basic notion that, after the change, the return on money invested in real wealth in Ireland will skyrocket. Why wouldn't you invest in these people?

STALINGRAD ECONOMICS

Critically, devaluation, like changing the clock, allows you to achieve your aims quickly and minimise, although not eradicate, pain.

At the moment, we are trying to achieve an increase in our competitiveness the hard way by forcing wages downwards and by firing people from jobs because the wage bill is too high. Over time, the logical result of this nut with a hammer approach to economics is that a cowed and highly insecure workforce will take their pay cuts like real men and Ireland will squeeze every last drop out of them to force wages down. The idea is that in time the bosses of Intel will realise that their wage bill in Ireland has fallen and they might re-commission a new Fab in Leixlip. But at what cost?

How high will unemployment have to be to achieve this increase in competitiveness—15 per cent or 18 per cent? Is that 500,000 or 600,000 people on the dole? And how far do wages have to fall? Let's drop our living standards by 30 per cent, why don't we? Sure isn't that why we educated all our graduates, so that they could get paid less not more? Let's do it the hard way not because it is the right thing to do but to do it any other way might affect the interests of the Establishment.

Think of all the emotional distress, the arguments, the families that will break up over money issues. All this can be minimised.

Instead of changing our currency to make our life easier and thus give hope to hundreds of thousands of our people, we will grind the life out of the economy, resulting in people losing hope. And while we do that we will continue to pay the interest rates of those who took a greasy punt on Anglo Irish Bank and the rest of the banking Mafia.

We are forcing the population to get up an hour earlier rather than change the clock and, just for good measure, we are asking them to devote the proceeds of their first four hours' work to pay for the bankers who are to blame for the mess.

There is an understandable and moral argument against changing the currency because we would be giving the two fingers to our creditors.

The crux of this objection comes down to the basic fact that when a serious country enters into agreements, it shouldn't lightly change tack at the first sign of trouble. There is some merit in this argument if you think like a lawyer. However, if you think like an economist or investor, things are less clear cut.

This is not the first sign of trouble. We are facing into an abyss and if we follow the current policies, we will cause people to abandon hope. We must do everything to give people the feeling that we can get out of this, that we are doing all we can and we are prepared to try whatever it takes.

The various arguments against the 'doing whatever it takes' approach that are bandied about have no real merit. Some people argue—indeed, I know the Minister for Finance believes—that it would be unprecedented for a country to come away from an exchange rate arrangement that has been set in stone and has been used by investors as the basis for lending to us in the first place. The worry is that to be so radical would cast us into the financial darkness for ever.

In fact, there are many precedents for change. The most significant is the US during the Great Depression but, as I have repeated exhaustively, practically every country has taken the devaluation approach when in trouble.

Let's look at the American example because it reveals the difference in mindset between the civil servant and lawyer on the one hand and the economist and investor on the other.

In 1935, at the height of the Great Depression, when America faced rocketing unemployment and mounting bank failures, President Roosevelt announced that he believed in heresy. He said that the gold standard was one of the main problems preventing the American recovery. He argued that the US economy needed to print money and loads of it. He proposed a New Dollar that was not backed by gold but by the technocratic ability of the Federal Reserve. This was, at the time, like the Pope doubting the Resurrection.

The gold standard was an article of faith for the US. It was like the euro for our believers. The US had had a currency that was backed by gold since the end of the Civil War. Telling your creditors that they would now be paid in something other than gold—a new currency— was a bit like us telling creditors that they would not be paid in actual euros but in new Irish punts.

The move prompted a series of lawsuits from irate creditors. Ultimately, the Supreme Court had to decide if this change was consti- tutional. Creditors claimed it was robbery; the government claimed that it was necessary to get out of the Depression.

In February 1935, the Supreme Court of the US upheld the govern- ment's decision to repudiate the debt by 5-4. It ruled that it was constitutional for the US to come off the gold standard. By coming off the gold standard the US was now changing the terms of its debts. It meant that the US government was no longer repaying the people who lent to it in gold, which had been the basis of the loans in the first place.

The conventional wisdom was that the financial markets would sell off on this news and no one would lend to the US government again. We hear similar arguments in Ireland from the financial establishment— which only serve to tie one hand behind our back. They contend that even thinking about devaluation and the possible implication for debts that were originally taken out in euro, but now will be paid for in a new currency, is heresy. They argue that the iron law of markets is 'cred- ibility' and that can be won only by honouring debts, no matter how much pain it causes, and by never changing course.

But one interesting aspect to financial history is that there is prac- tically no evidence to support this Stalingrad approach to economics. What I mean by Stalingrad economics is the all-or-nothing, no-retreat, victory-at-all-costs approach to finance. Seasoned investors know that's how you lose fortunes. Never become emotionally attached to your portfolio.

Let's go back to New York in 1935.

The *New York Times* reported on the day after the case: 'Court backs government on gold', '5-4 for bond payment in new dollar', 'Business surges forward, stocks rise'.

There was the usual moral outrage, the type of thing we would see here in Ireland following a decision to change the currency and devalue. For example, according to reports of the time: 'Justice

McReynolds, in a strident and emotional dissent, decried that "the Constitution is gone" and compared the actions of the government in these cases to those of "Nero in his worst form". The minority expressed "shame and humiliation" at the majority's decision and found the consequences of the decision upholding repudiation "abhorrent".

Yet the financial markets just got on with it. There is no room for fixed moral positions when we are in the business of making money and financing companies or betting on countries that have considered their options and chosen the most sensible one. Nobody wants to invest in fanatics.

Stock, bond, currency and commodity markets rallied after the decision and rallied for years after. This was the result of investors making a rational assessment of the facts on the ground.

The *New York Times* went on to report that: 'Trading in stocks and bonds immediately following the decision jumped to levels that had not occurred in months.'

Had America stayed on the gold standard, it would not have been possible for it to repay its debts. This is precisely why a risk premium was placed on the debts—the markets knew that a default was more likely with the gold standard. No one has any interest in mass default. Straight after the government had made a decision, however unpalatable, the market took it as a signal that it was time to move on. Lick your wounds and get back up.

The lesson from all such events is that there is always new money in the world looking for a home and if we in Ireland give this money a good reason to come here, it will come. Once the markets realise that the game has changed and the pointless policy of driving down the economy has changed, the risk falls and money returns.

The crux here is that if the situation is so precarious that enforcing debts threatens bankruptcy, both the bondholder—the person who lent money in the first place—and the borrowers have an interest in finding a solution. Bankrupt companies, bankrupt people or bankrupt countries are no good to anyone—everyone loses.

In the case of the us in 1935 and all the other examples of devaluations in Sweden, Finland, Thailand and Korea in the last chapter, when the governments made a proper decision, money flooded back into the countries.

But the funny thing is that you don't have to go abroad to see how devaluations work. We had our own successful devaluation in Ireland in 1992. It is worth revisiting this to see just how wrong the mandarins and the economic mainstream can be.

THE MANDARINS

To see why the people who make policy in Ireland—the civil servants, consultants and lawyers who preserve the status quo—don't understand the mindset of the investor and fail to understand these basic economic ideas, we have to get inside the head of the mandarins who are actively destroying this economy. They are not destroying the economy because they are bad people; in fact, the opposite is the case. Most of them are decent people who believe that they have the best interests of the country at heart, but they just don't get it—not because they aren't able, but because they don't think like a trader and so much of their own personal professional credibility is wrapped up in policies that might have been right yesterday but are not right today.

When they are faced with a challenge, the default position is to replace hard thinking with defending the status quo and replace the economics of the possible with the economics of Stalingrad. The first instinct of the mandarin is to burrow in the crisis, not to meet it head on.

I received a salutary lesson in this type of behaviour, its crass self-confidence and, ultimately, its extraordinary irresponsibility, in the early 1990s while working as an economist in the Central Bank in Dublin.

In 1992, the UK pulled out of an exchange rate arrangement that had sterling pegged to the German deutschemark. Investors calculated that the government in the UK was facing rising unemployment and a bursting property market and so it needed interest rates that were very low. In contrast, Germany was experiencing a post-unification boom and needed higher interest rates. Something had to give and it was sterling. Ken Clarke's description, outlined in Chapter 18, of the chaos in Downing Street revealed a government policy in disarray. Sterling fell like a stone. In the event and against unfounded superstitions about what happens when you devalue your currency, money flowed into the UK and its subsequent 15-year boom can be traced to this day.

I was in the Stag's Head in Dublin when I heard about the UK's shock exit from the ERM. It had been announced well after the markets had closed and it was confirmed to me by a colleague. We had had one of those days in the Central Bank, watching the British currency slide and knowing that we were next. My first thought was that we should devalue straightaway to prevent the nonsense that was to follow.

The next morning we were called into an emergency meeting and asked what we thought we should do. This was just preliminary stuff, sounding out the options that history and economic theory might offer. I was the junior of six economists in the International Relations Department, which would end up writing the briefs and advising on the exchange rate.

When it came to my turn, I said that we were caught, that people looked at Ireland's double digit unemployment, and its biggest market, Britain, on the skids and they'd question why we'd try to keep the same exchange rate as Germany. Events in the UK had changed everything and we should change accordingly. Otherwise we'd end up in a futile war with the financial markets, jacking up interest rates. Businesses would close and we'd eventually run out of reserves and thus run out of money and have to devalue anyway. I pointed out that we'd devalued twice in the past decade, so one more time wouldn't make a difference. And interest rates would fall not rise, eventually.

As I finished talking, I heard it, the death sentence for any civil servant.

'Ah, David, don't you think that would be unwise?'

With one word, delivered with that sickly weak smile, the facial equivalent of a wet fish handshake, I was doomed.

'Make sure and shut the door behind you, like a good young man.'

The 'young man' bit at the end was not without thought. Nothing in the mandarin's world of the Civil Service is. In the complex language that replaces straight talking in the public service, the 'young man' moniker was not an innocent, possibly even paternalistic, phrase from an older boss. I'd been inside long enough. I knew what it meant and so too did everyone who counted.

In a system that rewards age and service, the worst thing you can be is young with ideas. The description was supposed to underscore the silliness, the youthful lack of consideration, of any ideas put forward by someone under 30.

If the 'young' was a nasty little jab that could be masked as descriptive, the 'unwise' bit you could not hide.

'Unwise'. It reverberated in my head. The judge had put on his Black Cap and David McWilliams had just received a death sentence.

With that one word, 'unwise'—delivered with an assassin's calm—I realised that I was condemned to a blighted career of spiked Personnel reports, fatally scarred with the red scrawl of 'unwise' across them.

The Irish public service is broken down into two types of beings. There are those with 'horns' and those with 'halos'. Many careers are ruined by the acquisition of horns. Those with halos simply ascend into public service heaven, unfazed, as if gliding on gossamer wings of effortless success. Buoyed by nothing bar the bright lights of being the chosen ones.

In contrast, the horned ones are advised to maybe spend more time on their hobbies, cultivate other interests, because as long as the present management is in place they are going nowhere, fast. The fact that the Civil Service moves glacially, with death the only exit strategy for the senior ones, means those with horns could be waiting a lifetime for their luck to change.

The reason I was unwise is that I dared to question the mantra. The mantra was simple, and it was based less on economics and more on the endemic Irish insecurity of 'what will our neighbours think?' The mantra was that to devalue would be to bring scorn and ridicule on the country; no one would ever invest in Ireland again. This view was shared by all the senior civil servants at the Department of Finance and the Central Bank (as well as the other relevant economic departments like the IDA, Enterprise Ireland and the Department of Enterprise).

One part of me thinks that they just couldn't accept going to Brussels and facing the mandarins of the rest of the EU at the various committees which they attended every month and admitting they were not part of the big boys' club. It was the traditional petit bourgeois Irish concern about what they might think of us abroad, which influenced the thinking.

Of course they clung to the belief that if we devalued, we would never be taken seriously again. This yet again reveals the civil servant's inability to understand the mind of the investor.

The thing that the civil servant doesn't understand about free markets is that markets run on fear. If there is no fear, then there will be no innovation. If there is no fear, then everything will stay the same, and a market where everything stays the same isn't a market at all.

Perhaps it might help to explain why civil servants cannot understand markets. Markets cannot be controlled by a dirty look and a well-chosen word. Markets look for the bottom line. They don't care what you did yesterday; it is what you are going to do tomorrow that matters to them. And if they think that you are going to spend tomorrow flagellating yourself rather than addressing your problems in order to 'save face' amongst your bureaucratic peers, then the market will take itself and its money elsewhere. It will be back to pick up the bargains when your time finally runs out.

A year later I was working at Europe's biggest bank, UBS, and there I realised that the investor thinks in a totally different way to the civil servant. The investor wants to back a winning horse but also accepts that part of the game of winning is losing, so the key is to keep the future hopeful and accept some defeats, regarding them as organised retreats rather than catastrophes. Everyone wants to live to fight another day. So the thing that really scares investors is the Stalingrad scene, where an outnumbered and knackered army is led into the abyss by a fanatical general, losing good men and machinery unnecessarily.

During the 1992 currency crisis, Ireland was led by fanatics. These civil servants didn't seem to realise that every time they raised interest rates when unemployment was rising, it made the country look weaker, not stronger. They were scaring rational investors who know when the game's up.

But the mantra was repeated again and again. No devaluation. We were even told not to discuss the exchange rate outside the Central Bank lest we met friends who might work in the commercial banks. We were warned that if we devalued, it would be a disaster for Ireland.

In the end, like the last days in Hitler's bunker where the fanatics were moving around fictitious German armies that had long been defeated, the mad generals who made up the Irish war cabinet were moving money around that we had long spent. The devaluation came in early 1993. Inside the bunker, the place was a morgue. We had suffered a crushing defeat.

But outside on the streets there were celebrations. Not only did the economy not collapse, it took off. Before the devaluation, the mandarins had suggested that inflation would go through the roof in Ireland if we devalued. And guess what? Inflation actually fell in the following three years. They also argued that savings would be wiped out if we devalued. Well, measured in German marks, it is true that 10 per cent of the value of our savings was wiped out in 1993; did you even notice?

The mandarins said that interest rates would rise after the devaluation. The opposite happened. Interest rates fell dramatically and rapidly as investors saw that the madness was over and it was time to start again. This move signalled the beginning of the Celtic Tiger. Unemployment in Ireland dropped precipitously and American corporations started ploughing billions into the country. (In fact, since then, corporate America has invested twice as much in Ireland as it has done in the same period in China and India combined!) The bond investors, who had seen the value of their bondholdings fall by the amount of the devaluation, didn't sell all Irish assets and run away. They bought more, because the risk in Ireland had reduced. It was all upside for them and for us from then on.

Not only were the mandarins wrong, they were dangerously wrong. Many good businesses went to the wall during their pointless crusade and thousands of people were put on the dole during this episode. But guess what? What do you think happened to every one of those individuals who nearly drove our economy over the edge? They were promoted.

But let's not dwell on the idea that in Ireland you are promoted for failure, because that is the old regime, which has to change. What was a defeat for the mandarins, the insiders and advisors was a victory for the common people.

The same will happen again. This economy will boom and unemployment will fall if we tear up the script this time. All we need is the courage to do it.

The banking establishment is not the country. We are the country and they are the enemy within. The financial markets will support a putsch, as will our Diaspora. But have we got the balls? Have we got a T. K. Whitaker or a Sean Lemass?

Chapter 22

ON RIALTO BRIDGE

'What's the news of Rialto, man?'

'I dunno. My fella's gone fierce quiet,' said the Merchant of Ennis.

'Don't like quiet in this market,' responded Shylock.

'Eerie quiet everywhere.'

'It's as if we're waiting for something to happen.'

'Yeah, just waiting.'

Shylock lit up a Benson. He took a heavy drag, lagging behind the Merchant, who strode forward, still a hostage to hope.

Shylock knew it was over, but he was waiting to put the next phase in place. In Shylock's head it was 2011, when all these defaulted deals would be his for a song. The Merchant and all the eejits like him would be working in Maxol garages, tortured by regret, learning to live as bankrupts.

The Merchant, in contrast, couldn't think beyond this evening. He could barely see past the next hour. He didn't understand it. The Rialto deal had looked so simple. It was the last roll of the dice, doubles or bust. He was so sure, so very certain that he would get away with it.

How could he tell everyone? Elaine was at home with the children. She hadn't a clue. She'd be devastated. The banks would move on the house and they'd be pariahs in the town.

But that was just for starters. The lads in the club, what would they think? More importantly, what would they do? This last gamble was all the cash they had. He'd gone through all the details with them. He'd promised they would be out in two years.

How had he, fearing the whole thing was going belly up, taken money from them? But that's what happens when the creditors start calling. The desperate bankrupt will always try anything to keep himself above water.

And there was a charge over Richie's house. Richie, his best friend from school, his best man, Daddy of little Tom, Elaine's godson.

Maybe Shylock could get him out of it. The Merchant trusted Shylock. He was a good youngfella. Smart as paint, knew all the angles. Was there anyone out there now who could come in and buy Rialto from him?

The deal was supposed to be foolproof. He had bought a share in the site with the 200 new council flats planned for it. The builder who sold it to him was now in Australia. This builder had done a deal with the government, a 'land swap' is what they called it. All the rage in 2007, so it was. The builder was part of a consortium that bought the lease from the government. The top man in the consortium, Mr Big, was one of the biggest developers in the country. Totally blue chip. Mr Big had all the big developments in Dublin, worth billions and he was from Clare too. When the town heard the Merchant was in bed with Mr Big, that was it. There'd be no stopping him. They were all safe. Not just that, they were going to be rich.

Mr Big was going to knock down the old flats and rebuild much better ones in their place. He would put in a new community centre, a playground and shops. This blighted Dub estate would get some Clare fairy dust all right. The government would get new homes built on previously rundown 1950s council flat complexes.

In return, Mr Big would get land in the centre of the city because the new flats would be built on a tighter area of the original land, going up a bit higher, two more storeys, it was. A 'smaller footprint' went the jargon.

This left him with 'free' land on the original site on which he could build 100 new private apartments. The Merchant financed 20 per cent of the whole thing, putting him in line for a massive payoff. With all the young people wanting to move into the city, he would flog them easily and, as they came stuffed with tax breaks, they could charge much more for them.

Therefore, Mr Big and his consortium would do the State a favour, rehouse the poor and make a fortune for themselves in the process, paid for by the people who bought the private apartments who thought they were avoiding tax.

But for some reason, the original builder, despite going through two years' negotiation with the government, became uneasy and talked about making a lifestyle choice. That was when Shylock approached the Merchant.

Shylock had put the initial deal together and he had arranged for all the original buyers to buy off plans. This was back when Shylock was still working at the mortgage broker. By that stage he had moved from individual mortgage applications to bundling dozens of them together. In fact, this was the last batch of mortgages he sold, because he moved on to work with the Godfather, organising syndicates. The same work, just higher up the ladder—bigger loans and bigger fees. Bigger margins, too. He couldn't believe the amounts of money changing hands. All he had to do was make a call. The Godfather knew everyone in town—everyone.

Shylock knew the builder who wanted to sell his share in the site. So when the builder approached the bank saying he wanted out, the Godfather asked Shylock to find a new buyer. The Godfather assured him that if he put this deal together for Mr Big, the sky was the limit. Like the Godfather, Mr Big believed in loyalty. They were all very tight.

The builder, who had gone from being a chippy to quite a force in apartment building in just a few years, said he wanted a change of scene and wanted to move to Australia with his wife and new baby.

The Godfather had known this builder for years. They had got rich together. He was one of the new lads whom the Godfather had backed on instinct. The builder's success and the fees coming from lads like him was what sparked the turf war between the Godfather and the other Dons. By 2006 everyone wanted him—even the perennially snobby Bank of Ireland was inviting him to Cheltenham, all expenses paid—but the builder, Breakfast Roll Man, wanted out. Get out when you're ahead, his aul' fella always said, even though he'd never gotten out of anything, because he was never ahead.

But Breakfast Roll Man was ancient history to Shylock. He was on to the next thing. He knew the drill. The key was to lovebomb the buyer. Tell him the deal was 'off-market', for his eyes only. All hush, hush, all confidential.

'Just between you and me.'

'Not a word to anyone.'

'I can trust you, can't I?'

Once they had stars in their eyes, he reeled them in. He did the same to five bidders all on the 'nudge, nudge, wink, wink, say no more' basis.

There were plenty of suitors. After all, the deal was simple: build decent houses for the dirt poor paid for by fleecing the filthy rich. Then you throw them all in next door to each other and see how they get on.

Don't forget to stand well back. Shylock allowed himself a smirk. If they didn't get on, it was the coppers' problem. He'd still get paid before the first Audi TT was hotwired. Gentrification, it was called.

The Merchant of Ennis saw none of this. The development was his opportunity for the big time. He could refinance all his other deals, some of which were struggling. He worried once or twice about them, but was so far in that the only thing to do was keep expanding. After all, it was August 2007. There was money everywhere. Practically falling off the trees. Above all, he'd be in with Mr Big and all the banks would take this as a signal that he was untouchable. That's what Shylock said anyway. Shylock always had the little detail that appealed, the little push that got them to sign.

The Merchant only met Breakfast Roll Man once. He seemed like a good bloke, happy to leave something on the table for the next guy. A typical Dub with the faded Three Castles on the Arnotts jersey—*He's seen some disappointment in his time*, thought the Merchant.

He was a grounded fella too, loaded but still driving the dusty blue Ducato van. Breakfast Roll Man hadn't changed much over the years. His missus came along to that one meeting and she seemed like a decent sort, chatting about babies and stuff.

He told the Merchant that he was looking at deals in Australia, which is why he was selling. The Merchant of Ennis thought he was mad, but kept his mouth shut. He was getting a steal, after all. Breakfast Roll Man said the weather was getting on his nerves, always had done. He'd finally had enough of the Irish summer. All two days of it. They laughed over that one.

They had a few drinks together in the Submarine, Breakfast Roll Man's choice.

As they were leaving, Breakfast Roll Man's missus, now two vodkas past sober, giggled something about Pat Kenny. It went over the Merchant's head, but Breakfast Roll Man was furious.

The Merchant didn't get it, but he laughed anyway. It must have been something she saw on the *Late Late*. You know the way women talk? Sure you'd be on a hiding to nothing trying to figure them out.

HAVE YOU DONE YOUR EKKER YET?

At the start, the Merchant was a bit nervous. It was a huge amount of money, but Shylock assured the Merchant he'd double his investment, the way the market was going. Shylock had pre-sold half of the apartments on the Rialto site off plans. Miss Pencil Skirt was amongst the first he'd financed. She was enthusiastic and upbeat on the phone, if a little hesitant. In the end, he got her 100 per cent. All in. Shylock had even looked her up on Facebook, deciding he needed a hook to get her.

She looked like fun, beaming at the camera, surrounded by her mates at the inevitable barbeque. Somewhere warm of course—Maldives '07, apparently. Bit rich for his purposes. He checked out her top five musical acts: The Jam, Queens of the Stone Age, Dizzee Rascal, Brian Wilson, Bat For Lashes. Interesting mix for little miss university. But that was all he needed. He emailed her that day:

'Exclusive Competition Offer—Sign up to 100 per cent interest-only mortgage before 1 March and you could win four Electric Picnic tickets!'

He could see from her Facebook page that all her friends were the same, like an army of Stepford Wives with 'natural' highlights and matching BlackBerrys. She'd sell the idea to all of them before she'd even confirmed the deal with him. *Free advertising is a wonderful thing*, he thought.

He had her signed up within a week. Shylock always found that crucial detail to close the deal. That was his motto—'do your ekker, always do your fuckin' ekker, man'.

With pre-sales like Miss Pencil Skirt, Shylock's new bank was only too happy to back the Merchant to the hilt. Project finance, they called it. The mortgages would pay the interest on the loan and the capital when it was all finished. The Merchant of Ennis was on the pig's back, even making the property section of the *Irish Times* for the deal of the month. No longer a small player, he was the man. He was pictured with Mr Big—two Claremen. His mother was so proud. Secretly she wished her husband had gone for it all those years ago. She tore out the article and stuck it to the fridge door at home. His dad just told him to be careful and make sure everyone was looked after and be certain that no one in the town was getting into something they couldn't get out of.

Christ, he needed Dad now.

Over two dozen people in the town bought the apartments off plans. It was the talk of O'Neill's, how they'd all have to meet up on All Ireland weekend in their new 'pads' in Dublin. C'mon, the Banner.

Shylock organised a one-off deal for 48 apartments to be done with his former mortgage broker friends. He was always so helpful, thought the Merchant. He believed in Shylock. And they believed in the Merchant. Hadn't he led the village to county championship fame in the hurling in 1997? Wasn't he '97 Kevin? They couldn't go wrong with him. In early 2008, it still seemed bright what with Mr Big and all.

Then rumours started flying about Mr Big. He was in trouble and the Godfather was in trouble too. Mr Big was into all the banks for billions and the market had turned. The problem was that all the deals were cross-collateralised. This means that if one deal goes, they all go. The creditors come after everything. And as the Merchant of Ennis was a junior partner in the Rialto deal, he hadn't a leg to stand on. The apartments, if they were ever built, would be worth a fraction of the price his people paid for them. The Merchant's people were on the hook, legally. He was also on the hook because he'd borrowed €12 million for his share and now it was his share of nothing and everything was personally guaranteed—that's how Shylock and the Godfather worked.

Mr Big was closed down. The deal was off and the Merchant of Ennis was left picking up the pieces in Rialto. His world was in tatters.

Shylock barely flinched at the Merchant's agony. The Benson and Hedges smoke flared through his nostrils. He knew how he'd make money on it, Merchant or no Merchant. In fact, the way he saw it, things were going perfectly. They couldn't be going better.

SHYLOCK

Detached, Shylock observed the way the former captains of the boom now looked at him with pleading eyes, hoping for redemption. The swagger was gone now, along with the repossessed Lexus. He couldn't decide who was worse—these bankrupts with their impossible dreams, clutching at the economics of 2007, or the cowards at the bank, these tarnished knights of the free market, who were knifing each other in the back in a pathetic attempt to ingratiate themselves with the new government owners. None of them understood the game.

They were sheep. They had no spine, happy to stumble along with the herd, never joining the dots, never looking out the window. But that was just fine. Where these losers saw despair, Shylock smelled money. Opportunity was everywhere. He was going to make a fortune from their misfortune. In a few years, he'd be so big that they'd all be coming to him for work. They'd still avoid eye contact in the pub, but now it'd be because you don't look directly at your king. *There'll be no hard feelings,* he thought. *I'll pick the best of them. Everyone has a role to play, each one of them has a use and, most importantly, a value.* And unlike the Godfather, Shylock had no intention of taking his eye off the ball.

The minute the Merchant had walked into the room, Shylock knew he had one. The boom was still roaring, but it was starting to get a bit too wobbly for some of the seasoned players. Breakfast Roll Man could see the sums didn't add up. He was a builder; that was his job. He was nervous, waiting for a signal. Then the Pat Kenny story broke. It was all he needed. When a guy grabs some of his neighbour's garden, claims squatter's rights and gets involved in a scuffle, things are going off the rails. Breakfast Roll Man decided it was time to cash in and head to Sydney.

Shylock also knew what was going to happen. But he liked to play a much more dangerous game. He knew that the madder it got at the top, the more he'd make at the bottom. So he did everything in his power to sign off as many loans as possible at the top. The Merchant of Ennis was one of his most dependable victims.

Shylock knew how the country worked. The Establishment would never abandon the bankers. They were all mates, all part of the tribe. They were insiders, as though that mattered. The government wouldn't let the banks go bust, even though they were run by morons and had no right to stay open. There would be a plan hatched to leech ordinary people like his ma for the bill.

It was the same thing they'd done when the priests rode all those youngfellas back in the day, he thought. Those lads were the same as him, no das to protect them from the creepy perverts that go bump in the night. Poor little youngfellas with no mas or das to comfort them in the darkness. All alone, abused by the people who were supposed to be looking out for them.

So of course the government hands us the bill and the Church gets away with it. Shylock lit another smoke. It'd be funny if it wasn't so tragic. He knew that the same thing was about to happen again. The government would buy all this shit from the developers, that was certain. Shylock could see how it would all pan out. This is how it works in Ireland. All the bankers were petrified, swearing blind that they were never on the Godfather's side when they'd been lodged so far up his arse that they could describe the inside of his nostrils. Eejits.

No one took responsibility. What confirmed his suspicions was all the same creeps turning up time and again. This was the Irish pattern. If you understood the pattern, and Shylock most certainly did, you could make a mint. Why get angry? What was the point? Just work the pattern. Nobody got rich marching for fairness and equality. When he saw that the same lawyers who represented the pervert clergy were now advising the government on the banks, he knew. The people would pay. Same shit, different day, as they say.

His ma, who hadn't stepped inside a church since the Pope's youth mass, would be footing the bill for the priestly paedophiles. Those would be the same lads who had called her a slut for getting up the duff without a ring on her finger 30 years ago. That's how this kip worked.

Shylock didn't show anger about things like that. He could have—he never forgot it, any of it—but that was no one's business but his own. He didn't say a word. He kept it all inside and he made money. Lots of money. Success is the best revenge, he'd heard, years ago. It made sense to him.

His plan was based on the State buying all the land from the developers to save the banks. He knew they'd do that. He also knew that they'd have to sell the stuff cheaper in a few years, when he'd be waiting. He'd have done his ekker, all right.

First, they'd say that the State would trade the land to make the most money for the people. The spin would be: 'Trust us. We'll get your money back from those nasty developers.' *And if you believe that, I'll tell you another,* thought Shylock.

All the while, the banks' share prices would begin to recover. But it wouldn't be fast enough for the new generation of bankers who were going to take over. Those lads would want to forget about all these loans, the land and the mess that they'd created. They would have to get that land, now government-owned, back on the market double-quick if they wanted to enjoy another property boom in a few years' time. Same old, same old.

So the banks and their loyal lawyer mates would very quietly lobby their pals in government to sell the land at a large discount very soon, not tell anyone and put the difference on the national debt. *Sure they may as well,* he thought, *who'll notice another few million at this stage?* Shylock calculated that the difference between the price the government paid for the land in 2009 to keep the banks afloat and the price they would sell the land for in 2011 or thereabouts to enable the same banks to create another boom, would be picked up by the taxpayer.

For Shylock, the transactions and the market would evolve in a predictable way. Take (for example) the Merchant of Ennis's portfolio of property, which Shylock lent him the money to assemble. At the height of the boom, the Merchant had borrowed €18 million. The land, flats and apartments were now worth half that at €9 million, but to make sure the banks don't go bust, the government would buy the portfolio for €14 million. If the government bought the portfolio for €9 million—which it was worth—the banks would have to take a €9 million loss, which would bankrupt them. So Shylock reckoned the government would pay over the odds for everything.

But the government would soon realise that the only way it could get the market moving would be to sell the Merchant's portfolio and hundreds like it. This is how markets work. You need a seller and a buyer. So to lubricate the land market in Ireland it would have to start selling, and soon. Shylock's plan is based on the fact that the government would sell this portfolio dirt cheap to get it off their hands and it would do so quietly.

Shylock knows what it's like to have cash in hand when you're in trouble and believes that if he builds up a war chest now, he will buy the Merchant of Ennis's portfolio for 20 per cent of its peak value. The government will be forced to sell at that price, otherwise the property market in Ireland will remain frozen.

So now he's building his cash pile. He's going to speak to people like Breakfast Roll Man who got out when the going was good and who have cash. He will set up on his own, buy everything he can with as much money as he can possibly raise and then wait for the next generation of Merchants of Ennis to come along and buy it off him for twice the price he paid the government.

Yet again he is three steps ahead. And the poor Merchant standing beside him on Rialto Bridge hasn't a rashers.

It's a nice life, Shylock thinks. Success is definitely the best revenge. He might even buy a car, he thinks. There are some good deals at the moment.

THE MERCHANT'S LAST STAND

The Merchant of Ennis thought about the letter from the bank. It was notice of proceedings against him and Elaine as she was the company secretary for the company which owned the empty estate in Lahinch. The Rialto deal was all in his name because he got greedy and wanted to pay only 20 per cent capital gains on the upside. They'd come after him, the house, the car, the boat, everything. He'd be on the streets and so too would his friends.

What would his father have thought? The funeral was only four weeks ago and even then there was still a chance. Now it was over and Elaine didn't know anything. She questioned him the other day, when they were visiting the grave but he lied and said it was all under control.

He asked Shylock did he want a lift from Rialto to town. He was going down as far as the Four Courts to meet a solicitor. Shylock said he'd take the lift that far then hop on the Luas. They drove in silence around Heuston Station.

The Merchant thought of all the good times he and the lads had coming up to Dublin for matches, missing trains and hitching home. How they'd come up and won in '95 when he was still on the fringes of the squad. And, then in '97 when he won and the town went mad. Heuston Station had nothing but fond memories for him. When life was simple, when they were innocent, before this madness gripped them all.

Shylock didn't speak much. He jumped out at the Four Courts and told the Merchant he'd call him tomorrow. The Merchant watched Shylock as he moved swiftly towards the lights at the bridge where a crowd had gathered, trying to get across. The lights must have been broken. He watched Shylock, this strange character, as he slipped through the crowd. He smoked incessantly, like a human steam engine, puffing his way down the street. A queue formed at the lights. It must have been three deep. Barristers with double chins and funny collars awkwardly clutched bulky files. Soon the Merchant's life would be in one of those folders. It was the book of evidence that was about to be thrown at him.

Shylock stood behind the barristers who'd seen a good lunch or seven, at the back of the throng, beside a woman in a yellow dress holding a child with a blue balloon. Shylock was actually a lot taller than he seemed, a good head above most of the other people at the lights. The Merchant had never noticed it before. That was the way it was with Shylock, people only began to notice things about him when he had lost interest in them, when he had all his ekker done and when he decided it was time to move on.

In fact, Shylock was a good six inches taller than the barristers and about half the width. He was staring ahead at the next lights, oblivious to the overweight pinstripes around him.

The Merchant's hands-free on the dash rang and he glanced down. It stopped after one ring, before he could answer. 'Private Number'. When he looked up again the barristers were still there. So was the woman with the child, who was now looking up at the sky, his balloon taking flight. The people were still jostling for position at the lights.

But Shylock was gone. The Merchant looked everywhere, over the bridge, down the quay on the Liffey side. But there was nothing. Shylock had disappeared.

Later, on the drive home, the Merchant of Ennis turned off his phone for the first time in five years. The solicitor couldn't have been clearer and the implications were obvious. He didn't so much care about the law or the banks in Dublin, it was the people, his people, and what he had done to them. He understood what happened in Ireland when you fell, you fell far and no one picked you up. That's the way we were.

At the graveyard, his father's headstone wasn't up yet, something about the ground being too soft for four months after the funeral. All that was left was a little temporary cross, with his mother's latest wreath. This was it.

The Merchant blessed himself automatically and stared down at the mound of earth. At the funeral everything was so different. Everyone was there. The graveside was packed with friends, family and local people. They spoke of his dad as being a gent, a decent man who'd never, in all his years of business, damage the good name of the town, the people and, most of all, the family. The Rices were always good people.

He missed his dad. He hadn't realised how much in all this madness. He would never see him again. He was on his own. He wanted him back, just once, just for now.

But what could I do, Dad? They were falling over themselves to get involved. You know how it was. I didn't mean to get in this far. It wasn't my fault, Dad. I got swept away.

What am I going to do, Dad? Elaine knows nothing, nor does Mam. What would you do? Everyone's involved and it's all my fault. But everyone was doing it. They said it could never go down and the banks were throwing money at me.

Will they ever forgive me?

Can you forgive me?

Can you, Dad?

Back in the car, he switched on his phone. Six missed calls from home. Elaine must know now. She'd probably opened the post.

Poor Elaine. She'd never known the extent of the deception. She thought he was on top of everything. She knew nothing of the money taken from this account and put into that account. She didn't know about the last round of financing after Christmas when he'd gone back to his oldest friends, lads he played hurling with, and taken their money explicitly to pay Shylock's interest payment.

He'd told them, his closest friends, the new money was for a new project he was working on which was a dead cert. But it wasn't. It was for Shylock so that Shylock wouldn't pull the plug.

He, '97 Kevin, the local hero, the man who put the village on the map, had ended up robbing his own friends—the people who respected him—to pay this weirdo in Dublin who had disappeared at the lights as if he were never there.

He hadn't just taken his pound of flesh. Shylock had taken the Merchant's soul.

Chapter 23 ～

MISS PENCIL SKIRT
FIGURES IT OUT

Miss Pencil Skirt stopped at the door. She looked around at the remnants of her former life. Did it really have to be like this? Move back to her dad's, and lose her little apartment? She might even have to head back to London. Wherever she went, the black credit mark would follow, like one of those red 'a's they used to give adulterers. How could this happen?

Surely one of the politicians who lived on 'Prime Time' could answer those questions. Wasn't that what they were there for?

She stopped at the mirror. Well, at least the Pilates was still working. Pity she couldn't afford the classes any more. She was still in great shape, young, fit, intelligent and, like thousands of her generation— born around the time the Pope came to Ireland in 1979—she had so much going for her. Were we all about to give up now and accept that the last 10 years were a mirage? It was ridiculous.

She needed hope. They all needed hope. Some developers lost the plot and bet the farm on vanity projects, and for that everyone's future was shut down? It didn't seem logical.

She couldn't understand why they didn't just let the banks fail and set up new ones. You know, the way failed shops close and new ones reopen? That plan seemed to work for the rest of the planet, she thought. Clearly, 'Ireland is different', as they used to say in 2007.

Her dad had tried to explain it to her the other night but he was spoofing. She always knew when he was spoofing because he took in a big gulp of air before he answered and tended to inspect the back wall, while saying things like, 'It's very tricky, actually, love.' She did love him when he did it, though. He was like so many other Irish blokes she'd met, bullshitters—but decent bullshitters—our bullshitters. They'd sell you the sun, moon and stars, but in fairness to them, they wouldn't actually charge you for them.

The bloke she was with now had a touch of that. He was a dreamer, but a fun one, with good taste in music and funny in a soft kind of way. Typical type, lazy but clever—full of plans but found it hard to get out of bed on the weekdays for work. Never had a problem on the weekend when they were both up early for the surf. Could build shelves but had no idea what Toilet Duck was for. Your basic Irishman, in fact.

She loved looking at him as he drove them to Sligo early on Saturday morning despite only four hours' kip. Him unshaven, clearly knackered, squinting through his cheap €2.99 shades, making her laugh as they argued over the car playlist. She was falling in love with him. And that was another reason why the bloody recession thing was so inconvenient. She had plans. She was nearly 30, for Christ's sake. Her poor mother had had three kids by then. She missed her now more than ever.

Dad was tired too. She could sense it. He was sick of the banks and their new forms. They were tightening the credit lines for the small firm he'd built up over the years. The printing game was hard enough without having your working capital cut. What got on his nerves was that he hadn't got involved in the Mania.

He hated it when he heard people on telly say things like 'We all lost the run of ourselves.' No. We hadn't. Not all of us. This was just a way to spread the blame. He hadn't lost the run of himself, nor had most of his friends. They didn't have second houses. They didn't have apartments in Spain. What he did have was a file of school reports and orthodontic invoices and a mantelpiece full of athletics trophies. He spent his cash on his kids and ploughed it back into the business, so that the kids might take it over when he'd had enough, if it suited them.

Now, he had to pay to bail out the banks, who'd bet all their money and his money and apparently the money of any fool who would lend to them on a few flashy gobshites who wouldn't know how to run a real business in a month of Sundays. All these lads understood was the basic idea that if you borrow and borrow and borrow, eventually you are the banks' problem not the other way around. And now, worse, as far as he could see, the government was siding with these eejits because they were all mates and they were asking him to pay more taxes to keep these banks open. All his family's security was disappearing faster than Michael Lynn.

She checked her hair in the mirror. It looked good up. Was this the last Electric Picnic she could afford to go to? Actually, she thought, was this the last Electric Picnic that there would be because if she and her friends were now out of jobs, where would they get the money to go next year? More importantly, if they weren't going, where would the organiser get the money to pay for the bands next year?

She had a panic the other day when people started saying on Facebook that Electric Picnic was bust. The previous three had been such a laugh and she'd be disappointed if the festival wasn't going ahead. But then she heard that despite the company that ran the gig being bust, the gig was still on. She couldn't get her head around this. How could the company that ran the festival be bust, yet the festival continue? Were they paying in air?

Wasn't the whole thing real? The news said that the company had too many debts to continue trading. But if the festival was going on and people bought tickets and saw bands and had fun, what difference did it make? Either the festival was going ahead or it wasn't.

Her dad said that when you really think about it, debt isn't real. It's accountancy. Real stuff is going to the gig, having the stamp on the back of your hand, an overpriced pint and dancing to the music. What did they care if the company was bankrupt? Surely a new company would just take on the festival meaning that 40,000 people would have fun anyway? Then something else struck her. If Electric Picnic could be technically bust but continue and be even better than before, could the same thing happen with the country?

Real wealth was people, education, ability and work. Money was just something you used to pay for stuff. As long as you all believed it was worth something, then it was. But when you stopped believing it was worth what it said on the piece of paper, then it wasn't any more.

She thought about Electric Picnic. If it was going ahead, it was real. This was true whether or not the company that ran it was different to the one that ran it last year. She shook her head. Back to the money stuff. She'd done economics in first year in Arts at UCD. It wasn't that hard. She hated the sums—so she dropped it—but the logic of it was fairly straightforward.

In her head it was simple. Ireland borrowed too much money and couldn't pay it back. Either we spent the next 10 years trying to do so, turning ourselves into a large debt-servicing agency for creditors, or we didn't. What then?

The more she thought about money, the funnier it seemed. After all, in her brief lifetime, Ireland had had three currencies. The year she was born there was the Irish pound, then the punt for ages and now the euro. None of the changes had ever made much difference to her daily life. *So if we've had three in my time,* she wondered, *and nothing adverse seemed to happen, what's to stop us changing again?*

IRELAND'S BEST ASSETS

She checked her list: Cheapo McCheapo tent, two-man McGlinchy bomb shelter tent (just in case the weather got nasty), two sleeping bags, two pillows, a couple of yoga mats for cushioning, two fold-up deckchairs for chilling outside tent, lots of loo roll, two towels, crappy tent sheet, ear plugs and a pink flag to identify the tent whenever they crawled back from the main stage.

What else? Bikini for showers, comb, slides and bobbins for hair, hat, Puma top, hoodie, cardi, flip flops, trackie bottoms for Monday, knickers, socks, bras, green boob tube, white Roxy top, runners, jeans, wellies, Gore-Tex rain jacket, small mirror for make up, lots of beads and earrings, make up, moisturiser, cleanser, cotton wool, toothpaste, toothbrush, some factor 15, old Nokia charger, little bag for carrying stuff, disposable camera, shades, booze, more booze, bread and milk for brekkie, plastic plates, glasses, utensils, water, cooler bag, plasters, and Motilium and Solpadeine for hangover.

Had she left anything out? Torch, yes, they'd need a torch—particularly after getting lost last year. Oh and batteries, of course. They needed to set up a meeting place. Maybe beside the Burning Man tent or the Mindfield area—it was chilled and not too busy.

Her generation were born organisers. Her boyfriend said that if they were in charge, this economy would be sorted. All people had to do was see clearly and not panic.

A thought struck her when she was on her hands and knees, looking for hair clips. The first thing to do was what Dad always did in his business, she thought: identify the problem. Once you find the issue, you can sort it out. That seemed pretty straightforward to her.

The banks weren't lending money. So instead of there being loads of cash about like a few years ago, everyone was broke, or getting there.

Dad said the recessions in the 1980s were different. Back then, there was a big problem dating from the 1970s when he and Mum got married. It always seemed to be about the cost of everything. He remembered queuing for petrol with cars backed up past Sutton Cross and out towards Baldoyle. The price of oil went through the roof, followed quickly by everything else. Lots of firms went out of business.

But it wasn't because people stopped spending. There was never that much money around anyway and people had no debts. In the 1980s, though, the country seemed to get into huge debt very fast. Dad and Mum didn't pay much attention. They just got on with it.

Taxes were high. Her dad remembered that interest rates were high too but he was doing printing jobs for companies in England, which was rocking, so he was doing OK. Many of his friends were working in England and he used to go over and back on the B&I ferry from North Wall and get the train to London.

The business was helped by a devaluation of the punt at the time. Or maybe there were two devaluations, he couldn't remember at this stage. This made it easier to pitch for English business and cheaper to deliver to the people in Woking who were buying from him.

Originally, he'd got the contract because one of his friends from Joey's in Fairview was working there and introduced him to the boss. Dad had always thought that his mates who'd left would be a great marketing tool for Irish companies. That's the way business runs, it's about the network, who knows who and who can introduce you to who. We might need them again now, he had said.

Miss Pencil Skirt sat back, looking over her packing. She understood that if there was no cash around, that could explain why people weren't spending and why she'd lost her own job. Over the years she had noticed that what she did was affected by what other people did. So for example, if all her gang were going to Electric Picnic, she'd have to go too. It was the same with bands. The way bands became popular was something that always fascinated her.

Bands were contagious. Their popularity was fuelled by word of mouth and attitude. Obviously, they had to be halfway decent, but the way some rapidly went from being marginal to being huge was an exercise in group psychology as much as anything else. It was the same with money, she reckoned. If lots of people were spending that meant more would spend too, mainly because prices were always rising so if you didn't buy today, you'd pay more tomorrow.

Surely the opposite must hold too? If the banks weren't lending, then some people would stop spending. That would scare other people enough to slow down too. Then prices would start to fall. But as they started falling, people would begin to think that they will fall more again tomorrow, so why buy today? That's how the cycle worked, she thought. Bad news brings more bad news.

So something had to be done, by the politicians, to make our people think prices would not fall but would rise. How could this be done? She looked over the Comedy Tent line-up. She'd heard that Des Bishop's new set was hilarious. Tommy Tiernan was there too and that young guy, Jarlath Regan. He was brilliant. Maybe those lads might have an idea. It's not as if anyone else was coming forward.

She tucked the listing away in her bag, but couldn't stop turning the ideas over in her head. Could we just print new money to replace the old stuff that people were keeping under the mattress? It seemed obvious. But if it was yet it wasn't being done, maybe she was missing something.

The politicians said this was a global problem and if it wasn't for the rest of the world, Ireland would still be fine. They talked about it as if we'd caught something from Iceland, like the economic equivalent of swine flu. But she'd heard someone else from the government on the radio the other day, saying how brilliant it was that Ireland's exports were doing so well. They were up, she thought he said, by 6 per cent, while in other places like Germany exports were down by 30 per cent.

That sounded good for Ireland. But what Miss Pencil Skirt couldn't figure out was that if our whole problem, the dole queues and everything else, was caused by the rest of the world, how come they still had the cash to buy our stuff?

That argument didn't stand up. Obviously, she thought, if our exports were rising but our local economy was shrinking, then the problems couldn't have been caused by the rest of the world. If they were, then the opposite would be happening. Exports would be falling and local jobs would be increasing.

She heard on the 'RTÉ News' the other day that the Irish savings ratio had increased massively in the past six months. That meant her hunch on the postponed spending was right. The saving rate measured the amount people were saving, so now we were saving loads whereas before we saved nothing. That made sense. The less we spend, the less people want to pay for things like PR, which is why she had found herself down in the dole office.

WHOSE MONEY IS IT ANYWAY?

Miss Pencil Skirt dragged her bag down the stairs. It weighed a ton. Maybe she could lose something. But she couldn't think of anything that she could do without. Sod it anyway, it'd be grand.

Diarmuid was down at the car, fiddling with stuff in the boot. Typical. He always thought he could organise it and he hadn't a clue. Blokes. She whooshed him away and surveyed the damage. Sometimes she wondered how he managed to get dressed in the morning. This would take a while to sort out.

She pulled all the stuff out and started again, this time arranging it so that the big stuff—tent, sleeping bags—was at the back and her bag, which contained the tickets, was at the front. As she tidied it up, she wondered, *Why can't we just print new money? If we did, people would believe that prices were going to rise, not fall. Then, surely, people would start to spend again. Why is nobody asking this question?*

When Diarmuid came back with a cup of tea for her, she asked him. He laughed and made a joke in his infectious Tyrone lilt, then got serious. He said we were in the euro and it couldn't happen. Money was printed in Germany now so we'd have to ask the Germans to print all the new currency. They wouldn't do it, he said, because they were afraid of inflation.

'Do you remember those photos in your school history books of Germans before Hitler going around with wheelbarrows full of paper money in order to buy something real like bread? Well, that's why.'

But she couldn't figure out what a German history lesson had to do with her being out of work. She was clever and hard-working. She had a degree and seven years' work experience, for God's sake. What the hell did old Germans have to do with her?

The way she saw it, if we carried on like we were, most Irish people wouldn't be able to pay their borrowings anyway, so they might as well print new money because they were going to default on their old stuff in a few months.

I mean, she had just told the bank she couldn't pay her mortgage. Not because she didn't want to but because she couldn't. She was spending the last of her redundancy now. All the stuff they had for Electric Picnic they'd bought when they had jobs. Short of trying to flog it all on eBay, she might as well use it.

Like everyone else, she didn't buy anything new now because she didn't have the cash. So if she was defaulting, who else was? In the papers they said unemployment would go to 500,000 and it was being suffered mostly by people under the age of 35. So they'd all be defaulting soon enough.

Unemployment was going up and up and it was her generation that was bearing the brunt. They were the ones who'd bought the new houses and they were the ones who couldn't afford them any more.

GIVE US A BREAK

The car was loaded up, finally. Tea had been drunk and toast munched. Time to go. They'd better get a move on if they were going to miss the traffic.

Diarmuid drove as fast as he could until they were out of Dublin. Miss Pencil Skirt looked at all the 'For Sale' signs that lined the roads as they went by, wondering how many were voluntary and how many were repossessions. If the banks and the government really believed in the future like they said, why didn't they defer the mortgages? That would give people hope.

Why not say to people like her, 'Listen—we realise you can't pay the full amount now. Let's work something out that benefits both of us.'

After all, the same bank had given her a 100 per cent mortgage three years ago for the apartment in Rialto. They could do something like cut the total amount (the €380,000 principal) in half and say: 'You keep paying the mortgage on half of the total amount and we'll defer the other half and take it back from you when you sell the house in ten years' time. If the price in ten years is more than the mortgage, we'll take the full amount from you. We're both square then.'

She wouldn't be off the hook, but would have a breathing space so things weren't so desperate. Surely that made sense for everyone in the long run. It wasn't about dodging responsibility; it was about making lemonade, as her mum used to say.

The politicians were always talking about the genius of the Irish people and how, if we could get over this hump, the future was bright. Well, why not take a bet on the people and have a mass debt deferral—not forgiveness, just deferral?

After all, it seemed to be what they were doing for the big guys. Miss Pencil Skirt wasn't following it religiously, but from what she could make out, the government had set up a sort of financial skip for big debts. Like builders, they were going to chuck all the economic waste into it. Then it would be taken for recycling and hopefully someone would pay something for this stuff, so that all the money wouldn't be wasted.

What was it called? NAMA, that's it. Supposedly, it would allow the big guys to get off scot-free. The banks who had lent them money said in the paper that the bill for the difference between what the government was going to pay for all these sites and what the sites had been bought for would be picked up by the taxpayer! This meant her.

Well, not technically, because she wasn't paying tax any more.

And that's what didn't stack up, she thought. If all her friends were losing their jobs, who'd be left to pay the tax bill for the sins of the developers? If the people who were in work had to pay all this tax, they'd have no money left to spend. Prices would continue to fall and things would get worse.

And we couldn't print new money because those Germans wouldn't allow it. So, basically, she had to stay on the dole in Kilbarrack.

It didn't seem fair to Miss Pencil Skirt. Nor was it smart, she thought. It seemed as if the government was betting all it had left to keep the old banks in business and make sure that no one who invested in the banks would lose money. But had they not taken the gamble? They were happy enough to take the money from us when things were going well. Now that things had fallen apart, we were supposed to go on the dole, emigrate or stump up huge taxes to pay off the people who had taken a punt on us. *Surely*, she thought, *this is a win, win, win situation for the people who lent to the banks and lose, lose, lose for the average Irish person.*

Even the name NAMA was a bit of a cod, she thought. It stood for the National Asset Management Agency. But these bits of land weren't assets. Even with a semester of economics 10 years ago, she could see they were liabilities. If they were assets, we wouldn't need to worry about them. But they were worthless. Even in her most flamboyant PR moments, she'd never try to pull a scam like that. You can't call something an asset when it is worthless. That isn't PR. It's just lying.

It seemed to her that the interests of the banks and their property friends were the key anchors of economic policy. The government was bankrolled by builders who were bankrolled by bankers who were bankrupting us.

She checked under the seat for her rain jacket, because you never know with the Irish weather and camping. All there, just as it was 15 minutes ago. Outside, the weather had anticipated her thoughts and it was starting to pour, reflecting her mood. She thought to herself, *What the hell is actually going on in Ireland, in my country, our country?*

Liabilities are being called assets; banks that are bust are being bailed out; developers who blew colossal amounts on their vanity projects are being rescued; and it's all of us, who didn't go mad during the Mania, who have to pay for it? Not only did we not all go mad, but those of us who held back were ridiculed by the politicians who all said we'd better take out loans and mortgages to 'get on the ladder'.

It was crazy, but it wasn't the only thing that didn't make sense to her. If the people couldn't pay their debts, why did the government think that the State could pay its own? Wasn't the Irish State (or any State for that matter) just the sum total of all the people?

Ireland equals all of us put together. Why should the many pay for the mistakes of the few? Surely there must be a good reason why we couldn't just throw our hands up and say, 'Sorry we've no money, we can't pay'?

If we declared ourselves bankrupt, she thought, *we could pay what we could and start over. The people who lent to us would have to take it and, if we changed the way we did business, we could quite easily pay the money by deferring it for a few years until we got back on our feet.*

What was so wrong with that?

THE OPENING SET

It was good to be out of Dublin and on the road again. Diarmuid, like every Northerner she'd ever met, had a pathological hatred of traffic, so they had been out of bed before anyone and on their way to Stradbally by seven. He'd spent all last night figuring out different routes on Google maps. She'd never have bothered, but it was cute to see him take it so seriously.

He laughed as she tried to go back to sleep. She always dozed off in the car, listening to one of the CDs he'd made for the weekend, 'Electric Picnic '09' scribbled on it.

Everything was so right and yet so wrong at the same time. Diarmuid used the wheel as his imaginary drum kit as they bypassed Naas, Newbridge, Monasterevin and on towards Portlaoise. The countryside was beautiful in the early morning, kind of dewy, a little bit dreamy. That was the thing about the new motorways, she thought, they opened up the countryside so that you could really see it. She felt herself falling in and out of sleep, looking over to Diarmuid at the wheel.

And then they were there, parking in the field and setting up the tent. Diarmuid was right. Get in early and you're sorted. There were only a few tents, probably set up by other punctual Northerners, so they were able to find a good space on a raised section, and hopefully if it rained they wouldn't get too muddy. The sun was out at last, cutting through the clouds, and Stradbally felt like the best place in the world. Kilbarrack's dole queue was a million miles away.

Later on they strolled in, and decided to get a celebratory beer. Even at this hour the beer queue was pretty long, so Diarmuid told her to go ahead to the main stage while he went to get some drinks.

He was so handsome with his curly black hair all over the place. Omagh's answer to Che Guevara. And the lovely thing was that he had no idea how good he looked in his ancient Led Zeppelin T-shirt, jeans and runners as he walked back up the field, a pint in each hand, laughing.

She followed him as he tried to find her again, disoriented by the crowd. He saw her and attempted to wave with his head, beer flying everywhere. She was so happy, sitting with her knees up to her chin, above the main stage on the top of the little hill, looking out over the whole festival. There must have been 40,000 people here but it didn't feel like that. Losing her job and the stress of the mortgage seemed so far away. She dragged on a Marlboro Light contentedly and offered a smoke to the two girls beside her.

They all chatted—herself, Diarmuid and the two girls from Kilkenny—about the usual festival things. What bands were they going to see? Where? When? She couldn't wait for Basement Jaxx. She loved dancing and losing it. Diarmuid (of course) had his own list of obscure bands in little tents that he claimed were 'wild good'. Life was perfect. But she knew it was only fleeting.

THE EPIPHANY

Now the worst thing about being a girl and festivals. She had done her best to ignore it. But you can only delay the inevitable for so long. Two quick pints does it. She'll have to queue for the loo.

The smell hits her first. But she knows the drill. She's been here before. At least it was early so the smell was still just sickly disinfectant. Later on—well, it didn't bear thinking about.

Miss Pencil Skirt felt the ground around the toilets give way a bit. It is always sodden and mucky, even on a fine day like this. The organisers tried to soak up the moisture with straw but she couldn't help but think about overflow.

She stood beside three girls in coloured wellies clutching loo roll and packets of tissues. Behind her, an Electric Picnic virgin, who hadn't quite nailed festival chic yet, tottered in dressy platforms. She offered the virgin a spare packet of tissues. The younger girl thanked her profusely and said you'd never get that generosity at Oxegen.

The queue moved incredibly slowly. It was coming to her turn. She was three away and about to do the usual: take a deep breath, go in and do the business. Never look down. She had it off to a tee from going to gigs since she was a teenager. She could hold her breath like a pearl diver and only ever inhaled when she came out. In a portaloo, breathing in is not an option.

At that particular moment she hated men. She could see four of them pissing in a hedge. Christ, she hated them.

As she was about to take a deep breath, Diarmuid appeared out of nowhere. She was annoyed with him. She didn't like him to be around her when she was at unpleasant places like portaloos.

He grabbed her and dragged her off, putting his fingers to her lips, silencing her protests. They approached the bouncer at the artists' area. He flicked two passes at the lad in the bomber jacket and in they went. Through the door, around the back and into an old coach house, nobody around—a real loo, with loo paper, a basin, a mirror, soap and a towel, plus a lock on the door. She was obviously the first person to use it that day!

At that moment, she loved him, more than he could imagine. He had just ascended into heaven, her Ulster angel.

As they walked back, she looked at him with her 'seriously, tell me the truth' raised eyebrow.

'How did you do that? Where did you get those little tags?'

She examined their triple A—access all areas—stamp.

'My mate who's in Mindfield—who does the politics. You met him at Conor's party.'

'Northerners and their politics,' she joked.

'Well, he sorted us, babe. It's the same thing I told you before. It's about the system. You've got to subvert it, otherwise you'll end up queuing like the other eejits, in the pissing rain.'

'Access All Areas passes is hardly "subverting the system", Che Guevara,' she laughed.

Diarmuid got serious again.

'Yes, it is, love. The system is designed to make people act in a certain way. If you risk going against it, like telling the bouncer you're a performer at some political gig, you get to use the good loos. Do the unexpected and you'll get what you want. Do what's expected and you'll only get what other people want to give you.'

She loved it when he got animated like this. He sat her down and pulled out a smoke.

'It's like GAA, like Tyrone GAA,' he said, brushing his hair back.

She smirked.

'No, I'm serious, Grainne. Forget what happened this year in the semi-finals and just look at the trend.'

He was so animated when he talked about the Tyrone team. She remembered when she first fancied him he was being quizzed by some particularly earnest Ranelagh republicans. They were asking him about the Troubles and spouting dispossession and occupation. 'Tiocfaidh ár lá' and all that shite.

One politico asked him who was the real enemy, was it the UDR, the RUC or the Brits? He'd supped his pint and paused, while they sat back, expecting a pearl of wisdom or controlled thoughtful aggression from the oppressed.

With a serious face, he glared at them.

'The enemy was always Drumquin. They were dirty fuckers, two great half-forwards and lightning quick hand passes. If you beat Drumquin in the Devlin Cup, you could forgive the Prods and the Brits anything! In fact, the Brits could have the whole country if they wanted.'

He was forever taking the piss out of Southern 'chuckie heads'.

But when it came to the GAA he was deadly serious. He explained to her as they sat on the grass why Tyrone was successful in GAA and why their approach to beating the system applied to everything.

'Kerry, the Dubs, Cork, Galway, Mayo, these are the big teams. But Kerry now, they like to think of themselves as aristocrats.'

She normally glazed over at sport, but she had to admit she even fancied him in a Tyrone GAA shirt, which was, as every civilised girl knows, an unforgiveable fashion mistake. But he sounded like he was on to something. Besides, she could listen to that accent all day.

'Look, the emergence of Tyrone and particularly our humiliation of Kerry in 2003 was all about beating the system and getting the opposition to play by your own rules.'

Diarmuid warmed to his theme, his cigarette forgotten.

'This is how small teams and small countries beat the system and thrive. They do the unexpected. They show no respect for the pedigree and they gain huge plaudits for being brave enough to change.'

He put on his best Kerry accent, imitating an apoplectic Pat Spillane in a full force Sunday night rant against Tyrone's 'puke' football. Diarmuid explained that Tyrone just decided that they would not allow Kerry to play their game the way they always had. They would swarm around them, knock the aristocrats off their stride and play the quickest hand-passing game the country had ever seen.

'Basically, we changed the rules to suit ourselves. There was no point playing by someone else's rules. They were set to get the best out of the other team, not you. So you do the unexpected. It confuses people, but then they see that you are getting results. That's when they copy you and wonder why they hadn't been doing this all along.'

And why? Diarmuid said that it was because the big guys always make the rules.

'The systems are designed to make the big guys win and the little guys are always pathetically grateful for whatever crumbs come off the table. But if the little guy changes the rules, he can do anything.'

Getting into his stride he asked, 'How did you think Jack Charlton's football team won anything? All credit to them, but they weren't the best footballers in the world. They played the game the way that got the best out of their crop of players and didn't care about the system. They played the same against Italy or San Marino.'

And then he was back to Tyrone GAA.

'The people realised this wasn't just a one-off. It was a real innovation in the way the game was played. This success made the Tyrone management and players refine their own system. They learned by doing. Made the good things better and threw out the tactics that didn't work.

'Soon they weren't just a flash in the pan, they were the standard. Teams like Kerry were no longer looking down their noses at the upstarts, but looking to see what they could learn.'

Initially, Diarmuid said, the new ideas and ways of playing are like all ideas. First they are ridiculed, then they are violently opposed and, finally, they are universally accepted.

'That's the way the world works and the innovator—the person or the county or the country that does it differently—wins, always.

'Grainne, just think of what you were saying the other day about the economy and Ireland and how we run things and why you are on the dole. And I'll probably be following you shortly, from what the boss said yesterday.'

She saw it all clearly. She looked beyond him to all those young, smart people, having fun but realising that the wheels were falling off and the old regime didn't care. It was time for action, time to make a change.

The sun was going down over the main tent, the flags flying in the breeze, people were smiling, laughing, texting, dancing. Life was going on. It always does, no matter what happens to debts, taxes and money. Life always goes on.

She took Diarmuid—her boy philosopher—by the hands. She looked into his green eyes and kissed him. She hugged him, snuggled into him. It was getting a bit chilly. Good job she had her hoodie.

Miss Pencil Skirt rested her chin on his shoulder and looked down the hill at her generation, thousands of them in a big field in Laois. It was up to them to change things, to change the system. They had too much to offer, too much at stake. They had to make a move.

If not now, when?

NOTES

1 Father and Son (pages 1–13)
1. Census 2006
2. Wexford Chamber of Commerce report on Gorey, May 2009

3 Steak and Chips (pages 28–41)
1. Author's calculation
2. Deutsche Bundesbank Monthly Report, March 2008
3. P. Krugman, 'The eschatology of lost decades', 2009
4. Bank Annual Reports
5. *Ibid.*
6. Central Bank of Ireland
7. Irish Life and Permanent Annual Report 2008. Loan to deposit ratio of 260 per cent
8. Author's calculation
9. *Ibid.*

8 Breakfast Roll Man's U-turn (pages 98–106)
1. Author's calculation
2. *Ibid.*

9 Addicted to Money (pages 109–23)
1. Calculation referenced in S. Cassin & P. O'Mahony, 'Criminal justice drug policy in Ireland', Policy Paper 1, Drug Policy Action Group, Dublin, 2006
2. P. Krugman, *op cit.*

10 The Best Way to Rob a Bank is to Run One (pages 124–32)
1. UCD Alumni, President's Dinner

12 The Turf War (pages 146–55)
1. P. Honohan, 'Resolving Ireland's banking crisis', *The Economic and Social Review*, 40:2, 2009, pp.207–31
2. Bank Annual Reports
3. Bank Annual Reports, Central Bank Quarterly Bulletin
4. Minutes from meetings on 27 and 28 September 2008 between German private banks and the German government, published in July 2009
5. *New York Times* report on Depfa, 2 November 2008
6. *Ibid.*
7. *Ibid.*

13 Manufacturing Consent (pages 156–67)

1. *Irish Times*, 5 November 2008

14 Bent Cops (pages 168–81)

1. J. Kelly & M. Everett, 'Financial liberalisation and economic growth in Ireland', Central Bank Quarterly Bulletin, autumn 2004
2. *Irish Times*, 28 July 2005, *Sunday Business Post*, 26 October 2008
3. *Irish Independent*, 13 June 2009
4. *Sunday Independent*, 18 July 2004
5. Donations disclosed by TDs, Senators and MEPs for 2006, Standards in Public Office Commission (www.sipo.ie)
6. *Irish Independent*, 11 November 2006
7. Donations disclosed by TDs, Senators and MEPs for 2006, *op cit.*
8. *Ibid.*
9. *Irish Times*, 10 February 2009
10. Donations disclosed by TDs, Senators and MEPs for 2006, *op cit.*
11. *Sunday Tribune*, 19 April 2009
12. *Sunday Independent*, 25 March 2007
13. *Irish Independent*, 22 May 2008
14. Finfacts, 3 November 2006
15. Donations disclosed by TDs, Senators and MEPs for 2006, *op cit.*
16. *Irish Independent*, 20 September 2007
17. *Irish Times*, 10 February 2009
18. *Irish Examiner*, 18 May 2009
19. Institute of Chartered Accountants in Ireland Press Release, 25 September 2006
20. Statement by the Chartered Accountants Regulatory Board, 29 March 2009
21. *Sunday Tribune*, 8 February 2009

15 Down on the Street (pages 182–91)

1. At the opening ceremony of HSBC's fund administration and training centre in Sandyford, Dublin, April 2006
2. HSBC Annual Report 2006
3. *Ibid.*
4. *Irish Examiner* report on HSBC AGM, 26 May 2006

17 Ireland—Europe's Vietnam (pages 203–20)

1. P. Honohan, 'The banking crisis', Crisis Policy Conference, Trinity College Dublin, 20 May 2009
2. *Ibid.*

18 Ireland and the World (pages 221–30)

1. United States Department of Labor, Bureau of Labor Statistics, June 2009

INDEX